ISBN: 9781290623346

Published by:
HardPress Publishing
8345 NW 66TH ST #2561
MIAMI FL 33166-2626

Email: info@hardpress.net
Web: http://www.hardpress.net

DISTURBED DUBLIN

DISTURBED DUBLIN

THE STORY OF THE GREAT STRIKE
OF 1913–14

WITH A DESCRIPTION OF
THE INDUSTRIES OF THE IRISH CAPITAL

BY

ARNOLD WRIGHT

LONGMANS, GREEN, AND CO.

39 PATERNOSTER ROW, LONDON
FOURTH AVENUE & 30TH STREET, NEW YORK
BOMBAY, CALCUTTA, AND MADRAS

1914

PREFACE

THE great labour upheaval in Dublin in the latter half of last year was marked by such extraordinary features, and excited so large a share of public attention during the time that the struggle continued, that no apology will probably be deemed to be necessary for the publication of this volume. The author's aim has been to write a succinct and impartial history of the Larkinite movement in Dublin, from the period of its inception in 1908 until the resumption of the normal industrial life of the city early in the present year, in circumstances which marked the ignominious defeat of the attempt to establish a peculiarly pernicious form of Syndicalism on Irish soil. During a visit of several weeks' duration paid to Dublin in the Spring, the author had the opportunity of meeting many of those who had taken an active part in the conflict, and their views freely and courteously given were a valuable aid to a comprehension of the true character of the influences which brought about this memorable episode in Ireland's industrial history. But to a large extent in the accompanying pages Larkinism has been allowed to speak for itself, and it is hoped that the numerous elegant extracts culled from the press organ of the movement, together with the equally illuminating quotations from the speeches of Mr. Larkin and his chief lieutenants, will be held to justify the view taken as to the essentially revolutionary and anarchical aims of the Irish Transport Workers' Union.

In order to give completeness to the work and to allow of the labour position in Dublin being viewed in true perspective, the author has prefaced the narrative of the actual occurrences of the strike period with a sketch of the history of Dublin industries and an account of the modern industrial enterprises of the City. Attention has also been given to the slum problem, which it is widely considered was an important factor in assisting the development of the Larkinite movement. Generally speaking, the aim has been to furnish a complete picture of Dublin industrial life, with special reference to the circumstances of the disturbances of last year.

The author's special acknowledgments are due to Mr. Terence O'Hanlon, who rendered him much appreciated assistance in collecting and collating the great mass of published matter relating to the strike.

A. W.

LONDON, *September*, 1914.

CONTENTS

CHAPTER I

INDUSTRIES OF THE PAST

CHAPTER II

INDUSTRIES OF THE PRESENT

CHAPTER III

CONDITIONS OF LIFE AND LABOUR IN DUBLIN

CONTENTS

CHAPTER XIII

AN ORGY OF ANARCHY

CHAPTER XIV

THE AFTERMATH OF THE RIOTS

CHAPTER XV

ORGANISED REVOLT AGAINST LARKINISM

CHAPTER XVI

THE CONFLICT PROCEEDS

CHAPTER XVII
THE GOVERNMENT INTERVENES

CHAPTER XVIII
THE GOVERNMENT INQUIRY

CHAPTER XIX
FAILURE OF THE INQUIRY

CHAPTER XX
THE CHURCH AND LARKINISM

CONTENTS

CHAPTER XXI

A MARTYR AND HIS FIERY CROSS

CHAPTER XXII

THE ROUT OF LARKINISM

CHAPTER XXIII

A STUDY OF LARKINISM

DISTURBED DUBLIN

CHAPTER I

INDUSTRIES OF THE PAST

Introductory—The Dublin Strike—Aspects of Dublin—The City as an Industrial Centre—Beginnings of Industrial Ireland—Restrictions imposed on the Woollen Industry—Rise of the Silk Trade—Swift on the Wretched Condition of Ireland in the Eighteenth Century—The Linen Industry established—Disastrous Effect of Introduction of Machinery on Dublin Industries—Pernicious Influence of Labour Organisations on Trade—Characteristics of the Working Population of Dublin.

IN the latter half of 1913 Dublin was convulsed by an industrial struggle of a very remarkable kind. For several months the industries of the city, with few exceptions, were completely paralysed. The wharves, usually hives of industry, were for the most part silent and deserted. Very little trade came into the port and as little left it. Thousands of idle men swarmed the streets, from which much of the heavy vehicular traffic customarily seen in them had disappeared. The ordinary current of life was at several points entirely interrupted by ominous gatherings of strikers who, under the stimulus of inflammatory oratory, broke out into riotous disturbances, accompanied in one instance by pillage. It was a time more anxious for all involved, whether of the governing class or the governed, than any in the recent history of the Irish capital. Nor was it mere concern for the public peace that agitated men's minds. There were features in the struggle which differentiated it in a marked and alarming way from any previous industrial uprising in Irish history, or indeed in the history of the United Kingdom. The striker, by a vicious process of reasoning, became a revolutionary invested with all the revolutionary's powers of mischief. Not only was trade arbitrarily interrupted and the ordinary relations of life made difficult, but the whole fabric of civilisation was menaced by the promulgation and attempted enforcement of strange new doctrines which cut at the very roots of social order. The sinister character of the movement aroused the Dublin commercial world to a special effort to defeat it. There was a long and bitter conflict, but slowly common sense and determination carried the day. In the end Dublin was emancipated from a domination which, if it had been made effective, must almost inevitably have ruined the trade of the city for a generation. Such an episode in Ireland's industrial life is well deserving of more than the passing study given to the ordinary labour upheaval. While the latter is a mere ripple on the surface of industry, the events of 1913 in Dublin constitute an undoubted historic landmark. In this purely local quarrel a note was sounded which brought a new and vastly disturbing factor into the British labour movement, and which is probably destined in the future to have a wide-reaching influence on the course of industrial strife the wide world over.

For a complete understanding of the forces which produced this extraordinary movement we must cast a glance backwards into Ireland's economic past and analyse the conditions under which the industries of the Irish capital have been developed. The social problem, as it exists in Dublin, too, must be examined if we would appreciate fully the governing factors in the struggles.

The visitor is not long in Dublin before he discovers

that it is a city of vivid and, in many cases, startling contrasts. While it has unmistakably the grand air that distinguishes the capital from the mere provincial town—the spacious streets, the splendid buildings, and the pulsating life of a great social and intellectual centre—it has also, not less palpably, the dark, sordid aspect of the mean city steeped to its outermost fringe in the misery of industrial degradation. Sackville Street, one of the noblest of the Empire's thoroughfares, swarms with the miserable flotsam and jetsam of the darkest and dreariest depths of the social current. The Gothic pinnacles of St. Patrick's Cathedral, a stately fane of the most glorious period of ecclesiastical architecture, look directly down upon the quarter of the Coombe where the degradation of human kind is carried to a point of abjectness beyond that reached in any city of the Western world, save perhaps Naples. Hard by O'Connell Bridge, with its really magnificent vista of soaring monuments and noble buildings, is a maze of streets physically and morally foul. Yet with all the signs of degradation that are too painfully evident, Dublin is a likeable city. Not without reason was that facile piece of alliteration penned that assigns the attributes of dear and dirty to the Irish capital. The place grips you and fascinates you : you get to love its leisured life and its polite people, and, though you may begin with the rôle of the severely impartial critic, you end by being to their virtues very kind and to their faults a little blind. One thing at least we have to confess, and that is that Dublin's river is not so black as in our imagination it had been painted. Fresh from a perusal of Swift's poem to Stella at Wood Park, in which the great misanthrope writes of the lady's coming

> From purling streams and fountains bubbling,
> To Liffey's stinking tide at Dublin,

we had made our acquaintance with the famous tideway with anything but pleasurable anticipation. But the

stream seemed as innocuous as the Thames at Westminster Bridge. There may still be at certain states
of the tide and particular periods of the summer wafted
up from the blackish water scents which are not those
of Araby. Local opinion, indeed, is fairly decided that
the river has not yet outlived its evil reputation. Nevertheless, the completion of the main drainage scheme—
one of the things which counts unto righteousness for
a corporation none too highly in the odour of sanctity—
has indubitably changed vastly for the better the character
of the stream. That the local ediles may be induced to
go a stage farther in the work of purification and cleanse
the city of the moral blots that now so sadly deface it,
will be the wish of all who would have Dublin smiling,
not through her rags, but through the strong native
homespun that more closely accords with her simple
dignity.

It is in Dublin's character as an industrial centre,
pure and simple, that this work, however, is chiefly
concerned. Nature has denied the city some of the
conspicuous advantages that attach to the great manufacturing capitals of England and Scotland. She has
no coal mines at her doors from which to draw indispensable supplies of fuel. No iron deposits in her
neighbourhood yield the raw material almost equally
necessary for a large class of enterprises. She is out of
the track of the great steamship lines which carry manufactured goods to the uttermost ends of the earth.
Behind her are none of the great traditions which have
enabled captains of industry to build up within her
confines profitable concerns. Her position, industrially,
is one of a by no means splendid isolation. And yet she
is not entirely without advantages, and those advantages
of a substantial kind, too. In the river which bisects
the city and brings supplies to the very doors of the
mercantile houses and factories, Dublin possesses an
asset of incalculable value if it is properly utilised. On

both banks in the lower reaches of the stream there is vacant land sufficient to give house room to numerous additional factories and workshops. At comparatively small cost arrangements might be made for the establishment of a great shipbuilding industry, for which the river is well adapted, as some pioneers have, as we shall see later, already discovered. The admirably constructed wharves which are a notable feature of the city, and the supplementary docks at North Wall, make the landing of goods easy under existing conditions ; but if a growing trade should outstrip the present facilities, other dock accommodation could be provided without much difficulty at moderate cost. In fact, the situation lends itself admirably to the construction of a thoroughly up-to-date port, with all the adjuncts that belong to such a centre. It is, further, to the advantage of industrial Dublin that there is a plentiful supply of labour. So ample, indeed, is the amount of available human material for trade purposes that, as will be shown in succeeding pages, the circumstance constitutes one of the gravest features of the economic problem of Dublin. On a review of the whole position, it is impossible to avoid the conclusion that, with a due adjustment of means to ends, a reasonable amount of enterprise on one side— that of the employers—and a proper sense of responsibility and moderation on the other side—that of the employees—Dublin might in a few years' time be made as flourishing a manufacturing centre as any outside the greatest towns of England and Scotland.

In the past Dublin has had its share of manufacturing prosperity. Far back in the period of the Middle Ages it was an important port, as ports were estimated in those days. But it was not until the spacious age of Elizabeth that the city began to emerge from the obscurity of a remote outpost of English power. The foundations were then laid of the reputation which Dublin still enjoys as a great distributing centre for the supplies

of a considerable part of Ireland. The real beginnings of industrial Ireland are to be found in the early
seventeenth century, when the woollen industry, which
had existed in the country from quite early times, entered
upon an era of prosperity which marked Dublin out as
a commercial capital of importance. Attracted by the
advantages of cheap labour and an abundance of raw
material, many manufacturers migrated from the West
of England to the banks of the Liffey in those days.
They brought with them, besides a considerable amount
of capital, a welcome reinforcement of intellectual and
commercial ideas. Under this stimulus the industry
grew apace, until at the close of the seventeenth century,
according to Mr. O'Connor's 'History of the Irish
Catholics,' it was giving employment to no fewer than
12,000 Protestant families in Dublin. The conspicuous
success of the industry unhappily proved its ruin. The
period was one of rigid trade exclusiveness. Not only
as an outcome of the narrow economic creed in favour
in those days was district arrayed against district, but
town against town. The old municipal records afford
abundant evidence of the absurd jealousy with which
local interests were protected from the competition of
the 'foreigner,' as all who happened to be born outside
the favoured limits were customarily termed.

Ireland, almost necessarily from its geographical
isolation, came in for a full share of the jealous suspicion
with which local communities regarded each other in
Tudor and Stuart times. While her trading connection
was small, little notice was taken of her, but as soon as
she began to export in considerable quantities the products
of her looms, a great outcry went up from the English
woollen manufacturers, whose business was no doubt
injuriously affected by the Irish competition. Restrictions were imposed upon the trade by the English Government in the interests of the home traders. While in
Charles I's reign attempts were made to transfer the

attention of Irish manufacturers from the production of
woollen to that of linen goods by discouraging one branch
of manufacture and subsidising the other, Charles II's
Government absolutely prohibited the exportation of
Irish manufactures to the colonies which were then
growing into importance. The English market still
remained open, and the facilities were made the most of
in the ensuing years. But the time came when this
avenue also was closed by a despotic bolting and barring
of the door. In response to the clamorous demands of
the English traders for protection against Irish productions, voiced in addresses from both Houses of Parliament,
William III promised to do what he could ' to discourage
the woollen trade in Ireland and encourage the linen
manufacture there, and to promote the trade of England.'
What followed is well described by Lecky [1] : ' A Parliament was summoned in Dublin in September 1698 for
the express purpose of destroying the Irish industry.
The Irish Parliament was then, from the nature of its
constitution, completely subservient to English influence,
and, had it been otherwise, it would have had no power
to resist. The Lords Justices, in their opening speech,
urged the House to encourage the linen and hempen
manufacture instead of the woollen manufacture which
England desired to monopolise. The Commons, in reply,
promised their hearty endeavours to establish a linen
and hempen manufacture in Ireland, expressed a hope
that they might find such a temperament in respect of
the woollen trade as would prevent it from being injurious
to that of England, and proceeded, at the instance of
the Government, to impose heavy additional duties on
the export of Irish woollen goods. The English, however, were still unsatisfied. A law of crushing severity,
enacted by the British Parliament in 1699, completed
the work and prohibited the Irish from exporting their
manufactured wool to any other country whatever.'

[1] *History of England in the Eighteenth Century*, iii. 210.

' So ended,' says Lecky in a final note on the transaction ' the fairest promise Ireland had ever known of becoming a prosperous and a happy country.'

Dublin trade struggled on under the weight of the terrible disability imposed upon it. Towards the end of the seventeenth century, before the ruin of the woollen industry had been encompassed, a silk trade had been established by a body of Huguenot refugees driven out of France by the religious persecutions. It received much encouragement from the local authorities, and secured a strong foothold in the city. But it was on too small a scale to provide a proper substitute for the lost industry, and, under the depressing influence of the time, the population of Dublin and of a considerable part of Ireland fell into extreme poverty. Swift, in his ' Short view of the State of Ireland,' supplies a gloomy picture of the state of the country in those years. ' A stranger travelling in Ireland,' he writes, ' would be apt to think himself travelling in Lapland or Iceland, rather than in a country so favoured by nature both in fruitfulness of soil and temperature of climate.' ' The miserable dress and diet and dwelling of the people ; the general desolation in most parts of the kingdom ; the old seats of the nobility and gentry all in ruins, and no new ones in their stead ; the families of farmers who pay great rents, living in filth and nastiness, upon butter, milk, and potatoes, without a shoe or stocking to their feet, or a house so convenient as an English hog-sty to receive them. The houses of interest, in all other countries a sign of wealth, is in us a proof of misery, there being no trade to employ any borrower. Hence alone comes the dearness of land, since the savers have no other way to lay out their money : Hence the dearness of necessaries of life, because the tenants cannot afford to pay such extravagant rates for land (which they must take or go a-begging) without raising the price of cattle and of corn, although themselves should live upon chaff.'

Ireland, and more especially its capital, was, indeed, at this critical juncture in its industrial history, in the depths of despair. A belated perception of its responsibility for the mischief that it had worked by its restricted laws led the English Parliament to redeem in part the pledge given by William III to promote a linen industry. The financial support vouchsafed was inconsiderable, but it was not without influence in building up the present magnificent linen trade which to-day is one of the glories of industrial Ireland. Dublin, however, was not to find in the new interest the compensation it sought for its lost woollen trade. Though the linen industry in the initial stages had its seat in the capital and was directed from it for a long series of years, the manufacture never secured a permanent home there. Gradually the trade moved northwards, until Belfast usurped Dublin's position and completely dominated what has since become one of the most flourishing industries of the United Kingdom.

Dublin's industry continued more or less under a cloud during the greater part of the eighteenth and the early nineteenth centuries. Mr. J. J. Webb, in his interesting and scholarly essays for the Coyne Scholarship,[1] traces in elaborate detail the course of economic progress in the Irish capital in these years. He shows how, in spite of all drawbacks, the woollen and silk industries continued to exist, and how, as time went by, a cotton manufacturing interest was added to the trading features of the city. He further makes it clear that Dublin, in the latter half of the eighteenth and the early part of the nineteenth centuries, was the seat of a number of flourishing trades such as cabinet making and coach building, which ministered to the extensive needs of the society of what for a time was one of the most brilliant

---

[1] 'Industrial Dublin since 1698'; 'The Silk Industry in Dublin.' Two essays by J. J. Webb, M.A., LL.B. Maunsel & Co., Ltd., Dublin and London, 1913.

of the minor capitals of Europe. The introduction of machinery, as a substitute for hand labour, had the worst effect on those sections of the Dublin trade which were susceptible to the influences of the new agency. The woollen trade was completely extinguished, and the silk trade was reduced to inconsiderable dimensions. Many of the minor industries, which were not directly affected by the industrial revolution, suffered indirectly by the flooding of the market by cheap English productions, against which the native workmen could not successfully compete.

The handicap imposed by the drastic change in mechanical methods and the resultant increase in competition, was not the only difficulty which confronted Dublin manufacturers in the beginning of the last century. Labour at this period was stretching its limbs and feeling its feet. The old salutary influence of the trade guilds, which Dublin possessed in common with most important English and Scotch towns, had given place to the viciously exercised authority of a series of combinations of workmen. Inspired by a single-minded desire to raise wages, regardless of the capacity of the industry to bear them, these associations of artisans proved a very destructive element in Dublin industry. ' The members of the different societies,' says Mr. Webb, ' ruthlessly enforced the bye-laws for the regulation of their respective industries. Instead of the employers controlling the conduct of their own businesses, the different societies tyrannised over the masters. The various trade societies in Dublin were allied together, and were directed by a secret committee known as " The Board of Green Cloth," which was the terror of employers.' Mr. Otway, who conducted an official inquiry into the Dublin silk trade in 1838, made strong reference in his report to the evil effects of this system of trade combination. It had, he said, ' operated most injuriously on the silk trade, driven many of the most extensive manufacturers out of it, and deterred others from directing their capital and intelligence towards it, by which alone it could be preserved or enabled to compete with the other silk-weaving districts of the Empire.'

Some striking evidence, relative to the methods of these early Dublin trade unionists, was given in the course of the inquiry. Alderman Abbott, one of the leading silk manufacturers of the city, stated that up to 1829 he was engaged in the trade and employed a large number of looms. Owing to difficulties he called his workmen together, and they agreed to make a considerable reduction in the price of weaving. But, when the work was taken out for the winter's trade, the ' combinators ' took the shuttles from the workmen and would not let them finish their work in the looms until he agreed to give the full London prices. After this he did not think it safe to continue any longer in business, and consequently retired. Another silk merchant, Mr. McConnell, stated that about nine months previously he had made an agreement with men, at their own solicitation, to give them work under the usual price, trade being remarkably bad. As soon as the trade association heard of the arrangement, they passed a resolution prohibiting any workmen from working for him. To enforce the edict, vitriol was thrown through the windows into his works, and a system of terrorism inaugurated in other ways, which prevented the employees from continuing at their work. Mr. McConnell gave the following description of the methods of the associations : ' Part of the combination committee of each trade is in connection with a general combination committee, or body of all trades. To this, each trade that has formed a body or union sends its delegate, and, generally, when any of their laws are to be enforced against anyone who has come under their displeasure, the person to punish and the punishment is pronounced and awarded by persons connected with totally different trades and pursuits.'

Though the silk trade was the greatest sufferer by the tyranny of the combinations, perhaps because of the peculiar conditions under which it was conducted, the mischief was by no means confined to that interest. The greatest blow of all that the misguided activities of the associations struck, indeed, was quite in another direction. As has been stated, Dublin is peculiarly well situated for the work of shipbuilding. So it was thought a hundred years ago, when a brave attempt was made to build up an industry of the kind on the Liffey. If the fates had been propitious—in other words, if the labour organisations had been far-seeing—Dublin possibly might have vied with Belfast as a centre for shipping construction. But the narrow tenets of those who directed the combinations were opposed to that freedom of initiative without which the ablest captains of industry are helpless. The trade associations insisted on keeping the number of apprentices at an abnormally low level, and they, at the same time, forced wages up to an extraordinarily high one. What was even more disastrous in its effects was the interference of the ship carpenters' society in the working of the industry. Worthless men were foisted upon the management at wages equal to those of the best men ; then regulations were imposed upon the employers which were ruinous to discipline, and, if a trader dared to exercise his discretion and refuse work to a particular applicant, he might have to face a general strike amongst his workmen. A tyranny of this kind could have but one end. The employers, after struggling for some time against the combinations, closed their works and took their capital to another and freer market. With their departure Dublin lost the best chance she ever possessed of becoming the home of a shipbuilding trade. Her rightful position was usurped by Belfast, which, with inferior natural advantages, built up in the course of years an immense industry.

Mr. Webb, in his work, gives some amazing instances of the ridiculous lengths to which the spirit of combination was carried. ' On the Royal Canal a system existed whereby the crew were bound to the boat. The owners could not dismiss a man from his boat. No other would be found to take his place. The only remedy was to sell the boat and get a new one. A similar system existed amongst brewers' draymen. The men were bound to the horses and could not be parted from them. Violence was used to enforce the decrees of the associations. Employers and men who came under the ban of the secret committee which directed affairs, were beaten in the streets, and property was attacked and destroyed. At times a veritable reign of terror existed. Trade languished, as it was bound to do, under the influence of this oppressive system. While a good many businesses were completely extinguished, others were so severely crippled that they brought little advantage to the community. Dublin, in fact, went very near to losing her title to be considered a commercial city.'

It is a commonplace that history repeats itself. No one who has studied, even cursorily, the records of the labour upheaval of 1913 can fail to be struck with the remarkable resemblance between many features of these old-time struggles with the workmen's combinations and those of last year. It is not necessary here to unduly emphasise the point, as the reader in later chapters will be provided with ample material from which to draw his own conclusions. But before passing on to deal with the modern era which followed ' The reign of terror,' it may be permissible to suggest that no survey of Dublin as an industrial centre can be accurately made without taking account of the temperamental characteristics of its working population. Strongly emotional and highly

responsive to outside influences, they are easily caught
up by any movement which appeals either to their
pocket, their religious susceptibilities, or their sense of
patriotism.   Nowhere, perhaps, in the wide world is
there more plastic material for moulding by the hands of
the man who has a mission, or thinks he has, to reform
humanity.

CHAPTER II

INDUSTRIES OF THE PRESENT

The Industrial Dublin of To-day—The Brewing Interest—Guinness's Establishment—Distilleries—Manufacture of Non-alcoholic Beverages—The Poplin Industry—Paterson's Match Factory—Spence's Engineering Works—Shipbuilding Enterprise—Jacob's Biscuit Factory—Shipping Concerns—Bristol and Irish Steam Packet Company—The City of Dublin Steam Packet Company—The London and North-Western Railway Company's and other Services —Importance of the Dublin Shipping Trade.

IN its purely industrial aspect Dublin does not impress the writer as an English manufacturing town does. There is, happily perhaps for the æsthetic proprieties, no forest of chimneys belching forth black smoke, which hangs like a cloud over the buildings and blurs the outlines of the surrounding suburbs. If you mount the Nelson Column in Sackville Street you may, if you are particularly observant, count as many factory shafts as you have fingers on your two hands, but you will have to look for them. They are dotted about the city in isolated positions, some in localities where you would least expect to find them. Dublin in reality has no distinctively manufacturing quarter. The nearest approach to one is the Ringsend district, where the tramway power station, the gasworks, and a few other enterprises give a specious air of industrialism to a quarter sandwiched in between the business area adjacent to Westland Row Station and the residential district of Sandymount.

Nevertheless, the city has to-day a wider range of industrial interests than at any previous period in its history.   Scattered about the limits of the city and the districts of what may be termed Greater Dublin, are many enterprises interesting from their individual characteristics and important collectively as a testimony to the renaissance of the city's trade in modern times. A survey shows that while Dublin has preserved its character as a capital, and in particular has lost none of the air of leisured ease that has always pervaded it, it has become a real factor in the commercial life of the United Kingdom.

One industry which is pre-eminently racy of the Dublin soil is that of brewing.   Established in the early days of the city's trading history, this has weathered all storms, political and economic, and to-day confers upon the Irish capital a reputation for the production of a special description of alcoholic beverage—Dublin stout—which is world-wide.   There is said to be some special quality in the Dublin water, which gives to this popular drink its much-prized characteristics.   That may, or may not, be the case ; but probably the production would never have secured the position of extraordinary popularity that belongs to it, if there had not been exceptional commercial ability to push its claims to public attention in outside markets.   The great house of Guinness, whose heritage this branch of the brewery trade is, to a very large extent at least, has in successive generations produced men of the right type—merchants shrewd and far-seeing, who have been quick to seize advantages which have offered, and who have united to business capacity a public spirit which has done honour to Dublin.

The founder of the firm was Arthur Guinness, a member of a Dublin family, who in 1759 acquired a small brewery, in the vicinity of the present mammoth factory, for the purpose of producing the ' porter,' or black beer, which had obtained such vogue in London at that period.   It seems that chance largely decided the establishment of the Guinness business in Dublin.   Arthur

Guinness's first idea was to have a brewery built at Carnarvon or Holyhead, but as he was not altogether satisfied with the facilities there, he turned his attention to Ireland, with the result that an acquisition was made of the historic site in James Street.

How, from small beginnings, this enterprise has developed into the greatest brewing concern in the world is one of the romances of trade. ' Potentialities beyond the dreams of avarice,' Johnson's well-known estimate of the possibilities of Thrale's brewery, might, in a literal sense, have been applied to this Dublin undertaking in the later period of its existence. When, in 1886, the enterprise was converted into a limited liability company, the family interests were sold for £6,000,000. To-day the capital value of the company's interests exceeds £20,000,000.

Visitors who go to Dublin on pleasure are taken to the brewery as to one of the great show sights of Ireland ; and, indeed, it is a remarkably interesting place. Occupying over forty acres, and employing more than 3000 men, the establishment represents the last word in the adaptation of scientific means to commercial ends. It is o nly by this olicy that the enormous output of the firm, amounting to considerably over two million barrels per annum, can be grappled with successfully. Probably, if the wonderful progress of the firm could have been foreseen by the original founder, he would have chosen a site farther down the river, where seagoing vessels could have come alongside the brewery wharves for lading. But the drawback is minimised by the employment of powerful steam barges, which remove the barrels from the brewery to the quays below O'Connell Bridge for shipment. The spectacle of these well-appointed craft darting up and down the Liffey with their cargoes of casks, is one of the most cheerful that industrial Dublin presents. Watching their determined onrush against a swiftly flowing tide, one is constrained to hope that they are typical of the new spirit of Irish life.

c

Twin partner of the brewing interest in the ancient traditions of commercial Dublin is the distilling industry. Whether Ireland or Scotland is entitled to the honour of having discovered the virtues of usquebaugh is a problem which may be left for solution to the antiquarian. It is sufficient for our purpose to know that at a very remote period in Irish history, Irishmen were accustomed to find solace for their cares in the spirit which is recognised to-day as their national drink. There is some controversy as to the precise date at which Dublin became a centre for spirit distillation. One prominent authority gives the middle of the eighteenth century as approximately the time when the industry came into life ; but Mr. Webb thinks, and reason would appear to be on his side, that distillation of some kind must have been carried on much earlier than this, having regard to the fact that the art was generally practised throughout the country long before that. Whatever the truth may be as to the period of birth of the trade, the oldest record of a modern house goes no farther back than 1757. There are, however, as Mr. Webb points out, four existing Dublin distilleries which can claim a connection dating back to the eighteenth century. ' The Thomas Street Distillery, so long associated with the Roe family, holds the palm for antiquity. Next in point of age comes the Marrowbone Lane Distillery, which was purchased in 1779 by some members of the Jameson family. Power's Distillery, in John's Lane, was founded in 1791 by an ancestor of the present proprietors.'

Though firmly planted on Dublin soil, the distillery industry has in recent years been under a heavy cloud. A changed public taste in Great Britain and the colonies, and the abnormally heavy taxation imposed in 1910, have operated to reduce the exportation in a marked degree. A falling off in the home consumption, due to a large extent to the enhanced duty, has further contributed to the depression. Probably there is sufficient vitality in the industry to enable it to weather the troubles which beset it. At all events, if whisky is to be drunk at all, there will be few to deny that it is in the pure wholesome spirit which is manufactured in Dublin that the public will find its best stimulant.

If Dublin has suffered on one side by the wave of temperance that has been sweeping over the land in late years, it has profited on another. The taste which has developed for non-alcoholic beverages has greatly benefited the mineral water manufacturers of the city. This section of Dublin's traders is by no means a negligible quantity in the commercial life of the Irish capital. The firms of A. & R. Thwaites & Co., Ltd., and Cantrell & Cochrane are known throughout the world. The former claims to have been the inventor of soda water, and the latter produces a special brand of ginger ale, which has great vogue in America as well as in the United Kingdom. In the success of these firms Dublin may well find encouragement for the future. It is certainly in the establishment of miscellaneous manufactures, rather than of any single staple industry, that the best chance of the building up of a stable and adequate commercial structure lies.

It is impossible to deal with modern Dublin industries without a passing word in reference to the poplin manu-facture for which the city was once so famous, and which still survives, though now only a shadow of its old self. Poplin, a material made of pure silk as the warp and fine wool as the weft, is a relic of the Huguenot invasion of the latter part of the seventeenth century. It had, in old days, a great vogue, and kept thousands of looms in the city at work. But change of fashion doomed this, with many other glorious productions of the handicraftsmen, to neglect and obscurity, and it is only in late years, through the exertions of the Countess of Aberdeen and other friends of Irish industries, that it has been brought into favour again. The manufacture is carried on by Messrs. Atkinson & Co., of College Green, Messrs. Pim Bros., and Mr. Elliot, and, if society ladies were less wedded to the purely modern class of textiles, there might be hope of a flourishing trade on the old scale being established. As, however, the capriciousness of the Paris modistes is not at all likely to run in the direction of poplins, it is to be feared that the trade will have to be content with smaller achievements. Of late it has been making some headway by the manufacture of ties. The material is well adapted for this purpose, and the specimens of the manufacture on the market have won great favour.

The developments of the last half-century in the city's trade have been almost all in the direction of new industries. Soap manufacture, bottle making, patent manure making, boot and shoe manufacture, and cardboard box construction are some of the byways into which the enterprise of capitalists has penetrated. A peculiar product of the modern spirit is Paterson's Match Factory, hard by the Four Courts. In this establishment, with the most modern machinery, matches are being made in great quantities, not merely for the use of a patriotic local public, which desires to encourage native industries, but for export into the great world, to compete there with the products of older houses of long-established reputation. It is satisfactory to know that the enterprise of the founders has met its reward. Paterson's matches have become literally a household word in many houses far removed from the Liffey.

Of a different character, and dating to a somewhat older period, is the engineering works of Messrs. Spence & Co., in Cork Street. As this establishment was one of the storm centres of the strike hereafter to be described, a brief account of it may appropriately be given. Like many Irish businesses, Spence & Co. owes its origin to Scottish energy. Its founder was the late Mr. William Spence, whose parents came from Linlithgow in the early

part of the last century, and started this business in 1856
to provide for the engineering needs of the Irish capital
and its vicinity. Though severely handicapped by
freight charges on raw material, he managed by sheer
force of character to establish a flourishing business, on
lines which allowed of easy expansion should circumstances justify it. When Mr. Spence died his son, Mr.
Arthur William Spence, who had helped in the business
for some years, carried forward the traditions of enterprise and untiring industry which his father had
established. At the present time there is not a more
efficient firm of the kind in Ireland than that in Cork
Street. On a site of three or four acres there are to be
found all the appliances essential to the conduct of a
modern engineering and iron foundry business. Much
work is done for Dublin firms, notably for Messrs.
Guinness, but it is very far from being a mere local
enterprise. Commissions are executed for all parts of
the United Kingdom and for the Dominions, while
the house has also a good foreign connection. A concern
of this kind is an invaluable asset to a city situated as
Dublin is. If it were lost through labour troubles, or
other causes, it would probably not be easy to find
anyone venturesome enough to essay the task of replacing
the business, owing to the serious initial difficulties
which would have to be faced in regard to raw material.

Scotch pluck and perseverance are also responsible
for reviving the shipbuilding industry in Dublin. It
was in 1902 that two gentlemen from the Clyde, Messrs.
Scott and Smellie, established themselves on a site at the
mouth of the Liffey with the object of creating, if possible,
a profitable ship-constructing business there. They
brought with them, besides their native shrewdness, a
substantial stock of experience, which they were speedily
able to turn to good account, owing to the favour with
which the Government and the public authorities in
Ireland regarded their venture. Orders from many

quarters flowed in, and in a comparatively short space
of time the yard was firmly established. It has acquired
already such a reputation for the building of small craft
that it has not only secured commissions from England
and Scotland, but has been entrusted by the Canadian
Government with the construction of two high-speed
cruisers for protecting fisheries. These, it is hoped,
are the forerunners of a warship building connection
nearer home. Meanwhile several hundred men are
already employed in the yard, under wage conditions
similar to those which obtain on the Clyde. The future
of the enterprise will be watched with interest by all
who wish well to Dublin. If fortune smiles on it, it may,
to some extent, redress the disparity which exists between
the business fame of Belfast and that of the capital city.

It remains now to deal with what is certainly the
crowning instance of modern manufacturing enterprise
in Dublin—Jacob's Biscuit Factory. Unlike the venture
just referred to, this is Irish to the core. Its history
is a story which deserves to be given at some little length,
as, apart from its intrinsic interest, it is of importance
from the bearing it has on the main theme of the book.
Towards the end of the first half of the last century there
existed in Waterford a bakery and a flour mill, carried
on by Mr. William B. Jacob, a member of an old Quaker
family that had long been settled in that part of Ireland.
William Jacob was a man of enterprise and originality,
and was not content with the limited opportunities
which a small Irish town offered for the utilisation
of his energies and his capital. Migrating to Dublin
in 1851, he acquired some premises in Peter's Row,
and established there a biscuit factory. The firm's
progress was steady and continuous. Bit by bit new
premises were added, until the original insignificant
factory had grown to a huge concern occupying the
whole of a great site bounded by Bishop Street, Bride
Street, Peter Street, and Peter's Row, and extending

to other large blocks of property in the locality.   In the process of development the founder's three sons took an active part ; and they are to-day, with other directors and members of their families, carrying forward, with ever-increasing success, the work which was commenced over sixty years since by the Waterford trader.

Jacob's is a business of which not merely Dublin, but Ireland, has a right to be proud.   Built on Irish soil, with Irish money, and directed by Irish brains, it has carried the name and fame of the capital city to the uttermost ends of the civilised world.   It has been said by a great writer that the man who makes two blades of grass to grow where only one grew before is a public benefactor.   On the same principle assuredly the men who gave to Ireland this splendid industry, with its great capacity for the employment of labour on a large scale, are entitled to be regarded by all true friends of Ireland with respect and gratitude.   How widely different has been the view taken of their services to Irish commerce by a section of the people the sequel will show.   Maligned and calumniated to an incredible degree, they have been made the victims of a vendetta of a peculiarly shameful description.   In the proper place it will be the writer's duty to deal exhaustively with this singularly disgraceful episode.   Suffice it here to say that, while Ireland's economic history has much in it to bring the blush of shame to the cheek—records of wrongs perpetrated for selfish ends, and rights withheld under flimsy pretences —there is no cleaner or brighter page than that on which is inscribed the story of this great firm.

Bound up in the manufacturing interests of Dublin, and, to a large extent dependent upon them for its prosperity, is the shipping industry.   From the earliest times Dublin has been a port of note.   It was in the old days styled the ' Eye of Ireland,' and modern changes have not deprived it of its right to the title.   Indeed, the era of steam has, if anything, accentuated the claims

of the port to regard as a convenient centre for commercial purposes.   As has been pointed out, it is a great
distributing centre for southern and western Ireland.
In that character it is the head quarters of several
flourishing shipping companies.   One of these enterprises—-The British and Irish Steam Packet Co.—has a
quite historic connection with steam navigation.   It
goes back to the year of Waterloo, when a tiny steam
packet, christened the *Thames*, made the first passage
of any steam vessel between Dublin and London, carrying
as passengers Mr. C. R. Weld, the secretary of the
company, and his wife.   That voyage was remarkable
in shipping annals as not merely the initial step in
the history of Irish steam navigation, but one of the
earliest achievements in deep-sea navigation with steam
propulsion.

Many thousands of spectators assembled on the
banks of the Liffey on the eventful May 28, 1815, to
witness the departure of the pioneer steamship, and
high hopes were entertained of the prospects that were
opened up for trade by the venture.   But it was not
until eleven years later that a regular steamship service
was established with two vessels, the *Thames*, a name-
sake of the pioneer packet, and a sister ship, the *Shannon*.
One of the earliest vessels employed on the station was
the *William Fawcett*, which, after a short period of service,
was acquired by the Peninsular Steam Navigation Co.—
the progenitor of the P. & O. Company—and afterwards
became the pioneer of the famous company's trade in
the East.   In 1830 the British and Irish Co. had three
steamers—the *Thames*, the *Shannon*, and the *City of
Londonderry*—plying regularly between the Irish capital
and the Thames.   They were, according to modern
standards, insignificant craft of 513 tons burden and
150 horse-power, but they served their purpose of
providing an expeditious and reliable means of communication between Dublin and London.   In ordinary

weather the voyage occupied eighty hours, a record which to-day would be considered a poor one, but which, at the beginning of last century, appeared a remarkable achievement, contrasting as it did with the experiences of the period when sailing ships supplied the only connection, and when weeks were often consumed in the passage from the Liffey to the Thames.

The success which attended the service led, in 1836, to the formation of the existing British and Irish Steam Packet Co., with several of the best-known citizens of the Irish capital as directors. Under the new management the company upheld the traditions of public spirit and enterprise that the pioneers had established. It was one of the first shipping concerns to recognise the superiority of the screw propeller over the paddle wheel for driving seagoing steamships, and it also gave a lead in the construction of iron ships by putting on to the Dublin and London run a fine iron-built steamer called the *Foyle*. In 1848 the company had to face severe competition ably directed by the Messrs. Malcolmson of Waterford, but, after a fierce struggle lasting for three years, in which all the Irish companies became involved, an arrangement was come to by which Dublin and London traffic was divided. This agreement lasted until 1870, when the British and Irish company bought out Messrs. Malcolmson's competing interest, and thus were able to consolidate their position in such fashion that their supremacy in the London-Dublin trade has never since been seriously challenged. Their existing fleet consists of five passenger vessels, four of which are of about 1400 tons burden, and one—a stand-by ship—of about 1000 tons. They are admirably adapted for the service upon which they are engaged, and are in great favour with that large section of the public which finds pleasure in a sea voyage in a perfectly equipped ship. A fact worth mentioning, as evidence of the hold this oganisation has on Dublin life, is that Mr. Barry, the present secretary of the company, is only the third holder of that office, the two previous occupants being Messrs. Egan, father and son.

Another shipping company whose boats are familiar to travellers between England and Ireland is the City of Dublin Steam Packet Co., established in 1823. This company, like its predecessor in the Dublin shipping trade just described, was in the first flight of steamship companies in the British Isles, which is tantamount to saying in the world. Its earlier history presents points of interest to the student of Irish shipping industry, but it is with the modern organisation that the present narrative is chiefly concerned. The company to-day is one of the most vigorous and progressive commercial institutions that Dublin possesses. As the holders of the mail contract, the company enjoys a prestige which it thoroughly deserves, its quartette of steamers—the *Leinster, Munster, Connaught*, and *Ulster*—which ply regularly between Kingstown and Holyhead, being model cross-channel steamers, fast and well found and thoroughly comfortable. A second service between North Wall and Liverpool is maintained daily by a number of boats of slightly smaller capacity, but possessing the same much-appreciated qualities of speed, convenience, and safety; while a bi-weekly cargo and passenger service by other of the company's boats connects Dublin and Belfast. Tourists are specially catered for by the company. Indeed, it is due largely to the well-conceived measures devised by the management, both afloat and ashore, that the stream of holiday visitors to Ireland has reached the dimensions it has in recent years.

Apart from these two leading companies, a good many interests are associated with the Dublin shipping trade. The London and North-Western Railway Co. have a regular service of well-equipped steamers between Holyhead and Kingstown and North Wall. The Royal Mail Line runs boats twice daily to Belfast, one service being via

Greenock and the other via Ardrossan. In association with the company's operations the Laird Line runs from Dublin to Glasgow three times weekly. A regular connection with Liverpool is maintained by the Screw Steam Packet Co., the Dublin and Mersey Lines' boats, and the vessels of the Tedcastle Line. Finally, Dublin enjoys direct communication with Bristol through the agency of the Bristol Steam Navigation Company's steamers, and it is also in touch with Morecambe by means of a service kept up by the Laird Line.

The foregoing bare recital of the shipping interests of Dublin will serve to bring home to the reader the importance of this branch of the city's trade. On a capital basis the companies concerned are the most substantial of all the city's commercial assets outside the brewing industry, and with the various dependent trades they constitute a factor of overwhelming importance in the prosperity of the community. Like much else in commercial Dublin, the shipping industry is a tender plant. It is easy to injure it ; it would not be difficult to kill it, or a good part of it. So much of the trade is of the character of through goods that its diversion to other ports would present no serious difficulty. What remains—the purely local business—is associated with manufactories which could, and doubtless would, be transferred if there were persistent interruptions of the free course of trade by arbitrary and capricious intermeddling by irresponsible outsiders. These truths should be borne in mind by the reader, who will find them a valuable aid to the proper understanding of the events which have to be narrated in subsequent chapters.

CHAPTER III

CONDITIONS OF LIFE AND LABOUR IN DUBLIN

Tenement Houses and Social Degradation—Government Housing Inquiry—Depressing Facts—Appalling Character of the Housing Problem—Individual Testimony—Overcrowding and Unemployment closely related Factors—Great Predominance of Untrained Labour—Causes of the Phenomenon—Labour Responsible in part for the Economic Deterioration of Dublin—Trade Exclusiveness—Mr. John Good's Striking Testimony—Low Scale of Wages Current—Physical Deterioration reduces the Value of Labour—Good Qualities of the Dublin Slum-Dwellers—The Street Gamin a Merry Urchin—Wanted: a Training Ship in the Liffey.

IF an Irish Booth were to arise to survey the conditions of life and labour in Dublin, he would be able to produce as deeply fascinating a volume as the monumental work which is the classic authority on the life of the poor in the great Metropolis. Outside London there is no populous centre in the Empire where the problems which present themselves are more perplexing, or where a more poignant interest is excited by the life conditions of a large section of the population. Dublin is suffering from a combination of disadvantages, the most conspicuous of which, on a cursory investigation, is old age. In the central area of the city are districts in which, in a past day, the life of the capital flowed in some grandeur, and lofty dwellings with, in certain cases, considerable architectural pretensions, housed in comfort and luxury the members of the aristocratic and well-to-do professional and mercantile classes who made up the brilliant society of the period. But long since Ichabod was written over the portals of these roomy old residences.   With the decay of the city in social and political influence, the people who occupied them migrated, either to other quarters of the city or to places outside, leaving their old homes to fall into the hands of speculators, who turned them to the most profitable account they could by letting them as tenement dwellings.   This process, once started, speedily impressed upon the erstwhile fashionable localities the stamp of social degradation.   Under the pitiless influence of the low type of civilisation which had found shelter in their midst, they descended lower and lower, until finally their names became bywords as the cradles of the lowest and most wretched type of the city's outcast population. Much the same thing has happened in other cities for similar causes, but elsewhere mitigating conditions have operated to free the situation ultimately of its grosser elements.

The Dublin slum, in fact, is a thing apart in the inferno of social degradation.   Nowhere can there be found concentrated so many of the evils which are associated with the underworld of our modern civilisation.   To say that men and women live like beasts of the field is the merest truth.   In buildings—old, rotten, and permeated with both physical and moral corruption— they crowd in incredible numbers.   At the Government Inquiry into Dublin housing conditions, held in November and December 1913, some astounding facts were brought into public prominence relative to the extent to which human beings are herded together in the Irish capital. Altogether there appears to be in the city 5322 tenement houses, accommodating, if such a word can be used, 25,822 families, or a total population of 87,305.   No fewer than 20,108 families occupy one room each, 4402 of the remainder have only two rooms each.   But this is only a part of the terrible record.   In the official report of the inquiry, the houses are divided into three classes : (a) houses which appear to be structurally sound ;

(b) houses which are so decayed, or so badly constructed, as to be on or past approaching the border-line of being unfit for human habitation; and (c) houses unfit for human habitation and incapable of being rendered fit for human habitation. In the first category are included 1516 tenements occupied by 8295 families and by 27,052 persons. The second dubious class comprises 2288 tenements occupied by 10,696 families and 37,552 persons. In the last section of all are included 1518 tenements occupied by 6831 families and 22,701 persons. The most recent census of the city showed a population of 304,802, so that more than a fourteenth of the entire inhabitants of Dublin are living in dwellings admittedly unfit for human habitation, while about another eighth are housed in circumstances almost equally wretched. Probably we might say, without any over-statement, that the majority of the occupiers of these tenement houses—approximately nearly a third of the population—live under conditions which are injurious to physique and morality.

There is, in the simple citation of the figures given above, abundant evidence of the appalling character of the housing problem as it is presented in Dublin. But it is necessary to examine the testimony of individual witnesses called at the inquiry to realise, in all its horror, the extent of the overcrowding in these buildings, and the circumstances under which the inhabitants of them pass their miserable lives. A Roman Catholic clergyman, the Rev. P. J. Monahan, C.C., who gave evidence, mentioned an instance in which 107 human beings occupied one tenement house, stating that there were only two water-closets in the entire building for both sexes. His figures were challenged later by the corporation officials, who represented that the inmates numbered not 107 but 95, and that there were three and not two water-closets. But, even accepting the corrected figures, the position of the inmates is dreadful enough to contemplate. Mr. John Cooke, honorary treasurer of the

National Society for the Prevention of Cruelty to Children
in Dublin, gave striking testimony derived from his
personal experience, extending over a long period, of the
slums. 'In no city in these islands with which I am
acquainted,' he said, 'have the children such a freedom,
I might say, such possession of the streets as Dublin.
Many thousands of little ones throng the thoroughfares,
under no control, running moral and physical risks. Ill-
clad, ill-fed, ill-taught, ill-disciplined, how can they
become useful citizens, or fathers and mothers of healthy
children, serviceable to state and race ? Numbers never
rise out of slum life ; they rush into matrimony, and
the old process is repeated, five to eleven all told of a
family in a single room, and the only change they can
get is that to a neighbouring court or street, a rise
or fall of a few degrees in their condition, or a short
space in prison for drink or some petty offence. The
woman, left to herself in a single room with her children,
has no chance of cultivating the graces of life. She,
too quickly as a rule, loses any she ever had. In all
the rooms I visited I saw no woman with a needle in
her fingers, while there were plenty of tatters on her own
and children's garments for the use of it and thread.'

Mr. Cooke gave a number of characteristic examples
of tenement interiors. Here is one of his pictures :
'One room, measuring about sixteen feet square, with
a small closet off it ; contains absolutely no furniture.
The family of nine (seven children) sleep on the floor,
on which there was not straw enough for a cat, and no
covering of any kind whatever. The children were poorly
clad ; one was wrapped in a rag of a kind, and his only
other clothing was a very dirty loin cloth. The utensils
were a zinc bucket, can, a few mugs and jam pots for
drinking. 'Rent 2s. 3d. Wages in late weeks 4s. 6d.
Maximum for some time past 12s.' Another of Mr. Cooke's
vignettes was the following : 'A room, measuring fifteen
feet by twelve, occupied by parents and four children ;

a poor bed, table, no seats and no cooking utensils. The floor broken in patches, and has a list. The ceiling is patched, and the walls are dirty, with the paper peeling off. No proper ventilation.] Rent 4s. 1d. per week ; quite extortionate. A similar room on the same landing was equally badly furnished. Six in family, and the same rent.' As a final selection from the witness's depressing list may be cited this brief, but sombre, description : ' In another house is a room twelve feet by fifteen, one window, very bad light and air. It has a small closet. The family consists of a widow and six children. Bed, stretcher, and a few sticks of furniture. Rent 2s. 9d. There are ten families in the house ; two closets.'

It is impossible to read these details without being powerfully impressed with the depths to which the Dublin slum life carries its unfortunate victims.] Yet it must be stated that a number of witnesses expressed the opinion that the conditions were not now so bad as they once were. Mr. Cooke himself quoted an extract from *Saunder's News Letter* for 1774, which stated that there were then 18,000 beggars on the streets of Dublin ; and he supplemented this by citing from another old authority the fact that the death-rate of children in the Foundling Hospital from 1784 to 1796 was 68 per cent. A clerical witness, on a subsequent day, supported the view that things were improving by averring that, whereas in the early days of his acquaintance with the Dublin tenement houses it was a common thing to find a pig basking before the fire and chickens roosting on the bed, such incidents were never experienced in these days. The optimism of these authorities on slum life is refreshing ; but it must be confessed that the particulars given in their own evidence are too conclusive as to the reality of the magnitude of the existing evils to permit of any undue feeling of elation at the degree of improvement that has been registered.

Overcrowding and unemployment are closely related factors in Dublin, as in other great cities. In the Irish capital, however, the two influences act and react upon the other probably to a larger extent than elsewhere, because of the character of the population and the peculiar industrial position of the city. Taking the question of population first, it is noteworthy that, in 1911, as many as 169,736 people were classed by the Commissioners under the heading 'Indefinite and non-productive class.' The industrial class figures next in point of numbers in the returns with 73,175, but, as Mr. Webb shows in a careful analysis of the reports, the figures are misleading, as, by a pedantic system of classification, all persons dealing in various commodities, as well as those working in these directions, are assigned to the industrial ranks. The consequence is that the industrial class is swollen at the expense of the commercial class, and a quite wrong impression is conveyed of the size of the former. But the really important fact which emerges from an examination of the census figures is that no fewer than 45,149 persons belong to the unskilled labour class, or about one-seventh of the total population. The significance of this fact is too obvious to need elaborate demonstration. It is the root factor in the economic situation and must be steadily borne in mind if it is desired to obtain a true estimate of the labour movement, which has to be described at length in later pages.

The causes which have produced this large accumulation of untrained labour in Dublin are partly historic, partly economic, and partly social. The decay of industries, which has been traced in the preceding chapter, by closing the main avenues for skilled employment through which the youth of the city had previously passed to social competence, was a heavy blow, from which the working community has never recovered. The disastrous effect of free trade on the agricultural

D

industry accentuated the evil. In association with the famine the economic revolution drove the country labourers to the towns and abroad, to attempt to find the lucrative employment that was altogether wanting in the country districts. On the top of this movement came the modern craving of the countrymen for the excitements of urban life which has been manifested all the world over. These influences in association have helped to fill the Dublin slums with a body of workers whose only equipment is their muscle, a rapidly deteriorating possession in such an environment. The migration has been particularly pronounced in the last two decades. In these years the population within the old city boundary has increased by no fewer than 20,648. As in the same period there has been a marked growth of the population in the outer ring of suburbs, the attractions of the city have clearly proved of great potency to an exceptionally large class, and that, doubtless, for the most part, of the labouring type.

Labour must take her share, and a pretty full one for the economic deterioration of Dublin. In the past, as we have seen, it was the unreasonable and tyrannical action of the old trade associations that drove out of existence some of the most promising of the city's industries. The spirit which animated the workers' leaders of that period still, to a certain extent, survives in the policy and practice of some of the existing unions, more especially those associated with the building trade. A well-known Dublin merchant remarked to me that it was a mistake to suppose that caste was a privilege of the well-to-do; and he illustrated his point by the striking statement that, though a bricklayer's labourer might rise to the position of Lord Chancellor, he could never become a bricklayer. I recalled that the late Sir Richard Farrant, Lord Rowton's right hand man in the building of the Rowton Houses, had told me much the same thing in connection with an account he was giving of how separate arrangements had to be made for the meals of the bricklayers and their labourers because one would not sit down to dinner with the other. But I was not prepared to find that in Dublin the system was in such complete operation as it certainly is from the facts that have come to my notice.

My authority is a paper read some years ago before a professional society by Mr. John Good, a well-known Dublin citizen, who is the senior partner in one of the largest building firms in the city. Mr. Good, who was dealing with the apprenticeship system, mentioned that in the brick- and stone-laying trade an apprentice must be the son of a member of this particular trade. In some circumstances the trade society might relax the rule and accept a boy whose father did not happen to be a bricklayer, on his paying a £30 fee, half of which went to the man he was bound to and half to the society. The premium, Mr. Good stated, was practically prohibitive, as no father in working life can afford to pay so large a sum as £30 and, at the same time, provide his son with means of livelihood during the period of his apprenticeship. In consequence of this onerous restriction on apprentices, the number of such in the building trade is very small. At the period of which Mr. Good was treating, it was only 3·2 per cent., and, including the improvers, the figure was not raised beyond 4·2 per cent. The actual number that the trade ought to have for healthy development, Mr. Good calculates, is 33·33 per cent., or one to every three bricklayers, instead of one to twenty-four, as in the existing conditions of the trade. In the plastering branch of the building trade the apprentices are entirely in the hands of the tradesmen under the control of the local society, and it is an absolute rule, without exception, that both apprentices and improvers must be sons of plasterers. In the stone-cutting trade the rule with regard to apprentices is as follows : ' That no boy be allowed to be apprenticed

to the stone-cutting unless the son of a stone-cutter,
but that any lodge may apprentice a boy not the son
of a stone-cutter under extreme circumstances, after
getting the sanction of the majority of the members of
the union.' The effect of this restrictive system of
apprenticeship is described in words which, though
penned a good many years before the recent troubles
occurred, have a direct application to them. 'We are
not,' observed Mr. Good, 'training sufficient to fill the
gaps which the hand of time is making in the ranks of
our trades, so tradesmen come from elsewhere to fill
these positions; while hundreds, if not thousands, of
able and unskilled hands are to be found in all quarters
of our land, trying to get an existence on the wretched
wages at which such labour is valued; while hundreds
more are forced to emigrate, men who, if properly trained
in some of our trades, would doubtless have done credit
to themselves and their trade at home—conditions which
one would think would not for an hour be permitted to
exist in any civilised land.' With the views here expressed it is impossible for any intelligent observer not
to agree. Caste is bad in any walk of life, but it is
peculiarly pernicious in artisan circles, where freedom
of the individual to work out his destinies, untrammelled
by restrictive conventions, is as necessary to his full
existence as is breathing without restraint the pure air
of heaven.

With an enormous surplus of absolutely unskilled
labour as the primary factor in the industrial situation,
it is inevitable that the scale of wages in Dublin for a
very large class of the population should be low. How
intense the struggle for existence is in the bottom strata
of the workers is clearly demonstrated in the report of
the Housing Committee. There we find that of the
heads of families occupying tenement houses, 5604 earn
not more than 15s. a week, 9000 earn over 15s. to 20s.,
2585 earn 20s. to 25s., 1627 earn 25s to 30s., and 2384

earn over 30s. Necessarily the figures give only a partial view of the position. Not improbably, in the cases in which returns were not forthcoming, the wages were the lowest. At all events, it is abundantly clear, from the evidence given at the inquiry, that the earnings of many were a negligible quantity. These men were either of the unemployable class or were casual workers, who eked out a miserable existence by hawking, doing odd jobs in the streets, or working intermittently at the wharves or elsewhere. On the whole we may safely accept the general conclusion arrived at by the committee, as a result of their personal investigations, 'that a large number of the labouring classes, van drivers, carters, messengers, and such like, earn wages not in excess of 18s. a week.'

While it is impossible to withhold sympathy from classes so depressed as these slum-dwellers of Dublin are, it cannot be overlooked that the very nature of their mode of living tends to reduce their value in the labour market. One point upon which witness after witness insisted was the physical deterioration of men who find their way into these terrible hovels. Once drawn into this abyss, they speedily lose, not merely their sense of self-respect, but their capacity for sustained exertion. A sort of moral *malaise* overtakes them, which renders them subject to every passing evil influence. They work merely to secure the bare necessaries of existence, and when these are secured they are content to pass their hours in idleness. Recalling the dreary round to which they are doomed by a hard fate, we cannot be censorious of their failings : the best of men might go under in the face of the tremendous strain which life in a Dublin tenement house would put upon his moral fibre. At the same time, the thought of all that is implied in this vicious housing system in the way of demoralisation and decadence of physical powers, should make us chary of playing the rôle of critic to employers who have to utilise this damaged material. Inefficiency carries with it a penalty which cannot be altogether avoided while industry is conducted on commercial lines.}

In writing of the defects of the Dublin slum-dweller, it would be unjust to give the impression that he is a thoroughly bad subject. He is certainly not vicious with the viciousness of the low Londoner. There is no Dublin equivalent of the Paris Apache; it is doubtful whether there are many genuine hooligans. People in the Dublin slums do not stare and gibe at the well-dressed stranger as they would do in the low parts of the East End of London. And they are a kindly, as well as a polite, folk. One Dublin resident declared to the writer that there had never been a case of death from starvation in the Irish capital. Whether the assertion can be substantiated or not, it is undeniable that there is an immense amount of kindly feeling for the misfortunes of others in these drab, dreary streets. How good the poor are to each other was testified to by nearly all the expert witnesses at the recent inquiry. Indeed, it is the slum-dwellers' abiding sense of the virtues of charity which leads to the worst overcrowding in the tenement houses, for a family occupying a room never seems so large that it cannot take in another which has been evicted for non-payment of rent or some other cause. Summing up the qualities of the Dublin labouring class, Mr. G. D. A. Chart, M.A., in a pamphlet embodying a paper read in March 1914 before the Statistical and Social Enquiry Society of Ireland,[1] stated : 'It is deeply religious, as is shown by many indications. It lives, as a rule, a much more moral and respectable life than could be expected considering its surroundings. It exhibits, in a marked degree, the social virtue of kindness, cheerfulness, and courtesy. The inquirers of the Housing and Town Planning Association, though they went into hundreds

[1] *Unskilled Labour in Dublin : Its Housing and Living Conditions.* G. D. A. Chart, M.A., M.R.I.A. Dublin : Sealy, Bryers & Walker.

of dwellings during a great strike and asked a number of very pointed and delicate questions, rarely encountered suspicion or incivility.   Mentally and morally, this class is probably on a higher level than the labouring classes of most cities.   It is on the physical and economic sides that Dublin falls so far behind.'

Perhaps of all the products of Dublin slum life the street gamin is the most interesting.   He is a merry little urchin, who seems to embody in his tiny person all the careless, happy qualities of his race.   With wits prematurely sharpened by early contact with the realities of life, he bears himself with an amusing impudence which nothing appears to disconcert.   As the writer pens these lines a diverting picture arises before him : A stream of fashionably dressed people from Kingstown and the well-to-do districts adjoining is passing through the ticket barrier at Westland Row Station on a bright spring afternoon.   Suddenly, into the midst of them, dart a number of boys of the slum type.   Hatless, shoeless, with a few miserable rags as an apology for clothing, they walk past the ticket collector with an assumption of dignity copied from the better-class passengers.   The leader of the party, a mite of about ten, has in his lips a big cigarette, which he puffs with all the nonchalance of a man about town.   He is an inimitable actor, and plays his part as to the manner born.   It is only when some bystander makes a feint to snatch the cherished ' fag ' that his self-possession breaks down, and he rushes out with his motley following into the street, screaming with laughter as he makes his exit.   A Dublin resident, to whom the incident was described, capped the story with an experience of his own.   On mounting a tram-car one day near College Green, he threw away the stump of a cigar that he had been smoking.   Two boys rushed forward, and the smaller of the two picked it up.   The bigger boy annexed the prize and, putting it to his lips, commenced to

smoke. ' Let's have a syndicate,' said the smaller boy.
' Done,' replied his companion ; ' I'll be managing
director.' ' Where do I come in ? ' inquired the other.
' Oh, you will be the shareholder ; you'll do the spitting,'
remarked the possessor of the stump nonchalantly.
Another story from the same mint relates to two shoe-
blacks in Sackville Street. On the box of one a tall
guardsman, 6 feet 2 inches in his stockings, has planted
his ample foot. Before starting operations the owner of
the box, with a whimsical flourish of the hand towards
the huge boot in front of him, says to his professional
companion, ' Hi, Pat, come and help me ; I've a military
contract.'

It seems a thousand pities that material of this kind
should be allowed to run to waste as it does. A Dublin
gentleman lamented to the writer that there was no
training ship in the Liffey, of the type of those which
are to be found in the Thames and elsewhere, for the
benefit of homeless and friendless lads. The suggestion
is one which appears to be well deserving of attention.
A great Irishman, who is also a famous naval commander,
once publicly expressed a preference for ' scally wags '
as material from which to fashion the best type of handy-
man. It was a mere piece of rhetorical extravagance,
but there is a great truth underlying it. The boy who
has been turned loose into the streets from earliest
infancy is quick and resourceful, and courageous to
boot. He has probably a precocious knowledge of evil,
but his finer qualities are usually intact, to be
brought out by sympathetic treatment combined with
discipline.

The Dublin street boys certainly are of the type who
would shape well in a training ship. A wealthy philanthropist could hardly make better use of his money at
the present juncture than in providing the wherewithal
to place a hulk in the river for the equipment for life of
some of the unfortunate waifs and strays whose forlorn

appearance excites the pity of every visitor to the Irish capital.

When all has been done that can be done to alleviate the social ills of Dublin, there will remain difficulties of a substantial kind to be faced if the area of employment cannot be enlarged. This phase of the subject will have to be touched upon later ; and it is only necessary to say here that the crying need of the city is, not so much more wages as more work. The desideratum can be supplied, but not if capital is harassed and attacked and the foundations of credit are undermined by the propagation of the lawless doctrines of predatory Socialism.

CHAPTER IV

THE RISE OF LARKINISM

The Dublin Slums a Fertile Ground for the Propagation of the Principles
of Revolutionary Industrialism—Mr. James Larkin appears on
the Scene—His Birth and Antecedents—The Belfast and Dublin
Strikes in 1908—Mr. Larkin's Quarrel with the Dockers' Union—
Founding of the Irish Transport Workers' Union—Mr. Larkin
tried and sentenced—He is released by Order of Lord Aberdeen
before the Expiration of his Sentence—Mr. Larkin's Views in
regard to his Prosecution—Growth in Power of the Irish Transport
Workers' Union—Mr. Larkin's Extraordinary Personal Influence—
Distinctively Irish Character of the Larkinite Movement.

IT is a commonplace of sociology that discontent finds its
sturdiest growth amongst people living under conditions
of moral uncleanness and economic instability. Human
nature, being what it is, revolts against the tyranny of
circumstances which condemns it to existence in the
infernos of our modern civilisation. The feeling may
lie dormant for a long time, but it is always there to be
called into activity by demagogic influence. Dublin, as
will have been gathered from the facts given in the
preceding chapters, affords peculiarly fertile ground
for the propagation of the principles of revolutionary
industrialism. With little to gain and nothing to lose,
with stunted understandings wedded to impressionable
natures, the tens of thousands of unfortunates who go
to make up the bulk of the working population of the
Irish capital are easy prey to the glib orator of the street
corner who poses in the familiar rôle of the Friend of
Humanity. They are caught up readily by his windy

appeals and carried away by his specious arguments, while their fancies are tickled by the examples of capitalist cruelty and greed which are never wanting to paint the moral and adorn his tale. To most of the slum denizens the intrusion into their lives of a labour movement of the more strenuous kind—with its marchings and its counter-marchings, its shouting and cheering, and its periodic thrills—is a welcome change from the drab monotony of ordinary existence in which the normal excitement is provided by a wedding or a funeral or a drunken brawl on Saturday night. Therefore, when the great wave of industrial unrest swept over Great Britain in the period following the advent of the Liberal Government to power in 1906, it was inevitable that, sooner or later, Dublin should be drawn into the vortex. The people simply needed a leader. The occasion speedily made one of a remarkable kind in the person of Mr. James— or as he prefers to be called—Jim Larkin.

Who is Mr. Larkin? Many people are constrained to ask much in the spirit that prompted the late Lord Coleridge's query about a well-known burlesque actress. With a more genuine desire for information we may repeat the inquiry. Who is he? and whence does he come? It is not easy to give an answer off-hand—a full answer, at all events. One of his numerous Trade Unionist critics denies to him the right to call himself an Irishman. He describes him as 'a foreign adventurer from the slum recesses of probably some clog-wearing town,' and he asserts that his English origin is 'unerringly indicated by his frequent misuse of the aspirate.' Mr. Larkin himself has always denied the soft impeachment of a Saxon origin. He claims to be an Irishman bred and born, and there is no sound reason to doubt the accuracy of his statement. That, however, his early life was largely spent out of Ireland is very probable. In one of his public utterances he made reference to a voyage he once made to South America; and from his familiarity with shipping it may be assumed that he had a connection of a more or less permanent kind with the shipping industry ; for some years, at all events, he was in the employ of a large Liverpool shipping firm. According to a statement made by his counsel in the criminal proceedings against him, to which reference will shortly be made, he held a good position in this undertaking, and severed it in or about 1908 by going out on strike with other employees of the firm, ' thus,' his counsel said, ' making a sacrifice for the opinions he held.'

Mr. Larkin, after shaking the dust of the shipowners' office from his feet, became directly connected with the labour movement. He first came into public view in 1907 or thereabouts, when he was acting in the capacity of organiser at Liverpool and Glasgow, and elsewhere, to the National Union of Dock Labourers. Part of his duties appears to have been to keep an eye on the Irish ports in order to extend the ramifications of the union. He does not seem to have been a brilliant success, judged at all events from the standpoint of his colleagues. Mr. James Sexton, who was the general secretary of the Dockers' Union at the time, in a letter dated July 19, 1909, to the Irish Trades Congress, asserted that there was no port he (Mr. Larkin) had been in prior to the previous May, ' which would not bear testimony to his incapacity to conduct matters on a business footing.' Further on in this communication Mr. Sexton complained bitterly of the action of Mr. Larkin and a colleague in calling men out on strike at Newry and Dundalk and every port they could influence, without the slightest consultation with the head quarters in Liverpool, the only place where the money of the union existed to any extent. ' The inference,' he went on, ' is that those who pay the piper have, in fact, no right to call part of the tune, never mind the whole of it ; and that Tom, Dick, or Harry in Ireland may call a strike on his own and ask us to supply the money.'

These bitter comments were passed in connection with the conduct of the strike which devastated Belfast trade in 1908. Engineered by Mr. Larkin and a number of other fighting spirits, the movement ran on for weeks, and did an immense amount of mischief. The affair cost the workers' organisations £8000, of which £5000 came out of the coffers of the Dockers' Union. The disbursement of these funds was at first entrusted to the hands of a committee, but, under the masterful influence of Mr. Larkin, all power was speedily vested in himself and those whom he chose to honour with his favour. Money was spent so lavishly that Mr. Sexton crossed to Belfast from Liverpool and took over charge of the organisation. Subsequently Mr. Larkin's conduct was made the subject of complaint at the Dockers' Congress, and he narrowly escaped censure for his flagrant disobedience of the orders of the executive. The disfavour of the great, the wise, and the eminent of the dockers' organisation, however, had little effect on him ; we soon hear of him again at variance with the superior power in the union. On this occasion Dublin was the scene of the strife. Largely through Mr. Larkin's instrumentality a strike broke out amongst the shipping and riverside interests in the earlier half of 1908, and continued a violent course until a settlement was finally reached on July 23, in circumstances to be related in a subsequent portion of the narrative. Mr. Larkin played here the same irresponsible, reckless part that had distinguished him in the northern capital. He brought the men out on his own initiative, and it was only through the wise discretion of Mr. Sexton in assenting to terms of peace that the men's cause was saved from disaster. This fresh defiance of authority, as represented by the body which had the power of the purse in Liverpool, brought matters to a crisis. An edict, in the form of a resolution, was issued by the Dockers' Executive imperatively prohibiting any organiser from entering into any dispute 'which involved, or was likely to involve, the whole of the union funds.' Mr. Larkin snapped his fingers at the committee. He went to Cork, fished in troubled waters there, with the result that the union funds became very decidedly implicated in the dispute that inevitably arose.[1] The Dockers' Executive, incensed at the defiance, gave instructions to the secretary to suspend him in the event of further recalcitrance. Mr. Larkin showed the same contempt for this practical ultimatum that he had done for the earlier efforts of the executive to control him. In consequence he was, on December 7, 1908, suspended from office, and further financial support from the union was withheld from him. A virtual state of war now arose between the Dockers' Union and their masterful servant. When in the early days of 1909 Mr. Sexton went over to Belfast to assume control of the union's affairs, his authority was openly flouted, and a meeting he attempted to hold was broken up by a Larkinite faction who had obtained admission to it. After this a sub-committee of the Dockers' Union met and ratified the decree of suspension. The date of that meeting, January 20, 1909, may be said to mark the final severance of Mr. Larkin's connection with the Dockers' Union.

Months before this crisis was reached in the affairs of the Dockers' Union, Mr. Larkin had been laying his plans for the establishment of a distinctively Irish organisation. It was probably the knowledge of this fact that spurred the executive of that body on to the attempt to bring their irresponsible representative under effective control. They were quite willing, as Mr. Sexton made clear in Belfast at the time of Mr. Larkin's dismissal, that he should form an Irish branch of the organisation ; but they did not see the force of permitting their funds and their machinery to be used to bring into life a body

[1] A settlement was reached on December 8, 1908, as the result of a conference between the parties to the dispute.

which would have an independent existence and be directly under the thumb of their whilom servant. They, in fact, regarded his conduct as treacherous ; and it was not long before they gave striking proof of their feeling that the union had been badly treated by instituting criminal proceedings against Mr Larkin for the misappropriation of their funds.

The trial came on at Dublin in June 1910, and, after an exhaustive investigation, Mr. Larkin was found guilty and sentenced to twelve months' imprisonment. The presiding judge, Mr. Justice Boyd, in passing sentence said : ' You have been found guilty by the jury on evidence which has been fully considered. I don't mean to pass a heavy sentence, but you forgot your duty to the union which employed you, and you did acts which you should not have done. I think it was a very serious matter for the poor men, who considered that they joined a society of a recognised high standard both for money and otherwise, to conduct their affairs properly. I think it a very serious matter that you should have misapplied these monies to matters that you were personally concerned in rather than in the union which employed you.' Subsequently a motion for a new trial was made in the King's Bench on Mr. Larkin's behalf, but the application was refused after a three days' hearing of the arguments against and for the conviction. Mr. Justice Gibson, who pronounced the decision of the Court, emphasised the serious character of the offence which had been proved against Mr. Larkin. ' The charge made by the Crown,' he said, ' was that the defendant fraudulently cheated the dock labourers of their subscriptions. Every penny which was collected from the poor dockers in Cork was trust funds, and it would be a shockingly dishonest thing to collect that money as if it was for the National Union, and then send it on to another body. One circumstance was that no records or books had been kept. The Crown were entitled to say that Larkin was engaged in a criminal fraud. The money had been traced to Larkin's pocket, and it lay upon him to account for it. No doubt a balance sheet had been produced ; but what was it prepared from, when there were no books or vouchers ? Was that balance sheet a sham to conceal from these humble men in Cork that their money had been misappropriated ? The defendant had not made out a case to show that the conviction ought not to stand.'

The legal force of the conviction was thus doubly established ; but there were undoubtedly circumstances in the case which removed it from the ordinary run of frauds perpetrated for sordid ends. Many who are by no means sympathisers with Mr. Larkin or his methods consider that he was the victim of circumstances, some of which reflected little credit upon his discretion or even his scrupulousness, but which did not partake of the character of direct moral culpability. Lord Aberdeen, the Viceroy, apparently was of this view, for, when Mr. Larkin had served a little more than three months of his sentence, he caused him to be released. Mr. Larkin himself has always strenuously protested that he was more sinned against than sinning. The most recent, and perhaps most emphatic, disclaimer of guilty conduct was made on April 21, 1914, at what is popularly known in Dublin as the Pembroke Election Inquiry, when he was called to give evidence as to a compact said to exist between the Nationalists and the Larkinites relative to the support of candidates for election to the district council of Pembroke, an administrative area outside the limits of the city of Dublin. Mr. Larkin was cross-examined by the counsel (Mr. Sergeant McSweeney) who supported the petition, as to whether he had not taken money from ' Sexton's organisation ' and devoted it to his own society. His reply was a forcible denial. ' He had,' he said, ' been found guilty by a jury of employers and sentenced to twelve months' imprisonment, but was released after three months' imprisonment as he was

innocent.' 'I saw no declaration from the Lord Lieutenant that you were innocent,' remarked the counsel.
' If the Lord Lieutenant let me out before my time, and
I was not innocent, he should be put in gaol himself,'
retorted the witness. At another point in the examination Mr. Larkin said : ' I am secretary at the present
time of the society in Cork whom I have supposed to
have robbed.'

However the conviction of Mr. Larkin in 1910 may
be viewed from the standpoint of financial purity and
legal right, it is undeniable that its ultimate effect was,
if anything, to enhance his prestige with the class to
whom he looked for support in his new undertaking.
The circumstances of his release, the direct intervention
of the Viceroy, and the almost deferential way in which
his exit from Mountjoy Prison was arranged—circumstances which lost nothing in the telling—conferred upon
him the halo of the legal martyr, a character which in
Ireland never stands in need of popular sympathy.
Stepping quickly into the forum of the street, he drew
to his banner all the disaffected elements which were
lying in wait in the city for his call. The Irish Transport
Workers' Union, from a mere shadowy outline, became
before long a closely knit organisation, embracing
thousands of workers who had hitherto been either outside trade-union influences or only intermittently associated with labour societies. For a time the old trade
unions, in whose ranks were the ' aristocrats of labour,'
looked askance at this upstart body, with its leader
from the outside world. They disliked the propaganda
and they distrusted the man ; and, moreover, the heads
of the organisations had no desire to share their throne
with one so forceful as Mr. Larkin had already proved
himself to be. But before very long they found the
pressure upon them from Liberty Hall, the headquarters
of the Irish Transport Workers' Union, irresistible, and
the end of it was that the autocrat of the quays had the

Dublin Trade Council in the hollow of his hand.   There
are many remarkable things about this Dublin labour
movement, but none more extraordinary than the
complete way in which Mr. Larkin ultimately dominated
the older forces of Trade Unionism in the city, several of
which, as we have seen, are built upon lines of such rigid
exclusiveness that no one born out of the purple can
enter the charmed circle of workers in a particular trade.

From the very outset Mr. Larkin made the Irish
character of the union a leading, it may be said, *the*
leading principle of the organisation.   He never missed
an opportunity of enforcing the view that Ireland must
have her own labour movement, free from outside domination, and working on lines marked out only by her
own interests.   In one of the earliest issues of his paper,
the *Irish Worker*, he wrote : ' Whilst I agree that the
formation of the English Labour Party was, and is, the
best thing the English workers have ever done, so, too,
the formation of an Irish Labour Party would be the
best day's work ever attempted by the Irish workers.
The world cannot afford to allow the Irish nation to be
obliterated.   Internationalism   means   Internationalism
and not *one* Nationalism.   We, of the Irish workers,
are out to claim the earth for the world's workers, and
our portion as Irishmen is Ireland.   So hands off, all
predatory persons, no matter under what name or
disguise.   We are determined to weld together the
common people of the North, the South, the East, and
the West.'

The welding together of the common people referred
to in the last sentence constitutes another of the characteristic aims of the Larkinite movement.   This was a
distinctly new departure from the sectional lines on
which Trade Unionism in the British Isles had hitherto
moved.   Nowhere outside Dublin probably could a
project of the kind have had much chance of success,
and, even in the Irish capital, despite the immense

preponderance of unskilled workers, the task was a stupendous one, because of the difficulty of organising great bodies of people of diverse occupations and aspirations. Mr. Larkin, however, relied for his cementing material upon the common tie of poverty which bound the bulk of them together in a union of misfortune. His shrewd calculation of what could be accomplished by an appeal to this brotherhood of woe, couched in the appropriate socialistic language, was not belied. The wild talk of capitalistic tyranny and greed, which was poured out at scores of meetings, had its effect on the listening crowds. They dropped submissively into the ranks of the union, and, under the apt tuition of their master, became enthusiasts for the cause of social and economic redemption through the agency of the peculiar, but powerful, weapons which in due course were put in their hands.

CHAPTER V

The *Irish Worker*—Its Iniquitous Character—Patriotism called in Aid of the Industrial Movement—Elegant Extracts—Incitement to Murder—Malignant Attacks on the Police and on Employers—Defence of the Policy of the *Irish Worker*—Larkinite Municipal Campaign—Scurrilous Attacks on Political Opponents.

EVERY machine must have its driving force. Mr. Larkin's organisation found the indispensable agency in a Press engine of malignant power in the shape of a weekly newspaper called the *Irish Worker*. There was a time in England when, owing to the ferocity of controversial methods, a standing toast at public dinners was 'The Press without its licentiousness.' Even in that none too fastidious day probably this paper would have been voted outrageous. Its earliest issues were an extraordinary farrago of disloyalty, scurrility, and mendacity with an underlying note of intimidation. That some of the matter, containing direct incitements to violence, should have passed without official notice is one of the amazing facts of a remarkable episode in recent history. For saying—not printing—something far less mischievous some years ago in Trafalgar Square, a man was sent to a long term of imprisonment. The issues of this *Irish Worker* cannot be too carefully studied by anyone who would obtain a true perception of what the Larkinite labour movement is, and by what means it is kept alive.

At the outset it served Mr. Larkin's purpose to pose as a patriot of a specially robust brand. He was clever enough to see that no man who did not play to the political gallery had, as he himself would put it in his exuberant moments of oratory, a dog's chance. Hence we find him taking as the motto of his journalistic venture James Fintan Lalor's declaration—' The principle I state and mean to stand upon is : That the entire ownership of Ireland, moral and material, up to the sun and down to the centre, is vested of right in the people of Ireland.' Hence, also, it is that the earlier issues teemed with emotional appeals to patriotism such as are an important part of the stock-in-trade of the popular orator in Ireland. One characteristic effusion, a poem in the second issue, entitled ' Youth of Ireland,' struck the note which, with an indifferent degree of harmony, was sounded through many subsequent pages of the paper. The opening stanzas were :

> Youth of Ireland ! Youth of Ireland,
>   On your onward march to-day,
> For the freedom of your Sireland
>   Homage to the Old Guard pay ;
> To the men who marched before you
>   Over danger's deadly trail,
> They who struggled to restore you
>   To the freedom of the Gael.
>
> With their father's faith unshaken,
>   Lisp'd beside their mother's knee,
> Went they forth men to awaken,
>   And their country to set free ;
> Tho' the hopes their hearts were rearing
>   Led them to the rebel's doom,
> Tho' the tyrants' bands were bearing
>   Heroes to their living tomb.

In the concluding verse is the inevitable appeal to

those of the present to be worthy of the memories of the past :

> Then forget not, youth of Ireland,
>   That you yet may have to do,
> For the children of your Sireland,
>   As these brave men done for you ;
> Then like them be brave, be steady,
>   And for Ireland guard the way,
> And when God's right hand is ready,
>   Be you heroes in the fray.

This is harmless enough, and its only significance is that it was part of the propaganda which was avowedly revolutionary in its aims. It was probably thought that a mere dressing up of the social revolution would not suit the Irish workers' palates, and that something more racy of the soil was required to bring them into the fold. However that may be, all the early issues had a vivid patriotic colouring. But the blatant tones of the Nationalist harmonies were skilfully blended with dashes of the tints more useful for the organiser's purposes. For example, in No. 4 appeared an article of Lalor's in which figured his well-known declaration that on a wider field with stronger positions and greater resources than were afforded by ' the paltry question of Repeal ' ' must we close for our final struggle with England, or sink and surrender.' Accompanying this production was an exhortation to the *Irish Worker's* readers to act up to the principles preached by Lalor. ' Are you common people, you of the working classes, going to turn recreants ? ' asked the editor. ' Are you going to join the Amalgamated Union of loyal addressers, sycophantic Lord Mayors,[1] jelly-fish Councillors (Urban and Rural), scab labour employers like ——, J.P. ? If so, go home. Take down from your walls of the dwellings you exist in the pictures and photographs and all that recalls the

---

[1] A reference to the King's visit and the attendant functions in which the Lord Mayor took part.

men, the heroes and martyrs, men who despised all tinsel,
show, place, or profit, thought only of truth, honesty,
and loyalty to the land that bore them.' In another
part of the same number Mr. Larkin made it perfectly
clear that the political propaganda held a distinctly
subordinate place in his crusade. In the course of a
virulent attack on a foreman pavior employed by the
corporation, who had excited animosity by taking a
contract for paving work of a class which had previously
been in other hands, he wrote : ' If the granting of
Home Rule, and the opening of our own Parliament means
that the workers in this country are to be subject to the
tyranny of creatures like this fellow ——, with no chance
of redress, better far to exist under a Star Chamber of
Charles I, or the despotism of Cromwell.'

The markedly industrial character of the aims of the
organisation was emphasised by numerous contributions
describing the worker's hard lot. One of the earliest
published articles was a composition in which Mr. Larkin,
doubtless from his own experiences, painted a lurid
picture of the lot of the stoker. ' Think of him, one of
God's creatures, down below, with brains half burned
out of him ; with the open furnace before him, the eyes
bloodshot with the heat, the light of the flames dancing
around him, and a hard case engineer cursing him and
shouting to the already half crazy creature—" shake her
up." There is a saying " Hell has no terrors for a woman
scorned." What terrors, then, has hell for a creature
with the breath scorched out of him—the soul burned
up within him ? ' Contrasted with some of the men in
the stokehold—' white men,' the writer assures us—are
' magnates in the shipping world—men with an income
of £5000 a month, moral lepers, men whose very breath
breathed death.' These men, the article went on to say,
were the class who directed the Shipping Federation.
' A leprous crew,' wrote the editor in a final outburst.
' The earth would be well rid of them ; and they have

not a soul to be saved, and they have so managed to control the law that their bodies are to be saved from kicking yet a little while longer.' The menace in these concluding sentences is palpable.

In a different category to this scream of hate stands a poem which appeared in another column of the same issue under the title of ' The Winch, or the Dockers' Orchestra.' There is a grim humour in the treatment of the subject, and a swing of the rugged verses which compel attention. Here are some of the stanzas :

> It's not the pipe of the organ clear
> The engines play to an engineer ;
> It's not the carol of song birds gay
> Her cordage sings at the break of day,
> When a clipper's course is fairly laid
> Along the track of the roarin' trade :
> But just a grunt and a snaky hiss
> Of steam pipes leaking, an oily kiss ;
> A rusty rattle of iron gear,
> Or a new hydraulic lifting clear ;
> A grip, a strain or a patent clinch—
> And that's the song of the workin' winch.
>
> Up with the hardware, down with the bales,
> Under the gunwhale, over the rails.
> Tally clerk, tally clerk, where have y' been ?
> ' Jambing my thumb in the old machine.'
> Then tie it up with a bit of string,
> An' lower away like anything.
> *Now,* what's the matter down below ?
> Why are the stevedores trembling so ?
> Only the brains of a workin' man
> Bashed like a blessed old salmon can.
> Cover his face from the light of day,
> Send for a stretcher and heave away.

Geniality, even of the peculiar type disclosed in these lines, is not often permitted to have rein in the *Irish Worker's* pages. The commoner form is a brutal direct-

ness of statement without any softening feature.   Take
the fierce denunciation of a ' scab ' (a free labourer) in
No. 3 : ' A scab is to his trade what a traitor is to his
country.   He cares only for himself, but he sees not
beyond the extent of the day, and for a monetary and
worthless approbation would betray friends, family, and
country.   In short, he is a traitor on a small scale—he
just sells his fellow and is himself afterwards sold in his
turn by the master, until at last he is despised by both
and deserted by all—he is the enemy to himself, to the
present age, and to posterity, and deserves to be execrated
by all.'   Then are given verses, of which the following
is a specimen :

> Who shuns the face of the open day,
> Who wanders out in the gloomy grey,
> Who gets his price and sneaks away ?—
> The Scab.

An even more striking example of the *Irish Worker's*
characteristic mood is furnished in an article published
in No. 13 (August 19, 1911).   The writer, who had been
fired with enthusiasm by the vast industrial upheaval
that was at that time proceeding in England, wrote in
triumphant terms of the helplessness of capital in the
face of the emergency.   ' The people are starving ;
trains are not running ; boats are lying idle ; trams are
stopped ;   there is talk of a famine.   Why don't the
capitalists step in and save them ?   Why don't they
make the ships sail, the trains travel, the mill wheels
turn ?   Because there is a strike of workers, and capital
is helpless while the strike lasts.'   Further on in the
article the writer seemed to think that capital, after all,
might not be as helpless as he had pictured.   There
were the ' scabs '—otherwise the free labourers—to be
reckoned with.   He made it clear what he would do
with them.   ' They tell us,' he wrote, ' it is necessary
to call out the military to protect the lives of a few

miserable scabs. They are afraid the scabs would be killed. A scab is a traitor to his class, a deserter who goes over to the enemy in time of war to fight against his own people. When the capitalists go to war it is for the sake of robbery, as instance the case of the Boers. These men had right on their side—they were defending their country from invasion and robbery. England was in the wrong, yet, if a man deserted from the British Army to fight for the Boers and was afterwards captured, he would be shot. When a man deserts from our ranks in time of war (for a strike is war between capital and labour) he, on the same principle, forfeits his life to us. If England is justified in shooting those who desert to the enemy, we also are justified in killing a scab. If it is wrong to take a scab's life, it is right for British soldiers to desert to the enemy in war time. You can't have it both ways.' Mr. Larkin afterwards disclaimed the authorship of the atrocious article, and even personal knowledge of it before it was printed. But the sentiments expressed so completely accord with the general policy of the paper that his repudiation carries little weight. More especially is this so because he permitted the writer of the article to publish an explanation of his original statement, which was to all intents and purposes a repetition of the offence. ' We have never called on any man to shoot another,' he wrote in No. 21 (October 7, 1911). ' If we thought it would be a good thing to shoot scabs, we would not appeal to others to do it for us, we would do it ourselves. But it is unnecessary to shoot a scab in the interest of the working class, neither is it necessary to shoot down the workers for fear some poor soulless scab would get a black eye.' In another part of the article the writer says : ' We will, if necessary, meet violence with violence in self-defence. The working class is in revolt, and you will not ever be able to regain such a grip on their souls and bodies as you formerly held.'

Next to the free labourer the police had the chief

place in the venomous attentions of the *Irish Worker*. At an early period the members of the Irish Transport Workers' Union came into violent contact with the representatives of the law, and they bitterly resented the fact. ' What a skulking bully he looks as he lounges against the street corners of our city—how important he seems when the inspector appears in sight ! ' wrote the editor (No. 10, July 29, 1911). ' What a gigantic column of ignorance to be placed over the people of our Metropolis to administer law and order as it is known under the so-called stainless flag of British justice ! We are certainly a tame crowd in this ancient city of Dublin to remain so long under the heel of this most detestable creature. The question is, are we going to put up with it much longer ? Is the murmur recently raised against this savage breed of Cossacks going to develop into a mighty roar ? ' In the next issue of the paper the attack was made more personal. Under the heading ' Bullies Exposed—Behind the Scenes' appeared a letter from a correspondent who did not even adopt a pseudonym, bringing charges of a most offensive kind against individual policemen whose names and official numbers were given. Of one, who was described as ' lady killer ' and ' a bright light in the Plymouth Brethren crowd which meet in Merrion Hall,' it was said that readers of the *Irish Worker* would scarcely believe that he ' would stealthily creep into a police cell and wantonly kick an innocent man black and blue.' The editor appends to the precious contribution a note in which he coolly remarked, ' The writer of the above knows more about the private affairs of the police than we do. We are aware that hymn-singing covers a multitude of sins, but we thought that the last of the Plymouth Brethren had gone to heaven long ago.' Of course, from the point of view of the *Irish Worker*, the truth of the story was a mere detail. It was sufficient that it administered a series of poisoned pin-pricks.

The Dublin police are well able to take care of themselves, as the Larkinites have had only too painful reason to know on various occasions when they have come into collision with them. But the same cannot be said of many who were singled out for the invidious attentions of the *Irish Worker*. Employers, of course, chiefly suffered. They were fair game for attack, and there was an obvious trading on the fact that they could not retaliate without loss of dignity, and possibly also loss of trade, by entering into a public discussion on the details of the working of their business. The charges made were usually anonymous. In one issue nearly a column of contributions of this character appeared with the significant intimation : ' We do not hold ourselves responsible for all the statements made by correspondents.' As one of the letters stated that it would be ' decenter ' for the manager of a certain enterprise to put his hands into the girl employees' pockets and ' take out what they were after earning, instead of swindling them in such a bare-faced way,' we can understand the editorial reluctance to vouch for the truth of the horrible examples of capitalistic tyranny that his correspondents laid bare. But what an iniquitous system is this which gives currency to any wild story that the fancy or the malice of an anonymous contributor may concoct ! That the charges made were often without the least foundation is clear from the *Irish Worker's* own columns. For example, a correspondent brought against a certain laundry a series of accusations of oppressive conduct in dealings with employees. The manager of the concern in this instance took the trouble to show by indubitable evidence that the anonymous statements were either false or were gross misrepresentations. The editor published the letter with a note in which he said that he was glad to see that things were not so bad as he was led to believe.

Apparently it was thought, even in the *Irish Worker's*

editorial sanctum, that the strong meat supplied required
a lot of swallowing. At any rate something like a justification was offered (No. 10, July 29, 1911) for the matter
appearing in the paper. Briefly the apologia was an
appeal *ad misericordiam*. It was urged that the pillory
which the paper set up was necessary to bring home
the iniquity of the sweating employer. He might be
known as ' an exemplary family man, as a weekly com-
municant, as a benefactor of the Church, and as a sub-
scriber to charity.' But there was another side of the
picture. ' This self-same man,' said the writer, ' was
often known by his employees as a heartless tyrant and
as a sweater.' ' They fear to ask such a man for an
extra shilling a week to buy a little more food for a
half-starved family. Men are slaving ten and twelve
hours per day for a weekly wage of nine, ten, and twelve
shillings in this very city. They often enough have a wife
and a family, but God alone knows how they exist.' The
facts may be, and probably are, as stated, but they are
no excuse for the indiscriminate system of slander which
the paper encouraged by opening its columns to every
discontented member of the community who could put
his possibly malicious, and certainly exaggerated, complaints into writing. Though conducted with the best
intentions, journalism of this type inevitably breeds
rottenness. Mr. Larkin has good cause to know this,
for by an act of historic justice he is to-day being attacked
with the very same weapons that he brought into use
in Dublin. If anything, the pupil has advanced beyond
his instructor, for the *Irish Toiler*—the rival and antagonist organ—is a monument of scurrility and vituperation. Unhappily for Mr. Larkin, he is the victim of
the vitriolic stuff, and not the base capitalist.

An important plank in the Irish Transport Workers'
platform is purity of administration. Dublin, Mr. Larkin
asserts, is an Augean stable, and he holds that it is the
duty of the worker to cleanse it as a necessary and

indispensable preliminary to the enjoyment of a decent life. From what can be gathered from a study of official documents, to say nothing of enlightenment vouchsafed in the intimacy of private conversation, there is ample scope for this crusade. As the question will call for somewhat lengthened notice later, there is no necessity to go into it further here. Suffice it now to draw attention to the methods by which the Larkinite municipal campaign was in the first instance conducted, for they are highly characteristic of the moral intimidation upon which Mr. Larkin built his organisation.

In January 1912 seven labour candidates, including Mr. Larkin himself, were put forward for the then existing vacancies in the corporation. In No. 35 of the *Irish Worker*, issued on January 12, was published an article recommending the candidates to public notice. One of the most vital and momentous questions for the future of this race and the betterment of their common country, the editor said, was whether they were to have national and civic purity, or ' allow the present corrupt and inefficient creatures to use the administrative bodies of this and other towns for their own base purposes.' The article went on to show how a certain councillor guarded civic property—a sacred trust—by securing the appointment of his daughter, a girl of fourteen, to a position as teacher of typewriting at the Technical Schools at a salary of £40 a year, and by obtaining for her, after she had been less than three months in her office, a rise of salary. Then there was the case of his henchman, ' The notorious —— libertine and one of the most foul-mouthed blackguards, whose every word is an oath, whose breath emits blasphemy, and who, if the public knew a tithe of his guilt, could be hounded out of public life—aye, and private life, too. This beast, this stain on the earth's surface, actually appealed to the Dublin workers to return him on the grounds that, if rejected, they would not get Home Rule for Ireland. The name of ——

would bring the blush of shame to any man's face, never mind an Irishman's face.' There was a good deal more in this strain leading up to detailed descriptions of candidates and of their opponents, chiefly the latter. One of the anti-Larkinite workers was described as a ' pimp ' and ' lying slave driver—a thing, not a man.' A second as ' a lickspittle, time-server, place-hunter, and official hangman (sheriff) ' ; and a description was given of one who ' had to be carried home dead drunk ' after a certain meeting. The success of five of the labour candidates at the polls did not soften the asperities of controversy. A defeated candidate was consoled with the reflection that he was ' flouted by a pack of unhung scoundrels.' The battle, however, was undoubtedly to the strong—in votes and language.

CHAPTER VI

A MODEL FACTORY

Attack on Jacob's Biscuit Factory—Description of the Establishment —Contented Workers—The Factory's Roof Garden—Catering for the Workers—Arrangements for the Physical Welfare of Employees—A Disgraceful Campaign of Calumny.

As the Larkinite movement developed, it manifested an unmistakable tendency to syndicalistic methods. The most conspicuous indication of the influence of the subversive principles of the continental labour anarchists was shown in the dead-set made against certain employers whose reputation for dealing fairly with their employees was high. This was in accordance with the theory of Syndicalism that the good employer is the worst enemy of labour, because under him the working classes are apt to be contented and to decline to assist in securing that revolutionary change in economic conditions which, according to the extremists, is imperatively needed in the interests of the masses. Almost the first establishment to be put in the *Irish Worker's* pillory was Jacob's Biscuit Factory, the history of which has been sketched in an early chapter. The attack on this was conducted with relentless vigour and a malignity which never failed in its purpose to represent the firm in the darkest colours. The partners were held up to obloquy as oppressors and extortioners, who ground the faces of the poor and posed before the public as philanthropists. How false—how grotesquely false is the picture I found in the course of a tour I made of the factory during my visit to Dublin !

As the subject is one of great importance, I cannot do better than set out briefly my impressions.

Jacob's Factory is a tall building of several stories rearing its lofty head from a maze of streets in one of the oldest parts of Dublin. From top to basement it is a hive of industry. In its numerous well-ordered departments the various processes incidental to the business are carried on under conditions of scrupulous cleanliness. An appetising odour, diffused from the ovens through which are passing in rapid succession trays of the familiar biscuits, greets you as you enter the factory, and it accompanies you to the last stage as a fragrant reminder of the attractiveness and wholesomeness of an industry which gives steady employment to upwards of three thousand of Dublin's workers of both sexes. It is impossible not to be impressed with the cheerful atmosphere that everywhere prevails. Not a single sour, discontented face is anywhere to be seen : all are giving their services with that alert activity that is the best testimony to a willing disposition. I was particularly struck with the girls who ranged from the quite small damsel of perhaps fourteen summers to the fully-developed woman. A healthier, more attractive body of factory workers I have never seen. In their spotless white overalls, which set off their usually abundant hair—that ' woman's pride '— they gave, without exception, the pleasantest impression that I had in Ireland. Some of them had really beautiful faces of the true Irish type—black hair, grey eyes, and dark regular features delicately suffused with the glow of a healthy colour. Others there were of a different Celtic stock, whose masses of golden hair were associated with well-posed heads, bright homely faces, and substantial figures. ' And what do you earn a week ? ' asked my cicerone of one of the girls of the latter class as we passed. She paused at her task of soldering biscuit tins, and, looking up with a bright smile on her charming face, said shyly, ' Sixteen shillings.' ' And do you like

F

your work ? ' was asked. ' Very much, thank you,'
came the answer as she turned to resume her duties.
Similar inquiries put to other workers, selected at random
as we traversed the various departments, elicited much
the same replies. The wages varied, but there was a
never-failing assurance that the labourer was happy in
her toil—an assurance which carried conviction as to
its sincerity.

We climbed to the top of the building and found silent
evidence, more convincing than words, of the thoughtful
care of the firm for the well-being of its employees. The
whole of the flat roof of the great building had been
covered with shingle and converted into a ' lung ' for
this great working hive. Here the girls come during the
dinner hour, play games, read or otherwise recreate
themselves in the spare time left after their midday meal.
Perched high above the houses this roof garden has the
benefit of all the winds that blow. The girl, if she be of
an æsthetic turn of mind, may watch the changing lights
on the Wicklow Hills, note the effect of the golden
western sunlight on the dancing waters of the harbour,
or look into the brooding city and admire the picturesque
effect of the numerous church spires and monuments
which tower above the sea of bricks and mortar.
Probably very few of them do this, but that they make
the most joyous use of this playground is evident to those
who are in the vicinity during the dinner hour and hear
the merry laughter that floats down from the elevation.

Immediately below the roof garden is the great dining-
hall of the factory—a fine, well-ventilated and well-lighted
chamber with seats and tables placed in serried array from
end to end. In this apartment hot dinners are served,
consisting of a plate of meat and two vegetables for
twopence or threepence, according to the quantity. Other
prices are proportionately low. Thus, a cup of tea
costs a halfpenny, and a cup of cocoa a farthing. The
whole affair is worked by the firm on the principle of

giving the utmost possible for the money without making an actual loss. The value of the convenience to the worker need not be dilated upon. I can well recall here the harrowing stories once told me by the rector of a great slum parish in London of girls from factories who were driven to the streets in the dinner hour, and who, without a decent home to go to, turned into the public house to have a glass of alcohol, which was, as they put it, ' both food and drink.' Messrs. Jacob's critics might do worse than take a turn in some of the factory districts in England and see what is done there in respect of the creature comfort of the workers. If they did so they would, I think, hide their heads for very shame at the treatment they have meted out to this high-minded firm. But the cheap restaurant and playground are only a part of the arrangements for the care of the staff.

Not far from the dining-hall is a department exclusively devoted to the physical welfare of employees. In one room a medical man attends each day to give gratuitous advice to all who care to consult him; and in another room a dentist attends three mornings in the week, and extractions and fillings are done free of charge. In adjoining departments the lady welfare secretary, who is a qualified nurse, with the help of two assistants, looks after the health and well-being of the girls, and they can consult her at any time during working hours.

All injuries, no matter how trivial, have to be reported at once, as when immediate treatment is given they rarely become serious. At the time of our visit a lad with a swollen hand was under treatment. It was a pleasure to witness the deft movements of the nurse as she bathed the injured member and carefully adjusted the bandages afterwards. Again, I could not help drawing a contrast— this time between the youth and the boys I had seen in the streets with wounded or diseased feet and hands bound up with dirty rags which only served to accentuate the terrible neglect which was their lot. What end is served,

F 2

I may ask, by holding up to ridicule, as the *Irish Worker* did, these splendidly human and thoroughly practical arrangements of the firm for the well-being of those under them ? Even a high-minded trade union, if it had control, could not do more ; I doubt whether it could do as much, as there is an element of human sympathy visible in Jacobs' establishment which is as rare as it is precious.

It is difficult to understand the state of mind of the men who circulated these calumnies against Messrs. Jacob. They pose as the special friends and guardians of the workers—the chosen people who have a mission to uplift the fallen and strengthen the weak-hearted. But what would have been the effect of the success of their crusade ? Most certainly to throw out of employment hundreds of men and women who to-day are earning good wages under the happiest conditions ; for, let there be no mis-understanding on the point, a biscuit factory is a good deal of an exotic in Dublin. The local demand for biscuits is necessarily in the main for export purposes, and a con-cern of this character in the Irish capital, as has been pointed out, labours under exceptional difficulties. In the ordinary way, quite apart from the influence of the recent labour troubles, Messrs. Jacobs have been driven by the exigencies of trade to establish a branch of their business near Liverpool, on a site of ten acres acquired there for the purpose. It would not require much to overweigh the balance against the Irish factory to such an extent as to eliminate it altogether from the list of Dublin industries.

CHAPTER VII

MR. LARKIN'S BÊTE NOIRE

THERE was such a plentiful supply of vituperative material in the *Irish Worker* office that, while this campaign of calumny was being actively prosecuted in one direction, equally energetic measures of a similar type were being directed in a totally different quarter. The special target for abuse in this instance was Mr. William Martin Murphy, who had committed the unpardonable crime, in the eyes of the syndicalistic organisation which had come into existence in Dublin, of having shown exceptional capacity as a business man, notably in establishing, or directing, commercial concerns, which had obtained the unmistakable hall-mark of success. As Mr. Murphy will figure very prominently in the subsequent portions of the narrative, I shall deal at some little length with his career; but before I enter into biographical details, I will, by way of suitable preface, give a short account of an enterprise with which he has been closely identified from the start, and which illustrates in its successful working the rare commercial aptitude of the man.

If a visitor to Dublin after a lengthy sojourn were asked to name what appeared to him the most brilliant example of Irish enterprise in the city, he would unhesitatingly say the tramways. They are models of efficiency, comfort, and expedition. Nowhere else in the United Kingdom can you find a service which is so thoroughly comprehensive in its routes or so convenient in every respect as a passenger-carrying agency. From the far-flung confines of pleasant Dalkey in one direction, to the rocky slopes of the great Hill of Howth on the other side of Dublin Bay, the cars carry you over what is, all in all, one of the most interesting tramway routes in the world. No important part of the city and its spreading suburbs is left outside the range of the facilities offered by the service. From a point under the shadow of the Nelson Column in Sackville Street, in the very heart of the city, you can go to most of the outlying districts, while a skilfully devised system of cross routes enables you to get from one area to an adjacent one expeditiously and with a minimum of inconvenience. For some years the company—the Dublin United Tramways, to give it its official designation—has paid a dividend of 6 per cent. on both its £10 preference shares and its ordinary shares, which have stood in the market during the past few years at an average of about 12. Nor has this result been secured at the expense either of the travelling public or the workers. The fares are as low as on almost any tramway service in the United Kingdom. For example, a trip to Dalkey from Sackville Street, a distance of nine miles, costs only fivepence, and, if a return ticket is taken, the double journey may be accomplished for eightpence; the fare to Howth from the centre of the city, also nine miles, is the same as to Dalkey, fivepence; while the journey from Dolphin's Barn to Glasnevin, four and a half miles, costs threepence; from Donnybrook to Phœnix Park, five miles, fourpence; and to Rathfarnham, six miles, fourpence. As for the working staff, the scale of remuneration is fully equal to that in force in towns in England of about the same size as Dublin. Further, a good many of the traffic men are provided by the company with excellent housing accommodation at moderate rentals close to the depots where the day's work begins and ends—no small advantage in view of the scarcity in the city of artisans' dwellings of a suitable character.

Such was the enterprise upon which, from a very early period in its existence, the Irish Transport Workers' Union and its press organ concentrated their maleficent activities. The campaign opened in the familiar fashion by a persistent fire of personal abuse in the columns of the *Irish Worker*, and at the Larkinite meetings. In turn Mr. Murphy was called an 'industrial octopus,' a 'tramway tyrant,' an 'importer of swell cockney shopmen,' a 'political and social Captain Mick McQuaid,' a 'financial mountebank,' a 'blood-sucking vampire,' a 'pure-souled financial contortionist,' a 'capitalist sweater,' and 'this whited sepulchre.' The last-mentioned choice epithet was applied in reference to Mr. Murphy's ownership of a 'rag styled the *Independent*,' which had drawn the Larkinite fire by a criticism of the morality of some of the sentiments expressed in an article which appeared in the *Irish Worker's* columns. Not content with the freest use that could be made of prose to defame the object of their attacks, the Larkinite scribes dropped on one occasion into verse. The lines, which were headed 'It's Murphy's,' and were a close parody of a skit which appeared in an American publication entitled 'It's Morgan's,' satirised the wide-reaching character of Mr. Murphy's commercial enterprises. A wanderer of an inquiring turn of mind is supposed to be making a tour. The reply he invariably gets to a question as to who is the owner of a particular piece of property, or institution, is that at the head of the verses   Thus :

> I entered a tram and rode all day
> On a regal couch and a right of way
> Which reached its arms all over the land
> In a system too large to understand.
> 'A splendid property this,' I cried ;
> And a man with a plate on his hat replied,
>   'It's Murphy's ! '

After various wanderings and obtaining the same reply to his question, the stranger quits the earthly scene:

> I went to heaven. The Jasper walls
> Towered high and wide, and the golden halls
> Shone bright beyond. But a strange new mark
> Was over the gate, viz. ' Private Park.'
> 'What, what is the meaning of this ? ' I cried ;
> And a saint with a livery on replied,
>   'It's Murphy's ! '

One final scene remained for the investigator. His experience was the same there :

> I went to the only place left. ' I'll take
> A chance in the boat on the brimstone lake,
> Or perhaps I may be allowed to sit
> On the griddled floor of the bottomless pit.'
> But the jeering tout with horns on his face
> Cried, as he forked me out of the place,
>   'It's Murphy's ! '

This, of course, is mere fooling, but all the same it is not without its importance as a part of the design to represent Mr. Murphy as a capitalistic ogre who battened on the sufferings of the poor and waxed rich on ill-gotten gains. The Larkinite myth was too monstrous to excite in Dublin, where the facts are known, anything but ridicule. But it had its effect later, when the real clash of arms came and Mr. Murphy stepped into the arena to conduct his historic fight with the sinister force which was strangling Dublin industry. Then certain English writers, as we shall have occasion to show, grasped eagerly at the idea presented to them by the *Irish Worker*, and pictured Mr. Murphy as a sort of vulgar American boss whose domineering personality gave a fierce bitterness to a conflict which, under other direction, would have taken upon itself a less ferocious aspect. The impression then created has not been entirely obliterated, but how utterly false it is will be apparent from a brief sketch of Mr. Murphy's career.

Born some seventy years since, the son of a Cork contractor, Mr. Murphy commenced his active commercial career as far back as 1863, when, owing to the death of his father, he had to take upon his shoulders the full responsibilities of a business house. For some years his interests were chiefly confined to Ireland, where he projected and carried out several railway undertakings as well as tramways in Dublin, Belfast, and Cork ; but the time came when his far-seeing schemes took him beyond the limits of the sister isle. The possibilities of tramways as profit-earning ventures in the great populous centres of England and Scotland early attracted his attention. He acquired parliamentary power for, and financed and constructed, a tramway line which ran from Vauxhall Station to Norwood. The overshadowing of private enterprise by the policy of universal municipal tramways within the county of London, adopted by the London County Council, destroyed the value of the line as a nucleus of a larger scheme. It seemed, in fact, in danger of becoming a derelict, owing to the rise of rival means of communication. Mr. Murphy's financial acumen, however, was ultimately justified by the sale of the enterprise to the public authority on terms which were satisfactory. Checked in London, Mr. Murphy turned his attention to other populous centres where the mania for municipal trading had, happily for the ratepayers, as things have proved in most places, not penetrated. Apart from the Dublin enterprise, to which reference has been made, he was responsible for the construction of lines in a good many towns in the United Kingdom, ranging from Paisley to Ramsgate and Margate, in all of which he still has an important financial interest.

From tramway construction to railway building is an easy transition, and Mr. Murphy has made it by associating himself with the work of making a line in West Africa, which will help forward the wonderful development that is proceeding in that part of the Empire. But though Mr. Murphy has established a business connection that is almost world-wide, his closest ties are with Dublin. Some years ago, when the prospects of the paper did not seem particularly bright, he acquired the *Independent* and the allied group of journals. Under his skilled direction the enterprise soon entered on smooth waters, and is now the most flourishing Nationalist journalistic venture in Ireland. A great drapery business is another interest of his. Indeed, he has a finger in most Irish financial pies of any promise, and the fact that he is interested in a particular concern is accepted in Dublin as an excellent guarantee of its stability.

Mr. Murphy is a Nationalist of a type once more common than it is to-day. With O'Connell and Isaac Butt and other men of a bygone generation he sees no incompatibility between a strongly held conviction of Ireland's right to mould her own destinies and a complete loyalty to the King. He is of the great liberator's opinion that ' the golden link of the Crown ' is a valuable and necessary adjunct of a Home Rule system. His views on this subject have made him the object of the virulent criticism of extremists, but he has gone his way with characteristic independence. A striking example of his indifference to the clamour of the section who would make Irish patriotism a mere narrow sectionalism was afforded in the case of the International Irish Exhibition, 1907. When this enterprise was first mooted there was an outcry from the advanced party against the holding of any exhibition other than a ' national ' one. There seemed a danger of the whole project being ruined by this rather stupid squabble about a name, when Mr. Murphy, whose sanity of vision is one of his chief qualities, stepped into the breach, pulled the affair together by sheer force of personality, and with the aid of a strong committee of citizens of all classes and shades of opinion whom he got around him, turned what had promised to be a dismal failure into a brilliant success.

A visit paid to the exhibition by King Edward and Queen Alexandra on July 10, 1907, was in its way a remarkable episode. An early invitation sent to their Majesties to extend their patronage to the exhibition had been declined on the advice of the Castle authorities, who were of the opinion that the time was inopportune for a Royal visit to Ireland. By some means the King got to hear of the disappointment that the refusal of the invitation had caused ; and when, in the summer of 1907, he was visiting Wales he took the matter into his own hands, and, with Queen Alexandra, went across in the Royal yacht to Kingstown with the definite object of inspecting the exhibition. The visit was an immense popular success. It began and ended in a burst of popular enthusiasm.

King Edward was anxious to mark his cordial appreciation of the public-spirited efforts of the executive of the exhibition by conferring a title upon its chairman. This led to a curious little contretemps which attracted a good deal of comment at the time. Mr. Murphy, before the King's visit, had been publicly accused of being influenced in his work for the exhibition by a desire to secure a title. In reply he had declared that in no circumstances would he accept a title in connection with the exhibition, even if one were offered to him. In order that there might be no misconception on the subject he, some little time before the Royal visit, explained his position to the Lord Lieutenant, and, having done so, thought no more of the matter. Great was his surprise, therefore, when a short time before the King's arrival at the exhibition Mr. Murphy was informed that, at the conclusion of His Majesty's reply to the addresses, it was intended that he should receive from the King the honour of knighthood. Mr. Murphy at once reminded the official who brought this information that he had already disclaimed any desire for titular distinction, and he requested that the Lord Lieutenant should be at once informed accordingly. It then appeared that Lord Aberdeen had been as much taken by surprise as Mr. Murphy himself. Having been previously informed by Mr. Murphy (as already stated) that the offer of a title would not be acceptable, His Excellency had done nothing in the matter ; and it was not until after the arrival of the Royal party at the exhibition (whither His Excellency had proceeded in advance in order to receive their Majesties) that he learned from his private secretary, Lord Herschell, who had followed from Kingstown and who had been informed by one of His Majesty's personal staff as to what was intended, that he (Lord Aberdeen) became aware of it. The proceedings of a State ceremony do not provide much opportunity for conference, but Lord Aberdeen contrived to have a hurried *sotto voce* conversation with Mr. Murphy, and then ascertained that he was determined to maintain the view he had already expressed. Accordingly, when a few moments later His Majesty called for the sword in order that he might proceed to the next item on the programme, the Lord Lieutenant found it necessary to step forward and perform what must have been the uncongenial duty of stating that this part of the proceedings would have to be omitted. The incident was of course somewhat disconcerting, but His Majesty passed it off with characteristic external composure.

But it may safely be surmised that, when the Royal party had retired, Lord Aberdeen was asked as to how any misunderstanding on the point could have arisen ; and it is certain that His Excellency took care to explain that it had arisen through the lack of timely notice of what was intended. However, feeling that his action might be misconstrued, and perhaps be attributed to a political cause which had in fact been suggested, Mr. Murphy immediately wrote to the Lord Lieutenant setting out his reasons for declining the knighthood. He said that, so far from having any difficulty in accepting an honour on any political grounds, he had, as a Constitutional Nationalist, always held the view that the cause of Irish nationality would be greatly advanced by a frank acceptance of the common Crown for both countries—a principle which had been for years agreed to by the representatives of the Irish people. While adding an expression of his personal feeling of respect for the then occupant of the throne, he observed that he would be grateful if His Excellency would explain his position and views to His Majesty, stating that he did not like that the King should leave Ireland thinking that he had left one churlish man behind him.

In compliance with this request, on the following day, at the Leopardstown races, the communication was handed to King Edward. His Majesty, as one would expect, was most gracious and highly pleased at Mr. Murphy's declarations. He sent a message through the Lord Lieutenant saying that he quite appreciated the writer's position. That the Royal words were not merely formal was illustrated by the fact that His Majesty intimated that he wished to retain Mr. Murphy's letter. Thus the incident was thoroughly characteristic of both monarch and subject.

It is, perhaps, not surprising, in view of what has been stated, that Mr. Murphy enjoys the entire confidence of the citizens of the more substantial class. Uncompromising

Unionists and equally determined Nationalists sit under his presidency on public committees in complete harmony. They know and respect him, and, above all, they have entire confidence in his level-headed judgments of men and affairs. In any other city than Dublin Mr. Murphy would long since have been marked out for the chief magistracy, but the Dublin Corporation is a select body in the sense that it has no use for a man who will not ' toe the line ' politically in all respects. What political narrowness has denied has been compensated for by the bestowal of high positions in commercial life— like the Presidency of the Dublin Chamber of Commerce and the chairmanship of important committees charged with duties of a temporary character. His leadership of the Dublin employers in the recent industrial crisis was almost a matter of course. He is the type of strong, silent man who inevitably comes to the front on occasions of public emergency or national danger.

A first meeting with Mr. Murphy suggests to the visitor the impression he has formed of the typical family solicitor of the old school—the man who is the repository of many secrets and who blends the milk of human kindness with an unswerving rectitude of conduct. ' A tall, spare figure, slightly stooped at the shoulders, with a mass of silvery brushed hair framing a benevolent face in which two kindly but piercing grey eyes are deeply set ' is the word-portrait painted of him for an English paper during the recent troubles by ' One who knows him.' It is a faithful presentment of the man. The very last attribute that you would associate with this striking personality is tyranny, and you would be right. Few Dublin employers have a higher reputation for kindliness and perfect consideration for those who are not so well endowed with this world's goods as he is himself. But Mr. Murphy, as is often the case with men of his temperament, will not be bullied. He acts,

moreover, up to the spirit of Polonius's familiar advice
to Laertes :

> Beware
> Of entrance to a quarrel, but, being in,
> Bear't that the opposed may beware of thee.

Those opposed to him certainly had reason, before he had
done with them, to beware of him.   But that is another
story.

CHAPTER VIII

' TO HELL WITH CONTRACTS ! '

Repudiation of Agreements a Characteristic Feature of Larkinism—
The Settlement of July 1908—Mr. Larkin's Reasons for repudiating
the Agreement—Antagonism between Mr. Larkin and the National
Dock Labourers' Union—Conditions of Dublin Dock Labour
favourable to Larkinite Propaganda—Labour Unrest in 1911—
Formation of Dublin Employers' Federation—Violent Attack
in the *Irish Worker* upon Employers—The Settlement of July 1911
—Lord Aberdeen and Mr. Larkin—Conciliation Board Scheme
ignored by the Irish Transport Workers' Union.

IN the foregoing chapters readers have been given a
tolerably full impression of the working of the Dublin
labour movement under Mr. Larkin's direction. But
what is, perhaps, the most characteristic feature of
Larkinism—its contempt for agreements—remains to
be dealt with. 'To hell with contracts!' exclaimed
the leader of the movement in a burst of oratory during
the tour he made in England in the course of the strike.
The sentiment expressed with absolute fidelity the
spirit of Larkinism. No understanding, however definite
may be its terms and however clear its stipulations
as to the duration of the contract, is held to be binding
a moment longer than it suits the policy and interests
of the workers to acquiesce in it.

An early example of repudiation is supplied in the case
of an agreement made in 1908 relative to the payment
of work done at the wharves and in connection with
the maltsters. In the early half of that year there

was a strike of dock labourers and others of such considerable proportions as to seriously hamper the trade of the port. The Government, with a celerity which at the time was somewhat criticised, intervened and, with a view of securing a settlement, recommended a conference of the representatives of employers and employed at Dublin Castle. At this gathering Lord MacDonnell, then Under Secretary for Ireland, presided, and there were also in attendance on the official side Sir James Dougherty, Assistant Under Secretary, and Mr. Mitchell, of the Board of Trade. The employers were represented by Mr. Watson, of the City of Dublin Steam Packet Co.; Mr. Laidlaw, of Messrs. Tedcastle, McCormick & Co.; and Mr. McCormick and Mr. Hewat, of the Dublin Coalowners' Association. Representing the men were Alderman Gee, Vice-President of the General Federation of Trade Unions; Mr. Appleton, Secretary; and Mr. James Sexton, Secretary of the National Union of Dock Labourers.

After an exhaustive discussion of the points at issue, the parties entered into an agreement of a far-reaching kind. The leading principle of the instrument was the establishment of a Conciliation Board for the adjustment of all disputes that might arise, excepting those affecting individuals, which were left to be settled by the malcontents and the firms concerned. A somewhat elaborate machinery was devised to give effect to the arrangement. If no agreement was reached in the case of a dispute, the general secretary of the National Union might make further representations on the matter to the firm concerned, who would then consider them. Should no settlement still be possible, the question would be referred to the representative body of employers and employed, who would appoint an umpire. In the event of a difficulty arising about the selection of the umpire, the appointment was to be made by the Board of Trade. Other points were disposed of on lines which seemed to

G

promise more stable conditions for the trade. Subsequently,
in accordance with the agreement, a number of questions
relative to wages and working conditions were referred
for settlement to Sir Andrew Marshall Porter, Bart., late
Master of the Rolls, and Mr. P. J. O'Neill, Chairman of
the Dublin County Council, who were appointed joint
arbitrators. The award, which was made in February
1909, was a most comprehensive one. It set up schedules
of wages for various grades of employees, fixed the hours
and conditions of work, and generally smoothed the way
for the establishment of peaceful relations between
masters and men. A final recommendation of the
arbitrators was that the Conciliation Board which had
been set up for this particular dispute should become
a permanent institution.

Both the original agreement and the arbitrators'
award were received with public approval. Some
sanguine souls, indeed, detected in them the beginning of
a new era in which the lion would lie down with the lamb
and an idyllic calm would ensue. But all had reckoned
without their host—the host in this particular instance
being Mr. Larkin. At the time that the agreement was
entered into, Mr. Larkin, as will be seen by a reference to
an earlier chapter, was the servant—the somewhat
unwilling and, if his critics are to be believed, none too
loyal servant—of the National Union of Dock Labourers.
He was a party to it as much as were other officials of the
Union, and if they were bound by it, he was. It was
certainly understood at the time that the settlement was
a settlement, and not merely a docket of pious opinions
which were to be followed or not as fancy or expediency
dictated. Otherwise it is impossible to understand why
all this complicated process of Conciliation Board and
Arbitration Court, with the highest trained official intelligence, should have been brought into operation. Mr.
Larkin may have disagreed with the arrangement, but,
if he did, he did not then, so far as can be discovered from

the publications of the day, publicly say so, and in any
event his individual opinion counted for nothing against
the fact that he was the recognised servant of the only
organisation that then existed to uphold the interests of
the workers.   At a later period, when it suited Mr. Larkin's
plans to throw overboard the agreement with all that it
implied, he asserted (*Irish Worker*, July 1911) that the
men repudiated the arrangement and declared that ' it
was because that agreement, made against their interests,
that the men threw over the National Union.'   ' There
has [*sic*] been no members of the National Union of Dock
Labourers in Dublin, nay in Ireland except Derry, since
November, 1908,' he proceeded.   ' Publicly and privately
that agreement was repudiated.   They might as well say
that the silent dead in Glasnevin acquiesced in the present
government of this country, and their acquiescence binds
the living men of this town.   No—the living men of this
town are going to have their union.   They claimed the
right to appoint their own chairman and secretaries, just
inasmuch as Tedcastle McCormick claimed to appoint
Mr. McCormick as chairman to speak on behalf of the
shareholders—that, and no more and no less.'   But even
according to this partial view of the position the National
Union of Dock Labourers was *the* representative authority
for the workers when the agreement was concluded, and,
that being the case, it is difficult to see how the obligation
entered into could be set aside on right grounds.   Surely
the whole system of collective bargaining breaks down
if the principle is admitted that a change made subsequent
to an agreement in the representative body, either of
workers or employers, vitiates that agreement.

No doubt the antagonism between Mr. Larkin and his
old employers in the National Union of Dock Labourers
had a powerful influence in securing the ultimate nullifica-
tion of the 1908 agreement.   He was, as we have seen,
strongly at issue with the executive on matters associated
with the organising work of the union, and long before

the final severance came, at the end of 1908, he was working against their interests. The undermining of their work in connection with the settlement was to such a man an obviously facile means of consolidating the new power which he was striving to establish. It is always easy to upset a compromise : it is doubly so when one of the parties to it is a body of workers whose means of livelihood at the best are inconsiderable. There were, therefore, many only too eager to give ear to the counsels which were lavishly tendered by Mr. Larkin to strike a fresh blow for industrial freedom under a new organisation which took no account of the undertaking ratified on their behalf. By the policy he pursued, Mr. Larkin achieved a double victory. He scored off his old friends of the National Union, and he rallied to his side a substantial proportion of the unskilled labour forces of the Irish capital—a proportion sufficient to give vitality to his own organisation. An additional advantage, and one by which, perhaps, he set most store, was that he had an absolutely clear course for his peculiar propaganda. No longer was it necessary to consult, even nominally, an executive many miles away. He was the only Richmond in the field.

Events in Dublin did not take a definitely aggressive shape until the summer of 1911. By that time Mr. Larkin, having set Belfast and Cork well ablaze with his incendiary activities and incidentally served his term of imprisonment in the circumstances already related, had regularly established his organisation in Dublin and entered upon his campaign against Dublin industries. He found a rich soil for his revolutionary seed in the dock labourers' domain. At the Dublin quays and docks the work of loading and unloading ships is done very much on the lines which were followed at the London docks before the great labour upheaval of 1885, in which Mr. John Burns played an historic part. Men are taken on as the exigencies of the trade demand,

and they are paid by stevedores who are responsible
to the shipping companies. The work is necessarily
fitful, days of strenuous labour being followed by periods
of inactivity. Such a system tends to collect a mass of
unskilled labour, more or less of the unregenerate type.
Idlers, whose only desire is to keep body and soul together
and obtain money for an occasional carouse, are glad
to be able to put in a day or two at the wharves to secure
the few shillings necessary for a precarious existence.
Countrymen, who have been attracted to the capital
by glowing stories of the wages to be earned there, are
equally willing to earn pay which for them is exceptionally good. In addition to these there is a large class of
workers, men with wives and families, who obtain an
uncertain livelihood at the wharves failing more stable
employment. In the mass the dockers are miserably
poor. The majority of them, probably, on waking in the
morning scarcely know where their next day's dinner
is to come from.

Preaching the gospel of discontent in such an environment as that described, Mr. Larkin found ready listeners.
With his rough eloquence he stirred the dull imaginations
of the crowds, which were never wanting at his meetings,
to a sense of the degradation of their lot. In one of
his speeches about the period of the strike (reported
in the *Irish Worker*, July 22, 1911), he inveighed against
the snobbery which kept the workers apart. ' We have
men in this country,' he said, ' there are men even in
this crowd, who despise the docker—men who don't
recognise themselves as of the same blend as the sailors
and firemen, who think themselves a little above the
ordinary worker, and who sometimes get very less wages
and have far worse conditions of work. Snobocracy
cannot exist if the working classes are true to themselves.
You can't live without them. Who is going to load the
ships and railway trains, or what will you put in them
if you have not the fellows who work the land ? They

cannot be done without, but nobody cares about them, because these men do not consider themselves ; they are apathetic, they are ill-educated, they are unorganised ; they are a prey to every demagogue, whether labour or political ; they are a prey to every sycophantic person in the country.' Having thus castigated the weaknesses of his hearers, the speaker played upon their prejudices by drawing a dark picture of the Dublin slums. ' Those terrible conditions,' he argued, ' were due to low wages.' ' There are,' he went on, ' thousands in the city who do not attend their religious duty because of their bad clothing. The women were in a wretched, ill-clad condition—below the level of humanity ; and little children were brought up in surroundings of sin and misery. I know what slum life is, and I know the cause of emigration, misery and vice, which is the low wages that people are compelled to work for. Our aim is to change those conditions—to improve the lot of the toilers—and I do not know of any organisation in the world that in its time has done so much in the same period to improve the workers' condition as the Irish Transport Union.' In fine, the thing to do to bring about the social millennium was to join the speaker's organisation.

If the argument had been carried on throughout on these lines there would be little to object to in the movement ; but, simultaneously with the oratorical campaign, there was set in motion a system of ' peaceful persuasion ' which was probably a good deal more effective for the attainment of the objects in view. A series of disputes with employers was brought about, and when the breach had been made effective, the position was maintained by devices with which the modern history of trade unionism has made us painfully familiar. So prevalent was the intimidation, that in a short time the trade of the port in many directions was at a standstill.

The employers who had surrendered a good deal for

the sake of peace in 1908 were naturally incensed at the turn of events. They held a meeting on June 30, 1911, to consider their position. Many of the leading merchants attended and gave evidence in speech and vote of their appreciation of the seriousness of the situation. They came to the sensible conclusion that the best way to meet combination was by combination. They felt that, while it was easy for the Transport Workers' Union to coerce a single employer or group of employers, it would be difficult for him to browbeat the whole body of manufacturers, merchants, and others who make up the commercial body in Dublin. Before the meeting separated the foundations were laid of a strong organisation which, in an extended form at a later phase in the troubles, grappled successfully with the labour octopus which was squeezing the life-blood out of the city's commerce.

As the employers' organisation will figure very prominently in the subsequent pages, a few sentences may profitably be devoted to the subject. In the main the federation followed on the lines of a similar body which, a few years previously, had been set up in Cork to fight Mr. Larkin and which had successfully coped with the difficulties that he raised. A company, called the Dublin Employers' Federation, Limited, was formed and a provisional committee appointed to carry out the objects in view. These objects were stated to be ' to afford mutual protection to and indemnity of all employers and to promote freedom of contract between employers and employees.' A businesslike scheme in every respect, it started on its way with the active goodwill and support of the great bulk of the commercial community of Dublin.

At Liberty Hall, Mr. Larkin's headquarters, the significance of the step taken by the employers was not missed. In the *Irish Worker* of July 29, 1911, under the heading ' Employers' Secret Society Unmasked,' a violent attack was made upon the new organisation. Apparently the writer's point of view was that, while it was legitimate and proper for men to combine, it was rank blasphemy for employers to form an association for mutual protection. In a burst of fury the editor asked : ' Do these creatures (the employers) think that, because they succeeded for a time in Cork to browbeat the workers (assisted by traitors such as Simon Punch and backed by a corrupt Government), they will succeed in Dublin ? May I remind them that Dublin is not Cork ? Within this town are living men who have defeated—aye, and destroyed—a more corrupt organisation (if that were possible) than this suggested Dublin Employers' Federation. But forewarned is fore-armed, and the working class of this great city has too long submitted to the tyranny of the sweater and despoiler.'

' Some of these gentlemen,' the writer went on, ' seem to have forgotten that we had a land problem in Ireland, and that a few individuals, who claimed they owned the land, were taught a lesson. In the beginning of that struggle a large number of the dispossessed farmers blamed the tools of the landlords and dealt in a very summary way with them. Later on men arose in the land who made it clear to the minds of the exploited that it were foolish to blame the tools, the emergency men, and the grabber ; the people who were responsible were the alien landlord class, and in a few short years the problem was solved—as regards the tenant farmers. Some of the landlord class tried the self-same tricks that you in Dublin intend playing. Well, *some of them found themselves lying behind a ditch suffering from want of breath, and don't forget we are the sons of those men who enjoyed the gaol and trod the scaffold. Do you think we will be less worthy than they who went before ?* You will conspire ; your tools will perjure their dirty souls ; you will intimidate, you will starve us into submission ;

you threaten us and our wives and children with the whip lash of hunger. Eh ! that is your game. Do you think there are no brains, brawn, or muscle left in this land among the working class ? '

Readers will do well to take special note of this choice effusion, and especially of the words which I have italicised. Language has lost its sense if there is not here a direct incitement to murder. The landlords who ' found themselves lying behind a ditch suffering from want of breath ' were the assassinated victims of the land war, the men who were shot by ' village ruffians ' from behind hedges as they were returning home. No English reader can miss the meaning of the sentence ; to the Irish reader, especially if he belongs to the class from which the clientele of the *Irish Worker* is drawn, it has a terrible significance. Again, it is permissible to express amazement that incendiary matter of this character could be printed in a newspaper without bringing down upon the writer and publisher the stern attentions of the law.

Strangely enough, in Mr. Larkin's case, the publication of the denunciation of the employers followed upon an episode which brought him into close personal association with the Viceroy. Alarmed at the turn that the labour troubles was taking, and particularly at the threat of the employers to introduce free labour, Lord Aberdeen had, as many thought at the time, and not a few think still, compromised his high position by calling the arch-labour agitator to his presence. He did so with the object of securing an adjustment of the difficulty by bringing representatives of the employers into touch with those who spoke for the employed, and his aims were achieved to the extent that a mutual arrangement was come to at the conference (which was held in Dublin Castle on July 22) by which the employers, represented by Mr. Watson and Mr. McCormick, agreed not to introduce strike breakers, and Mr. Larkin and his fellow delegate Mr. Kelly, according to a memorandum made of the conference at the time and quoted by Mr. Healy in his speech at Sir George Askwith's inquiry, pledged themselves to acknowledge the principle of free labour.[1] Mr. Larkin had been given his inch—he promptly took his ell.   In doing so he probably had complete confidence in the inaction of the Castle, with whose interior he had, only a week previously, made such intimate acquaintance.

Whatever may have been the effect of the Viceroy's intervention on Mr. Larkin personally, the Castle conference only resulted in ameliorating the position of affairs temporarily.   One of the proposals which emanated from the gathering was that the conciliation board scheme of 1908 should be given vitality by the appointment of representatives of masters and men.   The employers promptly sent in the names of two delegates to act for them, but no move was made in the Larkinite camp, and to this day the board is non-existent because the workers' representatives have not been chosen.   The truth, of course, is that conciliation is not a desirable object from the syndicalistic standpoint.   Exponents of the creed of the type of Mr. Larkin do not want workers to be contented and relations between employers and employed to be harmonious and peaceful.   They have, consequently, no use for conciliation boards, and it is sheer futility to press them upon them.   One touchstone, and one only, they apply to the disputes in which they are involved—the test of physical endurance. It was not long before even the most enthusiastic of official conciliators came to realise this rather brutal truth.

[1] Mr. Larkin at a later date strenuously denied that he had assented to the principle of free labour on this occasion ; but the memorandum is on record against his assertion, and, moreover, the recognition by him of the principle is in keeping with his action in the Cork strike of 1908. In regard to this dispute the Rev. Patrick O'Leary, in giving evidence on Mr. Larkin's behalf in the criminal proceedings taken against him in June 1910, said : ' One of the points of the settlement (of December 8, 1908) was that unionists should work with non-unionists, and the men agreed to that on Mr. Larkin's suggestion.' (Report in the *Irish Independent*, June 18, 1910.)

CHAPTER IX

SYNDICALISM IN EXCELSIS

Railway Strike—First Application of the Doctrine of ' Tainted Goods '—
Collapse of the Strike—' We the People ' of Liberty Hall—The
National Insurance Act a Larkinite Asset—Mr. Larkin's Personal
Qualities—Harassed Employers—Dead Set on Messrs. Jacobs'—
Growing Strength of the Irish Transport Workers' Union.

THE Viceregal Conference at Dublin Castle had such
small influence that, before many weeks had elapsed after
the settlement of the dispute at the wharves, Dublin was
in the throes of another struggle precipitated by the malign
activities of the Larkinite organisation.   In this case the
storm centre was the railways.   The men on some of the
Irish lines had come out in sympathy with their English
colleagues in the great strike which occurred in the summer
of 1911, but they had gone back again when the settlement was reached with the aid of the Government, in
circumstances which are still fresh in the public memory.
Business was settling back into its old grooves when a
fresh source of trouble was created in Dublin by the raising
of a novel issue by the Irish Transport Workers' Union.
A distinctive feature of the operations of the organisation,
as has been seen, was to strike at individual trades.
Grievances, which are never difficult to discover, were
exploited, and the screw was applied in the belief,
not always without justification, that an isolated firm
would put up a poor fight against the forces of the Union·
    One of the industries thus attacked in the summer of
1911 was the timber trade.   As events proved, the timber

merchants were of tougher fibre than some of the employers with whom Mr. Larkin had had to deal. They
declined to be intimidated into surrender, and actually
had the audacity to continue their business in the face of
the veto of the autocrat of Liberty Hall. Such contumacy
could not be passed over lightly, so plans were laid for
putting a stop to the work of the various firms by cutting
off their communications. Now for the first time was
used a weapon in the Larkinite armoury which was subsequently to attain historic notoriety. This was the
theory of ' tainted goods,' having as its corollary the sympathetic strike. Of all the instruments fashioned by
syndicalistic ingenuity this is perhaps the most monstrous.
If carried to its logical conclusion it would mean the
complete paralysing of industry, the subjecting of the
community to a slow death by the withholding of
the necessaries of life. The original dispute might be
of the most trumpery description. A squabble over a few
pence a day, affecting a score of men, might start rolling
the ball which in its subsequent passage would involve
every trade and every interest in which there were
organised workers.

In the case under notice the trouble grew out of a
simple question of wages. When it was found that the
timber merchants were able to dispose of their timber in
spite of the Union, attempts were made to coerce the
railway companies into a refusal to handle their goods.
On the 15th September some carts arrived at the Great
Southern and Western Railway, Kingsbridge, with loads
of timber, accompanied by the Transport Workers' Union
picket, who ordered the railway goods porters not to handle
the goods. The men submissively obeyed, and the outcome
of the episode was a strike which involved many of the
working staff on this and other lines. It was impossible, of
course, for the directors to surrender on such a point as
that which had been raised. Railway Companies, as public
carriers, are bound under statute to accept all goods that

are offered for transport, and if they had been weak or foolish enough to have fallen in with the insolent demands of the Union, they would have laid themselves open to heavy pains and penalties. The misguided men, however, under the Larkinite domination, persisted in their refusal to work on the only possible conditions that could be offered them, with the result that the strike spread to Cork and other centres, and for some weeks the trade of Dublin and the districts served by the railways, comprising half Ireland, was dislocated.

Though the strike had been entered upon without sanction and upon wholly indefencible grounds, the Amalgamated Society of Railway Servants—the general union of railway workers—took up the quarrel, and the entire headquarters' staff of the organisation was transferred to Dublin, the more effectually to conduct the campaign. When the dispute had been running three weeks the Society realised that its funds were being depleted without any prospect of advantage, and it suddenly shut down supplies.

When the inevitable end came, with the unconditional surrender of the victimised strikers, both on the railways and in the timber yards, the *Irish Worker* soothed their wounded feelings with a characteristic outburst. ' My comrades,' said the Editor (October 7, 1911), ' this so-called defeat of a section of the workers is to become an historic landmark in the rise of the common people of this country. Mark what I say, from this hour a new factor enters into the problem of the destiny of Ireland. The basic factor, that which has hitherto been ignored, now has asserted itself, felt the power, realised the possibilities. Woe to you Scribes and Pharisees, you have roused into life and action, the greatest power on earth, the God-given power of the common people. No longer in this land of ours (mark you, ours not yours) will a small privileged class hoodwink the people. Defeat, you say ? Yes, the defeat of ignorance and darkness. The common people of this country were of the opinion up to and during the fight that there was no cleavage between the people who had and those who had not. Our friends the enemy have dispelled the myth. The working class has felt its own power and realised the forces opposed to them. The next move belongs to the sovereign people, by the Grace of God. Out of our way you clods, you reptiles, you sycophants. We, the people, are awake.'

This rhodomontade from ' We, the people ' of Liberty Hall was poor compensation for the loss of wages and position which the railway workers suffered, and it may be doubted whether the most enthusiastic of Larkinites amongst them ate the very unsubstantial mess of pottage offered them with relish. But it was no doubt true, as stated in the article, that the check given to Larkinism was only a temporary one. The penalties which had to be paid for the reverse fell largely upon those who were outside the Transport Workers' Union, and there was a distinct set-off to the effect which these had in the object lesson which had been given of the tremendous power for mischief of the organisation. People of all classes had in fact, by this time, been made to realise that the syndicalistic forces in their midst were a danger to the community, which some day would have to be seriously grappled with if the community itself was not to go under.

Fortune smiled upon Mr. Larkin in various ways in these days when he was building up his organisation. The supineness of the Government in dealing with the more violent phases of industrial unrest in England gave strength to his influence over the Dublin populace by propagating the belief in the infallibility of the *vox populi* and the invincibility of the organised workers. But by far the most helpful of the agencies which he had at his call at this period was the National Insurance Act. This measure, with its scheme of approved societies dealing directly with the insured, was just the instrument that he needed to bring into his fold the miscellaneous class of unskilled workers to whom he principally made his appeal. Under astute guidance the men were shepherded into the Irish Transport Workers' Union for insurance purposes, and once there good care was taken that they should associate themselves with all the objects for which the Union existed. The character of the inducements offered to insured workers to cast their lot in with the Union may be realised from the following notice in the *Irish Worker* (February 8, 1913) : ' Remember, the Irish Transport and General Workers' Union Approved Society, under the National Insurance rules, requires no medical certificates, except in cases of malingering. All genuine cases accepted on their merits ; no delay in settling claims. Maternity claims settled in 12 hours after application. Transfer now to the Workers' Insurance Society. Branches throughout the country. We paid the first maternity claim in Ireland ; no deductions, no delay ; not a profit-making society, but a genuine Insurance Society. No highly paid officials, no titled ladies and gentlemen managing this Society ; working women and working men control and manage this Society in the interests and for the benefit of the working classes.' This notice appears below a suggestive cartoon in which the artist seems to have embodied the cynical amusement of the managers of the Union at the certain results of their very free system of administering benefits. In the picture a groggy knock-kneed individual is shown entering the State Insurance Office, on the door of which is inscribed the injunction ' Cough here, please.' Next he is revealed at the counter, below which are the words : ' Advance three paces, clutch the counter and groan horribly.' In the succeeding stage he is enjoined to ' breathe in short gasps, stagger heavily, and demand a chair (in a trembling voice).' Afterwards he is told to ' explain (in a hollow voice) that you have a wife and nine children (all the latter under six years of age),' also

to ' tell any other plausible lies that may occur to you.'
The last scene of all—the applicant running hotfoot for
the ' Harp ' public house—is described by the words :
' When paid, throw away your stick, turn off the cough
and groan business, and run for it.'

Another contributor, a Larkinite Silas Wegg, dropped
into verse, and in a parody of the Charge of the Light
Brigade described the rush of ' the Sick Hundred,' how
' just like a December gale ' they charged up the stairs of
Liberty Hall to make their claims for sick benefit.   In
the last verse we have an appropriate *finale* to the episode :

> Homeward those sick ones went,
> With money to pay the rent,
> Which Lloyd George had kindly lent—
> Happy Sick Hundred !
> And tho' they're badly crushed,
> Into the pub they rushed.
> Later, with faces flushed,
> Homeward they went.

By adopting the methods so picturesquely set forth
in the *Irish Worker*, the Union drew into its ranks hundreds
of the labouring class who would not otherwise, probably,
have been brought under the Larkinite sway ; and what
was perhaps more important for the objects of the propaganda, it fixed them in their allegiance by the strong
bonds which the insurance system supplied.   It is, perhaps,
too much to say that without the invaluable aid of the
Insurance system the Union could not have existed, but
it is fairly certain that it would not, on its own basis as
a trade organisation pure and simple, have been the power
it ultimately became.

Mr. Larkin's influence also unquestionably owed a
good deal to his own personal qualities.   Associated
with the magnetism by which he hypnotised his associates and moulded them to his will, was a real genius
for the ruder form of diplomacy which promotes the
success of a policy of aggressive industrialism.   His

cleverness was notably shown in the manner in which he effected a lodgment in the strongholds of the capitalistic enemy. One of his methods was to employ, as missionaries of his peculiar views, men who had been dismissed from a firm's employ usually for good and sufficient reasons. These individuals, being well acquainted with the business system of the establishment and also familiar with the *personnel* of the working staff, were able to assist in the direction of his operations on the most effective lines. These accredited agents, once established in a workshop or factory, had little difficulty in creating unrest. A high-handed foreman, an irritating regulation, or an exercise of stern, if salutary discipline, supplied a fulcrum for the disturbance of the good relations which had previously existed between employer and employed. Under this dual system the spread of discontent assumed proportions which made it easy to push the claims of the Union to be regarded as the special instrument for the emancipation of the Dublin workers from the thraldom of a desolating and merciless capitalism.

Driven almost to distraction by the continued interruptions to their business, caused by the disputes engineered by the agents of the Union, the employers in some cases sought to make terms with the enemy. But this they speedily discovered was the very worst policy that they could have pursued. Before they had been whipped with whips ; now they were whipped with scorpions. Agreements verbally entered into were broken almost as soon as they were made. Every man with a grievance—and in every large factory there are many such—went with it to Liberty Hall, and peremptory orders were issued from that seat of autocratic authority for the removal of the cause of offence regardless of whether or not there was right on the worker's side. Discipline in such circumstances was impossible to maintain. The control of the employer's business was

H

no longer his. It had passed to an irresponsible tribunal which had no other interest than to convince the workers that its power was paramount.

There were many instances of the tyrannical interference of the Larkinite combination in the working of individual firms in this period which preceded the great strike. Mostly those attacked were small employers who could not defend themselves. They were usually assailed at the very worst moment for their business— at Christmas or some other period of stress and strain, when stoppage might mean ruin for the firm. Mr. Larkin also, however, went for bigger game—the great undertakings employing hundreds of workers. Messrs. Jacob's Biscuit Factory, as we have already indicated, was from an early date the special object of the maleficent attentions of Liberty Hall. After a series of attacks had been made upon the firm, an agreement was come to by the terms of which forty-eight hours' notice was to be given in the event of a further dispute. Relieved that the difficulty had been overcome, Messrs. Jacob paid their workers for the day that they were on strike. The amount thus disbursed was considerable, but it was no doubt felt that if goodwill could be purchased by a concession of the kind the outlay was thoroughly justified. But, alas, for the vanity of human expectations. Messrs. Jacob had not counted on the essentially irresponsible character of the force with which they had made their composition. Before a year was out another sudden stoppage of the operations of the factory occurred, owing to labour troubles. The crisis, in this instance, was not caused by the direct action of the Union : it was brought about in a somewhat roundabout way by a carefully manufactured grievance. A man professed that he could not work at a particular machine because the dough was too stiff. The foreman pointed out that the dough was as usual. Still the man persisted that he could not work the machine. Thereupon the foreman set another man to do the work, with perfectly satisfactory results. So conspicuous an instance of insubordination could not be passed over and, after the facts had been carefully sifted by a leading member of the firm, the recalcitrant employee was dismissed. His cause was immediately championed by the Union. A day or two subsequent to the man's discharge, when the senior partner was away in Liverpool, the workers at a given signal—the blowing of a whistle—left their employment. The fact that an agreement, duly ratified by the head of the Union, had been entered into that there was to be no strike without two days' notice weighed as nothing against the inconvenience and loss which it was possible to inflict upon the firm for daring to assert its authority. Messrs. Jacob were naturally annoyed at the repudiation of the bond which the episode carried with it, but, wishing for peace, they took the man back on his making a proper apology for his conduct. Instead of ensuring harmony, the concession was only an incitement to the Larkinites to strengthen their grip on the business. Messrs. Jacob, who are above everything employers who value the human tie, noted with concern the changed attitude of their workers. But at the moment they had not much time for vain regrets. The interference of the Union in the working of their business was having the most serious consequences. Harassed by the agency of the sinister power which had gained ascendency in Dublin, they looked on the future with increasing misgiving. How they, in common with other cruelly oppressed employers, found deliverance from the desolating Larkinite tyranny will be told later.

Meanwhile it may be convenient here to point out to what a complete extent by this time Mr. Larkin had realised his ideal of a Union which should embrace all sorts and conditions of workers. Welded into one whole were dock labourers, factory workers, tramway men, builders' labourers, shop porters, railway men, domestic servants, and farm labourers. The female element was especially encouraged, and not improbably the dead set made against Messrs. Jacob from the first was due to Mr. Larkin's perception of the peculiarly good facilities which the working staff of the factory offered for the pushing of his propaganda in a feminine direction. His movement obtained a great stimulus from the exposure of some cases of undoubted hardship amongst the minor trades of the city where employers had overworked and underpaid their workers, and especially their women workers. But these stories of oppression often exaggerated facts almost beyond resemblance, and they were adorned with an embroidery of scurrility of the most nauseous description. What Mr. Larkin seems to have aimed at was to make himself a sort of benevolent Napoleon who would hold the whole industrial world of Ireland in fee and dole out to his very obedient subjects rewards for their fidelity out of the spoils of the dynasties he had overthrown. It was a brilliant conception, but Mr. Larkin had reckoned without his Wellington. The Waterloo of his campaign was looming in the distance.

CHAPTER X

THE GOSPEL OF REPUDIATION

Larkinite attack on the City of Dublin Steam Packet Company—*Irish Worker's* Views of the Binding Force of Agreements—Mr. Larkin attacks Lord Aberdeen—His so-called Disclosures denied—Settlements effected with Shipping Companies—Breach of Agreement with the Clyde Shipping Company—Discontent fomented in the Building and Engineering Trades.

MR. LARKIN, while making his forays into the more obscure recesses of Dublin trade, never overlooked the fact that the primary object of his Union was the championing of the cause of the transport workers, and particularly of the class associated with the shipping industry. His restless energies found ample scope in the ever-present discontent of those who made up the motley community of the quays and the dockside for the pushing of his claims to an industrial dictatorship. In the early months of 1913 friction was generated amongst the employees of the City of Dublin Steam Packet Co. This enterprise presented an especially broad front for labour attack. As the holder of the mail contract it could not, without very serious loss, allow of the interruption of its service of steamers. Furthermore, as the recipient of a Government subsidy, it was liable to political pressure which, as a simple trading concern, it would not have been subject to. When, therefore, trouble arose of the familiar kind, the Larkinite attacks were pushed with a vigour and assurance which gained new strength as the fight proceeded, and it was made clear that powerful outside influences were at work to terminate the strike in the public interest.

In this, as in other crises of a similar kind which occurred under the Larkinite dispensation, the strike was called without previous notice or complaint. On the morning of January 30, no doubt by a pre-concerted arrangement, the quay porters at work for the company at North Wall suddenly quitted their employment. Attempts were made to replace them, but, owing to the intimidation that prevailed, it was impossible to procure substitutes. As a consequence the sailing of the company's ships had to be cancelled. The *casus belli*, it afterwards appeared, was the refusal by the company of a demand made that four foremen in the steamship service should belong to the Union. It was a matter of dispute at the time of the outbreak of the trouble whether the men wished to join or whether they were prevented from doing so ; but, whatever the truth may have been as to that, it was soon made clear that non-union foremen were only used as a stalking horse for the pushing of a claim of a comprehensive kind for increased wages and improved hours of working. It suited Mr. Larkin's purpose to pose at this juncture as an out-and-out advocate of conciliation. Though, as we have already seen, he had never responded to the invitations addressed to him to join in the setting up of the Conciliation Board, proposed under the 1908 agreement and further recommended in 1911, he had now the audacity to complain that the Board had not been constituted and cite the circumstance as a justification for the strike. His insincerity is attested, not merely by his course of action from the period he first appeared on the scene in Dublin, but by the definite attitude assumed in regard to agreements, both by himself and those closely associated with him. Thus, in the *Irish Worker* of June 7, 1913, a contribution appeared in a prominent position in which the true Larkinite faith is expounded in these words : ' Agreements come to between parties on equal terms should be enforceable, but in the case of agreements between Capital and Labour, there is wanting the fair and square dealing and that free discussion on equal terms that alone makes ordinary contracts legally and morally binding. For instance, why should I be bound by an agreement drawn up at a time when I might be in a condition of helplessness that gives to another man the power to rob me of the greater part of my earnings ? I would keep on signing such things as long as they suited me, but I would never admit they should prevent me striking or demanding better conditions when the opportunity offers.' The gospel of repudiation could not be more frankly preached or more lucidly set forth than it is here. In point of fact, as has already been said, if there is one feature more than another which has characterised this Larkinite movement it is defiance of the moral law, to say nothing of the statute law, which gives binding force to contracts in every civilised community.

There is no necessity to follow the City of Dublin Steam Packet Company's dispute through its devious course. Enough to say that, after several weeks' turmoil and interruption of trade, a composition was reached which gave the men a good deal of what they claimed. The responsibility of the directors was great, and they doubtless were constrained by reasons which seemed to them all sufficient to come to terms with their active opponent. But, as in the case of Messrs. Jacob, it was a case of ' Peace, peace, when there is no peace.' The foe had been bought off for the moment, but the spoils of his victory only served to whet his appetite for further conquest.

The temper in which Mr. Larkin conducted the struggle to its final stage is aptly illustrated by an incident which attracted great attention at the time, and which cannot be passed over in a history of the strike.

When the dispute was in progress, a meeting was held at the Mansion House under the presidency of the Lord Mayor (Mr. Lorcan Sherlock) with the object, if possible, of finding a basis for compromise. The proceedings proved abortive, but they were made notable by a speech by Mr. Larkin, touched with some piquant reminiscences relative to his intercourse with Lord Aberdeen, the Viceroy. Alluding to his imprisonment for fraud, Mr. Larkin said that, on his conviction, Mr. Samuel McCormick went straight away to the Lord-Lieutenant and told him that he (Mr. Larkin) had been unjustly dealt with.[1] Subsequently he was released and given a free pardon. ' The next time he saw the Earl of Aberdeen,' went on Mr. Larkin, ' he said he was glad to see him (Mr. Larkin), and said he regretted his imprisonment. He also said, " Would you mind shaking hands with me ? " He said he had not the slightest objection. Lord Aberdeen said : " Every man in the country is sorry for you, and only for the old duffer of a judge you would have been out three months ago." '

In the columns of *The Times* was published an authorised communique to the effect that ' when any respectable intelligent man in Dublin publicly declares that he believes that the Lord-Lieutenant uttered the words attributed to him by Mr. Larkin it will be then time enough for his Excellency to deal with the matter.' Mr. Larkin took up the implied challenge embodied in the official statement and filled two long columns of the issue of his paper on April 5, 1913, with details of his intercourse with the exalted authorities at Viceregal Lodge and the Castle. There was an allegation that, in the trouble of 1908, Lord Aberdeen ' importuned ' Mr. Larkin to go to the Castle to have a chat about the strike, and that his Excellency placed a special motor-car at

[1] Mr. McCormick denies that he ever stated either to the Lord-Lieutenant or any other person that Mr. Larkin had been unjustly sentenced.

his disposal for use in the subsequent negotiations. He also averred that he and several of his colleagues were invited to tea at the Viceregal Lodge, and that at the symposium, over which Lady Aberdeen presided, he, Mr. Larkin, made it a condition of a settlement that all the men who had been arrested in connection with the strike should be released. The sequel as told in Mr. Larkin's own words was this : ' " What do you mean ? " said the last of the Gordons, his Excellency. " I mean this," said Larkin ; " and if this is not granted the dispute continues—that every man who has been arrested or sentenced in connection with this dispute shall be released, and shall be with wife, mother, or family, as the case may be, on Christmas Eve." Will he deny that a certain gentleman, a responsible head of the Government, objected and said that such a request should not be made publicly to his Excellency ? Will his Excellency deny that Mr. Larkin has in his possession, where the Castle minions won't find it until it is necessary to produce same, the paper from Mr. Isaac Mitchell, of the Board of Trade, dated December 1908, written in black lead, " Your request granted ; kindly furnish list of men." Will his Excellency deny that he or his minions have or had in their possession a list of the men's names furnished by James Larkin : of men lying in Mountjoy and Kilmainham Gaols, either under remand or sentence, to the number of 53 who were released on December 24, 1908 ? ' In this interrogative form the list of allegations was considerably expanded, and the whole effusion concluded with a gross personal attack on Lord and Lady Aberdeen. In the House of Commons Mr. Birrell gave a general denial to the assertions contained in the article.

The whole affair afforded a striking commentary on Mr. Larkin's peculiar methods. As he is not bound by contracts, so he is not hampered by the honourable conventions that make social intercourse possible. He was ready to abuse the confidence of the Viceroy at the

moment when it appeared that some end could be
achieved by doing so.   The circumstance that to Lord
Aberdeen he owed his release from a long term of imprisonment seemed almost to add zest to the task of laying
bare the intimacies of private life.   Mr. Larkin gave
special prominence to details which he knew would cause
pain, and he dragged in perfectly irrelevant matter with
the special object of adding force to his brutal attack
on the great functionary who had befriended him.   His
parade of ingratitude was no doubt a calculated performance designed for the benefit of the ignorant crowd
who would not fail to see how puny are the Viceroys
when faced by his Majesty of the People in the person
of Mr. James Larkin.   It would be useless to waste words
in denunciation of the spirit of moral lawlessness that
runs through all this chapter in the history of Larkinism.

Mr. Larkin, we may safely assume, thought that the
world was going very well at this particular period
in his career.   He had harassed to a point almost beyond
endurance large employers of labour like Messrs. Jacob,
he had infused terror into the hearts of the whole of
the smaller traders whose businesses were exceptionally
dependent upon labour, and he had won in a stand-up
fight with one of the greatest of the Irish shipping companies.   He was, in fact, almost at the pinnacle of his
fame as a labour agitator.   One notable series of victories,
however, remained to be achieved.   These were sur-
renders wrung from the leading shipping companies
who had been drawn into the struggle with the City of
Dublin Steam Packet Company.   The capitulating firms
included the Dublin-Silloth and Isle of Man Co., the British
and Irish Steam Packet Co., the Bristol Steam Navigation
Co., the Clyde Shipping Co., the Duke Shipping Co., and
Messrs. Tedcastle, McCormick & Co.   Virtually the
whole of the Irish shipping interest had now been brought
to book by the Dictator of Liberty Hall.   The firms
concerned had been driven to the highly distasteful

course of making a composition with their tormentor by the tremendous force exercised by an economic situation of daily increasing seriousness. They had conceded much as the City of Dublin Steam Packet Co. had done, in the hope rather than the expectation that a more or less permanent peace might be thereby bought. If they had been dealing with an ordinary Trade Union of the English type they would almost certainly not have been disappointed, for the agreement to which the representatives of the Union—Mr. Larkin and Messrs. John O'Neill and Patrick Nolan—set their hands was a straightforward undertaking carrying with it the apparent assurance of lasting harmony. Its terms are so important for a full understanding of the true spirit of Larkinism that the essential clause may be given here. It runs: 'Any question as to interpretation of this agreement, or any dispute arising between the men and their employers, to be submitted to the latter in writing : no stoppage of work to take place pending negotiations regarding such matters. This agreement to be binding on all concerned, and at least one month's notice to either side to be given of any intention to terminate it—the terms of this agreement to come into force on Monday, June 2, 1913.' The language of the foregoing is so clear as to preclude any possibility of legitimate misunderstanding. 'Lightning strikes' were to be things of the past and complaints were to be submitted in writing. There was to be order and reason where hitherto there had been a capricious and arbitrary method of handling disputes. As a paper arrangement the agreement represented a distinct advance on what had previously been obtained from the same source. If it had been given a fair trial it might have inaugurated a new era in the relations of employer and employed in the port. It would assuredly have averted many of the calamities that ultimately fell upon the city. But the syndicalistic theory, already quoted, that an agreement is only binding upon the workmen just as long as it suits them to accept it, had too powerful an influence to permit of anything so just and reasonable as the testing of the machinery provided by the understanding.

Barely was the ink dry upon the document in which the terms of the concordat were embodied than a flagrant breach of the agreement occurred. Some men who were working on a vessel called the *Sandow*, belonging to the Clyde Shipping Co., without a moment's notice, ceased work. On inquiry by Mr. Young, the manager, it was found that the grievance was that the men were not receiving such large wages as the Company's employees in Belfast. This, it was represented, was the more important matter, as there existed in the northern port a union which was inimical to Mr. Larkin and which he regarded with a mutual feeling of aversion. The excuse put forward for the gross violation of the compact was too flimsy even for Larkinite impudence to uphold, and in the end the men were ordered back to work ; but as a consequence of the dispute the vessel lost a tide, a rather serious matter for the company. The incident just described, which took place in the first week in June 1913, boded ill for the maintenance of the peace of the port, even on the precarious tenure that an agreement, terminable on a single month's notice, supplied. If this easy renunciation of the responsibilities imposed under the contract was possible a few days after the sealing of the bond, what was likely to happen later, when the lapse of time had brought to the front new questions of real importance from the workers' standpoint ? The answer to this was not long in coming, as we shall see in the next chapter. Anticipating a little, we may say that the agreement was treated as if it were no more than waste paper.

After the shipowners, it was the turn of the builders to feel the weight of the Larkinite dictatorship. In the middle of June a demand was made from Liberty Hall for an increase of wages for the men employed by Messrs. J. & C. McGloughlin & Co., a well-known Dublin firm. All the Dublin builders and allied trades belong to a federation, the members of which have a common understanding as to wages and hours of work. In consonance with this arrangement, Messrs. McGloughlin informed Mr. Larkin that the application would be sent to the federation and duly considered by them. This, however, was a course which did not suit the policy of the Irish Transport Workers' Union. Combination, excepting on the men's side, as has been shown in earlier pages, was abhorrent to the Larkinite mind. The shrewd perception of the agitator doubtless made it clear to him that his system could not long survive if the threatened interests united in defence in a thorough-going way. Therefore, when he received a reply from Messrs. McGloughlin, he offered strong resistance to the proposal that the question should be dealt with by the general body of builders, and he ignored their invitation to a conference to discuss the matter ; later stating that he did not receive their letters, although one had been sent under registered cover.

Mr. Larkin, finding his way barred in this manner, now raised an entirely new issue. He accomplished this in characteristic fashion by causing, or at all events utilising, local friction in the workshops for the attack on the firm of Messrs. J. & C. McGloughlin. A man who was put on to manage a particular machine refused to work on some flimsy pretext. After it had been shown by the substitution of another workman that the machine was in proper order, the offender was dismissed. Thereupon, without notice of any kind, Mr. Larkin withdrew all members of the Irish Transport Union from the firm's establishment. Almost immediately he followed up this action by sending in a demand for a reply to the application of June 18 for increased wages, but was again referred by Messrs. McGloughlin to the agreement which all builders had as to common action. Ultimately the Masters' Association

decided to consult the Trades Council, and to invite them
to send delegates to a conference. This course having
been adopted, a meeting took place, Messrs. O'Brien and
Simmons, Vice-President and Secretary of the Trades
Council, and Mr. Larkin appearing to represent the
Trades Council. In the discussion Mr. Larkin resolutely
declined to allow the Association to treat with the Trades
Council on the subject of the increased wages, and he was
supported in his view by Mr. Simmons. Mr. O'Brien
held the opinion that Messrs. McGloughlin were justified
in dealing with the matter through the Employers'
Association, and frankly stated that he considered it an
advantage to be able to deal with such an association.
His views were afterwards reflected in the resolution
adopted by the Trades Council on the subject, which was
to the following effect : ' That this Council approves of
the idea of Collective Bargaining, and we believe that all
matters in dispute can be more easily dealt with by such
means than by dealing with individuals.'

In a letter sent to the Masters' Association embodying
this resolution, the Trades Council stated that they thought
that Messrs. McGloughlin should re-instate the man victimised, and that the question of wages and conditions of
work should be settled between the Association and the
men's Union. Mr. Larkin, however, persisted in his attitude, and the Association reluctantly decided that they
would have no alternative but to lock out all their employees until such time as the Trades Council insisted on
Collective Bargaining by one of its affiliated unions.
At the same time the Association were of the opinion
that it would only be fair to consult the various trades
unions which would be affected before doing so. In the
meantime they refused to employ any members of the Irish
Transport Union. Ultimately a settlement was arrived
at by the man who had been dismissed apologising to
Messrs. McGloughlin and agreeing to carry out all their
instructions, which apology was accepted and the man

re-instated.   The question of wages, it was arranged
should be referred to the Association and the Union.

Almost simultaneously with this dispute the Larkinite
policy produced a stoppage in the engineering trade.   The
originating cause of the trouble was a strike which had
been manipulated at the Savoy Restaurant in Grafton
Street.   In order to isolate the business, Mr. Larkin issued
his edict that no one should work for the company in any
shape or form.   A firm of carters who transacted the
carrying business of the establishment saw fit to ignore
the order.   Not to be beaten in this way, Mr. Larkin put
on an additional screw by prohibiting Messrs. Booth, a
well-known firm of engineers, from doing work for the
carting firm.   As Messrs. Booth in their turn declined to
be dictated to, the engineers were called out in the trade
generally.   An appeal was made to the head quarters of
the Amalgamated Society of Engineers in London against
this monstrous act of tyranny, and a reply came back
that the men were not to come out, but were to remain at
work as long as their lives were not endangered.   This
was satisfactory as far as it went, but unfortunately Mr.
Larkin was able to cut off the supplies of the engineering
firms by inducing the carters to decline to handle their
goods.   The stoppage of the trade was thus eventually
brought about, ' all because,' as Mr. Healy afterwards
whimsically said at the Government Inquiry, ' of this
little dispute in a sweet shop in Grafton Street.'   What
the interruption of business meant may be gauged from
the fact that Messrs. Spence & Co., the firm in Cork
Street to which we have previously referred, had at the
time a contract for £30,000 for Messrs. Guinness & Co.

The Puck-like activities of Mr. Larkin almost always
seemed to be in the direction in which the greatest mischief could be worked to the permanent interests of the
Dublin trade.

CHAPTER XI

METHODS OF THE YAHOO

Mr. W. M. Murphy begins to move—Scurrilous Attacks on Mr. Murphy in the *Irish Worker*—Purge of Larkinites from the *Independent* Dispatch Department and the Tramway Company's Traffic Staff—The Larkinite Counter-Movement—Messrs. Eason & Son Attacked —'Tainted Goods' again—Disorganisation of the Shipping Industry—Menaces of the *Irish Worker*—The True Character of Larkinism.

USUALLY where a tyranny is established it is from within rather than from without that the force which breaks the chains comes. In the case of the Larkinite domination this was peculiarly so. Dublin trade was saved from possible extinction and certain permanent injury by one of its citizens, and he a prominent employer. Those who have followed the narrative will not need to be told that the industrial Wellington who was pitted against the Larkinite Napoleon was Mr. William Martin Murphy. I have already told the story of this gentleman's antecedents, and I need not repeat the details here. It is sufficient for my immediate purpose to bring him prominently on to the stage at the moment when Messrs. Jacob and the shipping companies were desperately struggling to free themselves from the tentacles of the Liberty Hall octopus, which had them in its vicious grasp. Mr. Murphy, watching this unequal conflict and ruminating on the position, especially as it was revealed in the *Irish Worker*, came to the conclusion that the time had arrived for him to take a hand in the business. Though so far no attack had been made on his business concerns, he realised that the day was not distant when he would be called upon to face the Liberty Hall forces. Like a good general, he decided to choose his own time for the fight. For this he was afterwards criticised by labour apologists, but obviously he would have been singularly foolish if he had waited for the attack to develop in the fashion which had caused ruinous loss to not a few business houses.

Mr. Larkin himself, judging from the character of his writings in the *Irish Worker*, was, in the early half of 1913, spoiling for a fight with Mr. Murphy. Scarcely an issue of the journal came out without the vilest abuse of that gentleman and all who were connected in any way with his enterprises. An example may be given of Mr. Larkin's infuriate style of conducting controversy. One day during the strike of the City of Dublin Company's employees the *Independent* published a story, written by a member of its reporting staff, illustrative of the strain that the dispute was putting upon the men who had come out. It was headed ' My Daddy's on Strike,' and related how a forlorn, half-starved boy encountered in the street had replied, in the words forming the title to the contribution, to a question as to why he was begging. There is not the least reason to suppose that the facts were otherwise than as related by the reporter. At all events, Mr. Murphy probably had as little to do with the publication of the story as he had with the issue of a ticket of a particular number to a passenger travelling the same day on the tramway. But the episode was a good enough excuse for the pouring out of two columns of unmitigated Billingsgate upon Mr. Murphy's devoted head. The article (published in the *Irish Worker*, February 15, 1913) opened with the statement that ' throughout the past week every issue of the *Daily Independent* and *Evening Herald*, owned by the most foul and vicious blackguard that ever polluted any country—whose career has been

I

one long series of degrading and destroying the characters
of men who he was, and is, not fit to be a doormat for—a
creature who is living on the sweated victims who are compelled to slave for this modern journalistic vampire——'
So possessed with rage was the writer that he omitted
to finish his sentence.   But he made it clear afterwards
that it was the story of the starving child that rankled.
' Fancy,' he exlaimed, ' William Martin Murphy sympa-
thising with a hungry child, the Ghoul, the creature who
swated [sic] and starved a whole country-side during the
strike of the railway slaves in Clare, the Ghoul who has
sacked hundreds of men for trivial complaints, knowing
that such dismissal meant actual starvation for those
dismissed men's children.   Why, there is not a labourer
in the employment of this capitalistic vampire who is
not at all times in a state of semi-starvation.'   There
was much more of this incoherent vilification of Mr.
Murphy, accompanied by miscellaneous mud-throwing
at those who in the press or on the platform had dared
to criticise the Larkinite methods.   Mr. Larkin's vituperative vocabulary never seemed to exhaust itself, and
again and again he returned to the attack on these
' skunk journals,' these ' Murphyite rags.'   ' They are,'
he said on one occasion, in a very frenzy of hate, ' as rotten
as the heart of their owner, and it is as rotten as hell.'
Somewhat later he wrote of Mr. Murphy :   ' Will this
hypocrite never be tarred and feathered ? '

If Mr. Larkin had stopped at mere abuse, Mr. Murphy
would probably have left him to void his filth unchecked.
No one knew better than he what little effect this moral
sewage had if it was left in its obscurity.   It was only
when the labour dictator gave evidence of his design
to follow up his vitriolic attacks by action of the familiar
kind that Mr. Murphy came to the conclusion that
the hour had arrived for him to move.   The particular
manœuvre of the Liberty Hall contingent which had
convinced him that a strike was maturing, was the

incorporation in the Union of the boys engaged in the dispatch department of the *Independent,* and of the youths who were employed in somewhat analogous duties in the branch of the tramway enterprise which has to do with the delivery of parcels. These youngsters are in the humblest ranks of the workers employed in both concerns, but they play a comparatively important part in the organisations to which they belong, since upon their active discharge of their functions depends the success of the whole operations. Realising, from the character of the Larkinite preparations, that the plan of campaign was to cripple his enterprises by calling out these lads at the moment when their services would be most valuable—which he calculated, accurately as it proved, would be during Dublin's great social festival —the Horse Show Week—Mr. Murphy boldly took the initiative by summoning a meeting of all the employees in the dispatch department of the *Independent.* At the gathering, which was held on August 15, Mr. Murphy made a business-like speech, putting before the workmen in plain language the policy that he had decided to pursue. While repudiating any hostility to legitimate trade unionism, he declared that he could not retain in his service any who belonged to Mr. Larkin's organisation, which was an irresponsible wrecking concern with which it was impossible for employers to work. When he had finished he asked pointedly who were prepared to obey his orders and who were anxious to enrol themselves under Mr. Larkin's banner. A show of hands revealed that the assembly was about equally divided. ' Very well then,' said Mr. Murphy in effect to the Larkinite section, ' you can take a week's wages in lieu of notice. If you mean to go on strike when Mr. Larkin calls you, you are no longer any use to me, and you may go now.' This direct manner of dealing with them took the malcontents somewhat aback, and they pleaded for time to consider their positions. The concession

was readily granted, but the result was a foregone conclusion. As soon as the Liberty Hall fraternity discovered
what was in the wind, they took good care that the lads
should not go back save to announce their adhesion to
the Union. It appeared from the sequel that most of
them were so anxious to shake the dust of the *Independent*
office from their feet that they did not wait to take
their wages.

Mr. Murphy, having effectually laid bare the position
at the *Independent* in the manner described, turned his
attention to the tramways. On discovering that Mr.
Larkin, preparatory to a strike, was getting the members
of the traffic staff (drivers and conductors) by persuasion
and intimidation into the Transport Workers' Union,
he himself called the men together to ascertain how
far he could rely upon them in an emergency. Mr.
Murphy found that, though a large number had become
connected with Mr. Larkin's organisation, the majority
were loyal to the company, and having given notice that
any man intimidating others to join the union would be
dismissed—a notice which was acted on—he was content
to await the development of events.

The Larkinite attack was not long delayed. It
took the form, in the first instance, of an organised effort
to prevent the sale and distribution of the paper. No
great difficulty was experienced, with the employment
of the intimidatory practices familiar to Liberty Hall,
in temporarily interrupting the free circulation of the
journal. Newsagents are, from the very nature of their
occupation, widely scattered, and the task of ' peace-
fully persuading ' them not to display the *Independent*
contents' bills, or to sell the paper over the counter,
was one well within the range of the activities of the
indefatigable and unscrupulous pickets. But it was
not enough to terrorise the smaller fry of shopkeepers
into compliance with the Union's edicts. If the end
aimed at was to be fully achieved, it was imperative that

the higher game, represented by the great newspaper distributing agency of Messrs. Eason & Son—the W. H Smith & Co. of Ireland—should be reached. Messrs. Eason & Son are one of the firms of which Dublin citizens are justly proud. From small beginnings the business has been built up to a great enterprise with many branches and a clientele which embraces every class of the community. The headquarters' establishment is in Middle Abbey Street, in direct connection with an extensive retail business in Lower Sackville Street, while an important manufacturing enterprise is carried on in large premises in Gloucester Street. But the feature of the firm's operations which is most in evidence to the visitor to Ireland is the railway bookstall trade. At every station of any importance in and near Dublin, Messrs. Eason & Son have a newspaper and bookselling business of the familiar kind, at which travellers can obtain all the leading journals and periodicals of the day. Manifestly no blow struck at the *Independent* could be effective without the support of this firm. Mr. Larkin, with a ready perception of the fact, at an early period brought his heavy artillery to bear on the house. Mr. Charles Eason, the head of the firm, who had already had a sample of the mischievous power of the Union in a series of attacks made upon him in the *Irish Worker*, was disposed at first to temporise with the enemy ; but as soon as the true character of the campaign which had been entered upon was revealed, he took the only course which a self-respecting firm could adopt when faced with a dictatorial demand to cease doing business for a customer—he resolutely declined to be a participator in the operations against the *Independent* by excluding their paper from his list. This open defiance of the decrees of Liberty Hall drew down upon the firm the unwelcome attentions of the organisation.

Out of the well-stocked armoury at his head quarters for the coercion of the unwilling employer, Mr. Larkin

drew out once more that now familiar weapon—'tainted
goods.' This he applied with a characteristically reckless disregard of the effect that might be produced in
quarters which were quite innocent of offence, even
regarded from the peculiar standpoint of Larkinite
ethics. His first blow was struck at the shipping industry,
in whose affairs, as we have seen, he had always displayed
an unwholesome interest. It was the easiest thing in
the world to pick a quarrel in this direction. In the
nature of the things hardly a ship came into port without
bringing a consignment of papers and periodicals for
Messrs. Eason & Son. The crisis was reached on
August 23, when the dock labourers, acting under Mr.
Larkin's orders, refused to unload the *Lady Gwendoline*
of the British and Irish Steam Packet Company's service
because she had on board goods for Messrs. Eason. A
more paltry excuse for a strike was never tendered on
the Dublin Quay, though interruptions of work on the
most trivial grounds have long been experienced there.
But even if there had been a justification for the objection of the men to carry on the task of unloading, they
put themselves in the wrong by ignoring the terms of
the agreement of June 2, by striking without notice. Mr.
Larkin was appealed to to secure the due enforcement
of the contract, and after some delay he condescended
to issue orders for the resumption of work. Two days
later, however, fresh trouble arose when the Silloth
Company's steamer *Yarrow* came into port, and further
'tainted goods' offended the susceptible nostrils of the
dock labourers. On their flat refusal to handle the
cargo the masters called a conference at Messrs.
McCormick's, and invited Mr. Larkin to attend. Mr.
Larkin put in an appearance at the meeting, and, when
the infringement of the agreement was brought to his
notice, he gave his personal guarantee that there should
be no more trouble, whether there were 'tainted goods'
on board the ships to be unloaded or not. Apparently

he afterwards repented of his adhesion to the bargain, for two days later he intimated to the employers he could not get his men to handle 'tainted goods.' When taxed with bad faith, Mr. Larkin replied: 'When an army rebels, what is a commander to do?' He received the answer that might have been expected from a body of hard-headed business men. He was told that the revolt of the men was a mere pretence, that he could bend them to his will if he wished; but that he did not wish, because it suited his purpose that they should come out in order that he might embarrass Messrs. Eason & Son and hit through them at his arch enemy—Mr. Murphy.

Apart from the modest satisfaction that comes of speaking one's mind freely, the employers got nothing out of their interviews with Mr. Larkin. They were left with the uneasy reflection that they could no longer rely, to the slight extent that they had hitherto done, on the *bona fides* of the labour leader or upon agreements in which he had the smallest part. This view was borne in upon them the more strongly by the stories they heard from the lips of many of the workers on the quays —their old servants—that they were anxious to work on the ships but that they were prevented from doing so by the system of terrorism maintained under Mr. Larkin's direction. It was asserted by the men that they were attacked in the streets, that pickets visited their houses and frightened their wives, and that the malignant influence of Liberty Hall even extended to the schools, where their children were denounced as 'scabs' and otherwise insulted.

While the shipping magnates were facing the extremely unpleasant vista opened up by the violation of the agreement which they had hoped was to inaugurate an era of peace, the fight against the *Independent*—or, more properly speaking, against Mr. Murphy—was being prosecuted with all the resources that Mr. Larkin could

command.   His pickets were active, and not a stone was
left unturned by him or them to secure adherents to
the Union and to intimidate those who dared to continue
at work for the enemy in defiance of the orders of Liberty
Hall.   Meanwhile, the columns of the *Irish Worker*
bore witness to the savagery with which the aims of the
organisation were pushed.   ' Every dog and devil, thief
and saint,' wrote the editor, ' is getting an invitation to
come and work for the Dublin Tramway Co.   Every
man applying is asked : " Do you belong to Larkin's
Union ?   If so, no employment."   " Will you ever join
Larkin's Union.   If so, no employment."   Well, Mr. Wm.
M. Murphy will know—I hope to his and Alderman
Cotton's satisfaction and the shareholders' benefit—who
is in Larkin's Union, and who will have to be in it.
Every man he is employing is known to us.   What say
Howard and Paddy Byrne ?   What say Scab O'Neill ?
What say Kenna, Lawlor, &c. ?   We have them all on
the list.   Mr. Wm. Martin Murphy's satellites, Gordon
and Tresillian, have discharged some ten men for being
in the Union.   Right, William the Saint.   We have not
moved, will not move until we are ready.   Woe betide
scabs then ! '   The old note of intimidation rings here
as blatantly as ever.   No man was to dare to act in
opposition to the Union.   If he did, woe betide him.

Larkinism, as we now see it, stands revealed in its
true colours.   Masquerading as a trade union, it had
little in common with the trade organisations of England
and Scotland but the name.   The sense of responsibility
which, with few exceptions, has marked the modern
history of those organisations was entirely wanting.
The sole guiding principle of Larkinism was the will
of the founder, who arrogated to himself despotic powers
and exercised them with an absolutism which few
monarchs would dare to emulate.   Agreements were
flagrantly broken.   There was a contemptuous disregard,
even of the ordinary conventions of industrial warfare,

in the manner in which strikes were called. Employers were struck at indiscriminately, the good with the bad ; and the most vindictive vendetta was carried against one firm which was especially distinguished for its humane and considerate treatment of its employees. The methods of controversy followed were those of the Yahoo. In gutter language of the vilest kind, anyone and everyone who crossed the path of the arch-agitator was traduced and held up to ridicule. The myrmidons of the Union were ubiquitous, carrying on their crusade of intimidation with a callousness which is happily rare in the annals of militant industrialism. The propaganda was ostentatiously revolutionary in its character. Betterment of the workers' conditions was a mere stalking-horse for a far-reaching scheme of Red Republicanism, in which the elimination of the capitalist by a drastic process had a conspicuous place. In fine, the movement had the worst qualities of syndicalism with the added drawback of a personal ascendancy based on the skilful exercise of an elaborate system of moral and physical terrorism.

Such being the character of the organisation, it is not remarkable that it aroused in Dublin feelings of the deepest anxiety amongst those who were in any way dependent upon the maintenance of the trade of the city. It was increasingly felt as the weeks went on that, if a check were not given to the sinister power which had established itself in their midst, irremediable injury would be done to many important branches of Dublin's industry.

CHAPTER XII

THE STRIKE THAT FAILED

The Dublin Season—Horse Show Week selected for a Tramway Strike—
Mr. Larkin's Miscalculation—Failure of his *Coup*—Inflammatory
Oratory in Beresford Place—Arrest of Mr. Larkin and his four
Principal Associates—Police Court Proceedings—The Prosecution
a Mistake—Incendiary Speeches—Police charge the Mob—A
Frankly Anarchical Crusade.

THE Dublin social season is an attenuated version of the
London season and a mere shadow of the spacious period
of the city's life as a capital a century ago.   It is practically confined to a single week at the end of the summer,
when the horse show, for which Dublin is famous, draws
visitors from every part of the world.   But this Horse
Show Week is a time of glorious life, when Ireland for
the nonce forgets her political troubles and gives way to
gaiety and the mild form of dissipation which shows
itself in a constant round of dinners, garden parties, and
balls.   During the period a fructifying stream of money
flows through every artery of Dublin's trade.   The hotels
are crowded to the utmost limit, the car drivers and
livery stable keepers are overwhelmed with patronage,
the shops are thronged with customers, and all the members of the humbler fraternity of the streets—the news-
vendors, the street hawkers, the luggage porters, and the
beggars—are made happy by the liberality of the pleasure-
seeking crowd.   At no other period in the whole year
would disorganisation of the ordinary machinery of life

produce more widespread inconvenience and loss to the community.

With the eye of a tactician who cares nothing for the consequences of his action so long as the end he seeks is achieved, Mr. Larkin selected this supremely important juncture in Dublin's life for the delivery of his *coup*. The position, as it existed on the eve of the Horse Show Week, was that he had got into his Union a certain number of the tramway traffic men in addition to about 120 of the parcel department who had been dismissed when Mr. Murphy made his purge of Larkinites a few weeks earlier. He had a leverage for a strike, and a very powerful one, or one which would have been powerful if he had had to reckon with ordinary conditions. But, as has been indicated, he was confronted with an exceedingly able antagonist who, all the weeks that the trouble was brewing, had been quietly perfecting his arrangements to meet the crisis whenever it should arrive. Every precaution that could be taken against attack was taken. Extra men were engaged and held in reserve to supply the place of the road repair men who, it was surmised— accurately as it proved—would be drawn out at the first summons from the Larkinite head quarters. The power house, with its delicate and indispensable machinery, was carefully surveyed and arrangements were made for dealing with any emergency that might arise, and stock was generally taken of the resources that were available to supply deficiencies in a time of crisis.

Mr. Larkin, like a good many schemers before his time, proved in this business of the tramway strike ' too clever by half,' to use a popular phrase. He conceived the brilliant idea of calling a strike at an hour when the tramways were fully working. The edict was to go forth like a flash of lightning from Liberty Hall, and lo! and behold, as a testimony to the power of a master mind, the whole tramway system was to be brought to a standstill at the same moment.

The course of events on the first day of the strike—August 26—may be briefly related. At a quarter to ten o'clock in the morning, at various points in the city, and notably in the central area, cars were deserted by their drivers and conductors and left derelict. In a few cases passengers were bluntly told that they had better get out as no more cars would be run ; but, generally speaking, no explanation was vouchsafed. The men simply got off the cars and donned the badge of the Irish Transport Union—a red hand—as a sign of their revolt against constituted authority. Posting themselves at convenient vantage points they awaited the development of the crisis with an assumption of confidence which their nervousness belied. They were not long before they discovered that the Larkinite strike had conspicuously failed. With a celerity which did credit to the perfection of their organisation, the tramway management got into the sheds the derelict cars, and reorganised the service with the aid of the emergency hands drawn from the clerical and executive staff. Within a little over an hour of the calling of the strike the service was in full swing again. In view of the fact that about 150 men out of a total of 750 had been enticed from their allegiance, the tramway directors were reasonably proud of the manner in which they had met the crisis. But it was perfectly clear that, though the Larkinites had been badly worsted in the first action, they had not by any means abandoned the fight. Although the day closed without any serious incident, it was obvious that there was an ugly temper abroad which, on small provocation, would manifest itself in disturbance of the peace. Sullen groups at street corners greeted the men on the running cars with execrations, and in out-of-the-way portions of the routes open intimidation was practised. The next day brought no real relaxation of the strain. The cars were run with fair regularity on almost all the routes, but they had at several points to encounter a hostile mob, who threw stones freely, and in a few cases broke the windows of the cars with their missiles. The defection of a small number of motor men on the Kingsbridge line and a brutal assault committed on an elderly driver were further indications that the Larkinite influence was still active.

Mr. Larkin himself had already given impressive proof that he did not accept the defeat of his plans against the tramways as more than a temporary check. In addressing a meeting of strikers, held at the accustomed labour rendezvous in Beresford Place on the night of August 26, he used the most violent language, apparently to cover up the discomfiture of the morning. Declaiming against ' police brutality,' he urged his supporters to adopt Sir Edward Carson's advice to the men of Ulster. ' If,' he said, ' it is right and legal for the men of Ulster to arm, why should it not be right and legal for the men of Dublin to arm themselves to protect themselves ? You will need it. I don't offer advice which I am not prepared to adopt myself. You know me, and you know when I say a thing I will do it. So arm, and I'll arm. You have to face hired assassins. If Sir Edward Carson is right in telling the men of Ulster to form a Provisional Government in Ulster, I think I must be right, too, in telling you to form a Provisional Government in Dublin. But whether you form a Provisional Government or not, you will require arms, for Aberdeen has promised Murphy not only the police but the soldiers, and my advice to you is to be round the doors and corners, and whenever one of your men is shot, shoot two of theirs. Now we will hold our next big meeting in O'Connell Street, come what may, and we will show them that we can use the property for which we pay.'

At any time a naked incitement to violence of this

character would have been reprehensible ; but, uttered as it was at a moment of public turmoil when the passions of the mob were aroused by the necessary measures of the police for the preservation of order, it was peculiarly mischievous and even dangerous. The Government, who had been watching with increasing anxiety the spread of the spirit of lawlessness and were only too well aware how speedily in Ireland the spoken word is followed by action, felt that so daring and outrageous a challenge to their authority could not be allowed to pass unnoticed. Within twenty-four hours of the delivery of the speech, orders were issued for the prosecution of Mr. Larkin and his four principal associates—Messrs. P. T. Daly, Wm. Partridge, Wm. O'Brien, and Thomas Lawlor. The arrests were quietly effected early on the morning of August 28, and later in the day the defendants were brought before Mr. Swifte, police court magistrate, to answer the charges. In the course of the proceedings attempts were made to shake the evidence of the police witness who took a note of the incriminating speech, but the substantial accuracy of the transcript was established. Mr. Larkin, who defended himself, at the close of the evidence made an excited speech in which he denounced the Government for taking proceedings against him which it was too cowardly to institute against Sir Edward Carson. ' Is there a law,' he asked, ' which says that we must not meet in O'Connell Street, or to say that a peaceful procession cannot be held through it ? ' He went on to observe that anything he said he stood by. He called the soldiers hired assassins, but he did not describe the police in that manner. He told the respectable people to come to the O'Connell Street meeting with walking sticks. Was there anything unlawful in that ? he asked. The Government might put him in jail, he added, but they could not stop the meeting on Sunday. In the result the defendants were all returned for trial, but were admitted to bail on the understanding that they would not attend illegal meetings or make inflammatory speeches in the interval before the final hearing of their case.

In the light of after events it may be doubted whether the action of the authorities in arresting the strike leaders at this juncture was a wise one. The language used by Mr. Larkin in the impugned passages of his speech was beyond question outrageous. His general conduct and attitude also showed an intention on his part to defy the law and produce a condition of public anarchy. But it was worse than useless to take proceedings against him if they were not to result in an immediate curtailment of his power of mischief. In point of fact the only effect of the Government's action was to give Mr. Larkin a splendid advertisement, of which he stood at the moment sorely in need, and to rally to his side bodies of workers who in other circumstances might have been at best lukewarm supporters of his extreme propaganda. Cheering crowds bore him and his associates, on their release, in triumph from the Police Court to Liberty Hall, where exultant speeches were made to a dense mass of spectators of the working class who had been attracted by the always compelling spectacle of victims of Government oppression relating the tale of their afflictions. A note of defiance ran through all these utterances—a note which gained in shrillness and confidence as the hours sped by and the growing excitement evoked by the operations directed from Liberty Hall appeared to give a surer guarantee of adequate popular support for the contemplated flouting of authority involved in the attempt to hold the Sunday meeting within the prohibited limits of Sackville Street or, to give it its popular name, O'Connell Street. The orgy of exultant oratory culminated, on the evening of August 29, in a great demonstration in Beresford Place attended by some 10,000 persons, at which the Government proclamation prohibiting the gathering, issued a few hours previously, was publicly burned by Mr. Larkin with every manifestation of contempt, to the accompaniment of the frenzied cheers of the crowd which packed the square to the last inch of standing room.

The speeches made at this gathering on the night of August 29 were pitched in a specially violent key. There was a reference at the beginning to action on the part of the strikers which, in Kruger's words, would 'stagger humanity.' Mr. Larkin himself adopted a deliberately provocative and inflammatory style. 'I care as much,' he said, alluding to the proclamation, 'for the King as I do for Mr. Swifte the magistrate. People make kings and people can unmake them; but what has the King of England to do with stopping a meeting in Dublin? If they like to stop the meeting at the order of Mr. Murphy, Mr. Wm. Murphy will take the responsibility; and, as I have previously told you, for every man that falls on our side two will fall on the other. We have a perfect right to meet in O'Connell Street. We are going to meet in O'Connell Street, and if the police or soldiers are going to stop or try to stop us, let them take the responsibility. If they want a revolution, well then, God be with them.' In another portion of the speech Mr. Larkin advocated a no-rent campaign and got the meeting to recite after him a pledge to this effect : ' I will pay no rent until the tramway men have got the conditions they demand.' A characteristic remark by Mr. Larkin, the significance of which we are told by a reporter was not lost upon his hearers, was : ' A man who would starve while there is food in the shops is an idiot and deserves to die.'

The vast audience responded to the mood of the moment. The cheering was fierce in its intensity and excitement was at fever heat. There were some ugly moments when it seemed that the combustible elements lying about amongst the crowd in over-generous profusion would explode with lamentable results. But the Larkinite leaders had the men well under control, and their exertions, coupled with the tactful action of the police, saved the situation, temporarily at least.   It was only when the meeting was over and the crowd was dispersing that any disturbance occurred.   Then the long pent-up feelings of the demonstrators found vent in attacks on the police, which were promptly met by a succession of baton charges. Before these charges the rioters fled like chaff before the wind, but some of the less agile of them received blows from the policemen's weapons which sent them home sadder and probably wiser men.

Affairs had now reached a stage at which it was evident that trouble of a very serious kind was unavoidable. Authority had been trampled underfoot with a calculated insolence which could not have been disregarded, even if the maintenance of respect for the law had been the only issue to be settled.   But it was clear that something a good deal more vital than the vindication of the power of the executive was involved.   The movement had assumed the character of a frankly anarchical crusade, in which all the disorderly elements of the population were banded together to establish a local version of the Reign of Terror, through the instrumentality of which the hated power of the capitalists, and particularly of their champion, Mr. Murphy, might be broken.   Those who have followed closely the story of the development of Larkinism related in the earlier chapters, will not be greatly surprised at the turn that events took.   The violence, both of action and language, which distinguished the policy of Mr. Larkin and his colleagues in these closing days of August, was the natural and almost inevitable outcome of the system which had been deliberately pursued from the first days of the establishment of the Transport Workers' Union. That organisation sprang into power by feeding the passions of the mob with a diet of highly spiced socialism, and it could not have lived if it had not kept up the supply of its peculiar provender by a course of antagonism to constituted authority.   The check given to Larkinism

K

by the failure of the tramway strike made the assertion of the ill-omened power of the Union the more necessary. If the wavering forces of the Union were to be held together, it could only be by the boldest assertion of the majesty of mob law with its corollary of the most open defiance that was possible of the edicts of the Government.

CHAPTER XIII

AN ORGY OF ANARCHY

Description of Sackville Street—The Larkinites Determine to Hold a
Meeting in the Thoroughfare—Rioting in the Ringsend District—
Attack on the Police in Beresford Square—Disturbance near the
Abbey Theatre—Savagery of the Mob—Terrible List of Casualties—
Sackville Street on Sunday, August 30—Melodramatic Appearance
of Mr. Larkin on the Balcony of the Imperial Hotel—His Arrest—
Outbreak of Rioting—Terrible Baton Charges by the Police—
Attack on the Inchicore Tramways—The Military called out.

DUBLIN'S citizens are properly proud of their great central thoroughfare, which is popularly known to strangers
as Sackville Street. An unusually broad street with
wide pavements, ample roadways, and a convenient
open space in the vicinity of the famous Nelson Pillar
to afford a centre for tramway traffic, it attracts to it
all the varied elements of the life of the city. On week-
days it is for the best part of the business hours thronged
with people shopping, and when night falls the youth
of both sexes takes possession of the pavements, which
they convert into a promenade. Sunday is the great
day of the week for this parade of Dublin juvenility. The
young people, in incredible numbers, then come out to
take the air, to see and be seen, and to enjoy the
opportunities of unrestrained companionship that the
meeting-ground offers. The street is rarely without its
crowds ; and all the time, week in, week out, a constant
stream of tramways is passing outwards in both directions
from the terminus under the shadow of the lofty monument
which dominates the position.

The selection of this important thoroughfare for a public meeting by the Larkinites could scarcely have had any other object than to foment disorder. They were already in possession of an admirable meeting-place in Beresford Square—a position at once central and spacious and free from objection on the score of any interruptions to the traffic by the assembled crowds. Here the members of the Union had for a long time previously met periodically to listen to their leaders, and here they might have continued to do so unmolested as long as they preserved the peace. There was involved, therefore, no question of the suppression of free speech, as was afterwards impudently asserted by the Larkinite apologists. All that was at issue was the right to assemble a disorderly crowd in the most frequented thoroughfare of the city, where its mere presence would constitute a source of grave public inconvenience, if not of actual danger. Challenged on such a point, the authorities could only use the full strength of the Government in the assertion of the right of the general body of the citizens to the unrestrained use of the street. They were under no illusions as to the character of the struggle that they had become involved in by the Larkinite action. The ferment visible in all the lower quarters of the city, and more especially those about the quays, told only too plainly the tale of the dangerous temper that was abroad. Under the stimulus of the anxiety caused by the popular symptoms, the Government caused the police force to be reinforced by considerable bodies of the Royal Irish Constabulary, both mounted and foot. These were disposed about the city in such a manner as to allow of the concentration of an overwhelming force on the Sackville Street area at any desired moment. At the same time the military were held in readiness to assist the civil arm in the event of the police finding the task of suppressing disorder too much for it.

Saturday, August 29, was a day of great anxiety for

those charged with the maintenance of order. Isolated acts of violence directed against tramway officials showed that the incitements of the previous night had not fallen on barren soil. In the earlier hours of the day the police found no difficulty in dealing with the situation; but, with the approach of evening, it speedily became evident that rough work was ahead.

The opening scene, in what was to prove a prolonged and sanguinary drama, was enacted in the Ringsend district. In his speech on Friday night Mr. Larkin had referred to a football match which was to be played on Saturday on the Shelbourne Ground at Ringsend between two local clubs. 'There are " scabs " in one of the teams, and you will not be there except as pickets,' he said, in language whose menacing character was understood by those who heard him. In obedience to the implied command, a large body of members of the Transport Workers' Union gathered at the time announced for the match near the entrance to the grounds. The Larkinites vigorously hooted the teams as they passed in; but, apart from this and an occasional scuffle between the pickets and those who entered the enclosure, there was no actual disturbance of the peace. A little later the temper of the demonstrators underwent a change. They gathered in considerable numbers on a bridge in the locality and indicated a clear intention to resort to violence against those who had excited their animosity. The small force of police present attempted to disperse them, but without success. Shortly afterwards, when reinforcements arrived, including a body of mounted officers, the attempt was renewed and the bridge was cleared. Now ensued some lively moments. A flower-pot thrown at the police from an adjacent house was a signal for a regular outbreak of violence. Tramway cars, crowded with passengers, were attacked by a howling mob, who broke the windows and assaulted the drivers and conductors. One occupant of a car, who had been struck by a stone, jumped off into

the roadway and threatened the rioters with a revolver—
a course which, in that instance, produced a cessation of
hostilities.   But soon the fight was raging as fiercely as
ever.   The police, finding that the crowd was rapidly
getting out of hand, drew their batons and charged.
They were, however, too few in number to make any
great impression on the mob, which had been augmented
by new arrivals.   At one point there seemed a danger
of the rioters getting the upper hand.   A ruffian seized
an inspector's sword, drew it from its scabbard, and
was about to use it upon the police when the weapon
was recaptured and the daring individual was arrested
for his pains.

Scenes of wild disorder followed.   The police were
savagely attacked and a number of them were injured
by the missiles thrown by the crowd.   A substantial reinforcement of police, sent to the scene of the disturbances
about six o'clock, had to fight their way through masses
of rioters at strategic points ; and when, later, prisoners
arrested in the various encounters were sent to the College
Street police station, the escort were stoned from the side
streets.   About an hour later Brunswick Street became
the scene of a hot encounter between the police and the
rioters, owing to attacks made on the tramway cars.   It
was only after a series of baton charges that the street
was cleared.

Nightfall brought an addition to the anxieties of the
harassed guardians of order.   Excitement increased every
moment, and it was manifest that a spirit of lawlessness
was abroad which would not be easily quelled.   Beresford Place now became the centre about which the conflict raged.   Here, about eight o'clock, a crowd gathered
in anticipation of a meeting announced for that hour.
Liberty Hall, with its doors heavily barricaded and its
windows mostly in darkness, presented an ominous appearance of calm.   About twenty policemen were on duty in
the vicinity of the square at the time, and, as the outlook

was apparently peaceful, the officer in charge considered that he might safely dispense with half his force. The detachment thus relieved had not long quitted the square before a fierce attack was made upon the squad left on duty. Stones and bottles were thrown at them, some from the crowd, but the larger number from the windows of the Transport Workers' Union building, which offered a safe vantage-ground for an attack of this kind. The police were ordered into the open by their superior officer, Inspector Campbell, and the word was given to charge the mob. One constable in the mêlée received a bad wound from a stone thrown from the window of Liberty Hall, and a bottle projected from the same quarter, doubtless intended for a constable, felled a rioter with whom he was engaged in conflict. Inspector Campbell himself was wounded in the face by a bottle and had to go off duty. Repeated charges were necessary before the rioters were dispersed ; and, so desperate was the fighting while it lasted, that the ambulances were kept busy for some time in removing the injured to the hospital.

The outbreak in Beresford Square was quickly followed by a still more dangerous disturbance near the Abbey Theatre. A riotous crowd which had assembled here was driven off by police charges, but the mob again collected in more formidable dimensions in Abbey Street. Sir John Ross, the head of the executive, who arrived on the scene at this juncture, impressed with the seriousness of the position, gave orders for the street to be cleared. The police in great force charged down the thoroughfare against the dense mass of rioters. At first the ground was stubbornly contested, viragos from the slum districts actively assisting the men in assaults on the hated representatives of the law. A number of constables dropped out of the attacking line with nasty wounds inflicted by the flying missiles. Disciplined force, however, eventually carried the day to the extent of dislodging the mob from the position it had taken up.

For some time the contest raged in adjacent localities. One particularly violent ebullition occurred as three injured constables, whose wounds had been dressed in hospital, were being escorted by their comrades back to the Store Street station. They were set upon in a most cowardly fashion by a howling mob of both sexes, who assailed them with volleys of stones and broken bottles. A small body of policemen emerged from the Store Street station and attempted to clear the street. Their appearance was the signal for a renewal of the attack with increased violence. Under the concentrated fire of glass and stone the little band quailed and eventually retired. A shriek of triumph went up from the frenzied mob. Another charge and another repulse, and another wild howl from the rabble. ' So furious was the rain of bottles—broken and whole—and bricks,' says a newspaper representative who was a spectator of the scene, ' that the place seemed more like the haunt of howling demons than a Dublin street within a few hundred yards from the cathedral. The shameful, filthy expressions, shouted at the top of women's voices, formed a very painful feature of the melancholy exhibition.' A baton charge down Talbot Street by Inspector Campbell with twelve or fourteen constables sent the mob down Mabbott Street towards Tyrone Street. ' To the accompaniment of hoarse, ribald execrations and shrieks from the rioters,' says the writer, to whose exceedingly graphic account I am indebted for these details, ' the combined police force charged up towards Tyrone Street, but had to withdraw owing to the hail of bottles and stones. Each time the police drew back, the howling rabble followed them and made havoc in their ranks with the hail of missiles that poured on them from all directions. The little barefoot urchins—girls and boys—more daring than their elders, rushed out every now and then and gathered up fresh stores of " ammunition " for the mob. Darting out into the street, they had little trouble in finding plenty of broken bottles and bricks which had been used on the police a moment before. Women, with dishevelled hair and looking like maniacs, were even more persistent than the men and youths in belabouring the police. One of them would rush out of the mob with a shriek and fling a bottle high in the air to drop on the head of a policeman or one of the foolish crowd of onlookers, or to fall with a crash on the street.' So great was the fury and determination of the mob, and so slender, comparatively speaking, were the resources of the police, that it looked at one time as if authority would be deposed. It was only towards midnight that the situation was got well in hand and that a proportion of the exhausted constables could be sent home to secure a much-needed rest.

When the tale of casualties came to be made out, it was found that hundreds of people had received injuries. The wounds in some instances were serious ; and one man, named James Nolan, died in the early hours of Sunday morning from the effects of a fractured skull received in the street fighting. A second individual, named Byrne, subsequently succumbed. Eloquent evidence of the fierceness of the fray is supplied by the fact that over thirty constables received injuries which necessitated medical treatment. The circumstance deserves to be borne in mind in view of the allegations afterwards made by the Larkinites as to the inoffensiveness of the crowds with whom the police dealt.

No need exists to emphasise the highly dangerous situation which by this time had been developed in Dublin. Lawlessness was everywhere rampant. The mob had tasted blood, and they were ready for a display of violence at the smallest provocation and in any direction that a favourable opportunity might offer. For the moment the police had triumphed, but it had been by so slender a margin of force that the dangerous lesson had been given of the tremendous power of a determined mob operating from several points. Not without many forebodings must the authorities have awaited the events of that fateful Sunday, August 30.

The morning broke in summer sunshine. A soft breeze blew down from the Wicklow Hills tempering the heat and dispersing the mists which had gathered about the river. As the day wore on, the streets filled with the usual Sunday crowd of worshippers. They went to their churches and returned from them, possibly not without giving some thought to the tragic possibilities of the immediate future. About Sackville Street gathered after midday an unusually large crowd of idlers, including a considerable contingent of the class from which Mr. Larkin drew his supporters. The police were not at first in great force, but about midday strong detachments appeared on the scene from various directions and proceeded to occupy the principal strategic positions. A fair proportion of them were members of the Royal Irish Constabulary, many of them were probably strangers to Dublin, or at all events not over familiar with its population.

Attracted by the police preparations numerous additional spectators arrived upon the scene. They, for the most part, were influenced by mere curiosity and were certainly not intentionally supporters of the Larkinite propaganda. But their presence of course, to some extent, had the effect of strengthening Mr. Larkin's arm in his fight against authority. At all events, nothing was better calculated to serve his interests than a great gathering on the very spot where the authorities had prohibited the holding of a meeting. The police were in due course instructed to disperse the crowd, and they did so without serious difficulty. About one o'clock a stir in the vicinity of Beresford Place appeared to suggest that some Larkinite move was under way. Observing the commotion, the police quietly made their preparations in O'Connell Street for dealing with the emergency which seemed to be at hand. Soon several hundreds of men wearing the red hand badge gathered in O'Connell Street in the front of the Imperial Hotel. They were in an excited state, and cheered and shouted without any obvious cause other than a desire to make a demonstration. A great crowd, attracted by the noise, gathered in the roadway and about the Corinthian pillars of the post office opposite the Imperial Hotel to find out what the meaning of the ebullition was. They had not long to wait for an explanation, for at about 1.30, almost to a minute, a French casement on the first floor of the Imperial Hotel was thrown open and a man, attired in a tall silk hat and a frock coat, appeared on the balcony and immediately commenced to address the crowd. Momentarily there was silence, as if the people below were puzzled as to the identity of this black-bearded man who was haranguing them. But the tones were too unmistakably those of the arch-agitator to cause long hesitation. A great shout went up, ' It's Larkin ! ' ' It's Larkin ! ' accompanied by a hurricane of cheering from the ranks of his supporters below. Through the din were heard the words, ' I am here to-day in accordance with my promise to address you in O'Connell Street, and I won't leave until I am arrested.'

It was in some respects an ingenious manœuvre that had thus reached successful consummation. A dramatic —it may even be said a melodramatic—touch never fails to appeal to a popular Irish audience. Probably there was nothing which contributed more to Parnell's hold on the Irish masses, through all the years of his ascendancy, than the air of mystery in which he enveloped himself. When he shaved off his beard, for purely personal reasons which are now understood, his followers saw in it the indication of some plot of superlative cleverness that was forming in that master mind. They came at length to have an almost superstitious belief in his powers and to regard him as quite apart from the ordinary run of

mortals.   Mr. Larkin, who is a close student of political
history as well as an astute judge of human nature,
had doubtless taken due note of Parnell's methods when
he entered upon his own campaign to secure the succession
to his post of uncrowned king.   Therefore, though he
knew that the club men and the society people, and even
the business men, would smile contemptuously at his
theatrical ruse, the people he cared for—his followers—
would discover in it a heaven-sent inspiration and would
be bound the closer to him accordingly.   However that
may have been, even his colossal vanity must have been
satisfied with the sensational consequences which followed
upon his melodramatic defiance of the law.

Immediately the identity of the figure on the balcony
had been established, Superintendent Murphy, with
about twenty men under his command, rushed into the
hotel to secure the person of the labour leader.   They
arrested him near the room which he had been able to
secure by giving a fictitious name and representing
himself as an invalid.   To the police officer he said :
' It's all right : I am satisfied,' and walked quietly by
his side downstairs.   Meanwhile, an immense crowd had
gathered in the street awaiting with eager curiosity the
development of events.   As far as the Larkinite section
of it was concerned, it was an excited mob plainly ready
to explode on the smallest provocation.

After a period of suspense Mr. Larkin, bareheaded
but still wearing his false beard, appeared in the door-
way of the hotel surrounded by his captors, whose drawn
truncheons suggested ominous contingencies.   Almost
simultaneously a car drove up containing two foreign
admirers of Mr. Larkin who had been conspicuously
identified with some of the later phases of his movements.
Cheers were called for Mr. Larkin by the couple, and were
given with zest.   Before they had died away the police
had turned round the vehicle, in which the newcomers
were, and had given an order to the driver to go into

an adjoining street. As the man showed some disposition to question the order, the police essayed to force him from his seat. This action was resented by the Larkinites in the crowd, who hooted vigorously. Every moment the excitement increased, and the patter of stones upon the shop-fronts and the breaking of the great plate-glass of one of the windows of a drapery establishment near the Imperial Hotel told only too plainly the story that the forces of disorder were at their old work.

The expected crisis had undoubtedly come. How was it to be met otherwise than by the dispersal of the crowd by the usual methods ? Spectators, who from secure vantage points saw the scene, as a whole thought that tact rather than force was the quality needed to deal with the situation. But, unlike the police, they had not been recently in intimate contact with the Dublin mob and tested its true quality. Nor had they the responsibility which belongs to the guardians of the law, who have to decide when the point is reached at which inaction becomes dangerous weakness. The police officials in charge at the time deemed that the hostile attitude of the Larkinites betokened a disposition on their part to renew the conflict which had been commenced with such lamentable consequences overnight. The police by this time had been formed into a long line in Sackville Street, extending from the post office to the O'Connell Monument. With drawn batons they awaited the order to charge. When the word was given the constables fell upon the crowd with an energy which created momentary surprise but which ultimately produced a panic. Individuals fled in all directions in their attempt to escape the blows which were dealt with fierce intensity by the infuriated members of the police force. Innocent sightseers along with rowdy demonstrators shared in the terrible punishment that was meted out by the guardians of the law. A number were knocked down and trampled upon in their vain efforts to escape. Again and again the police charged

up and down the street.   One section of the flying crowd
made off down Princes Street, only to be met here by a
body of police who were held in reserve and who, joining
in the fray, dealt out blows indiscriminately to the
wretched fugitives.   The piteous cries of the injured and
the shrieks of the frightened women filled the air.   'Terror
and panic were let loose,' observes a spectator, 'and a
state of frenzy seemed to possess police and people
alike.'   The scene of the disturbances was strewn like
a battlefield with the bodies of injured people, many of
them with their faces covered with blood and with their
bodies writhing in agony.   The whole episode only
lasted a few minutes, but in that brief space of time
hundreds were injured, some seriously.

Though at heavy cost the clearing of Sackville Street
had been effected, the riotous crowd had not been disposed
of.   The force escorting Mr. Larkin to the College Street
police station was repeatedly attacked; and in the evening,
after the labour leader had been removed to the Bridewell, the station itself was assailed by a furious crowd,
which was only dispersed after repeated charges had
been made by the police who were guarding it.   Another
serious outbreak occurred outside the Jervis Street
hospital during the conveyance into the building of a
police sergeant who had been injured in the afternoon's
operations.   But the worst rioting of the whole day
was experienced on the tramway route from Christ
Church to Inchicore, where fierce mobs assembled and
attacked the cars.   The police did their best to afford
protection, but they were too few in numbers to cope
with the demonstrators, who, gaining confidence as the
evening advanced, made desperate efforts to establish a
complete mob ascendancy.   When at length it became
clear that the police could not suppress the rioting, a
battalion of the West Kent Regiment was called out
from the Richmond Barracks to assist in the restoration
of order.   The appearance of the military had a salutary

effect upon the roughs in this particular area. Elsewhere, however, the contest raged almost without intermission for hours, and it was not until the night was far advanced that the last stone was thrown and the last charge made by the police.

CHAPTER XIV

THE AFTERMATH OF THE RIOTS

Sackville Street Riots cause a Sensation in England—Mr. Handel Booth, M.P., intervenes—Censure of the Police—Trade Union Congress send a Deputation to Dublin—Fierce Rioting at Redmond Hill—Funeral of a Victim of the Riots of Sunday, August 30—Collapse of Tenement Houses in Church Street—Calamity used as an Object Lesson by the Labour Representatives—Employers not Responsible for Tenement House Evil.

A TREMENDOUS sensation was caused throughout the United Kingdom by the events recorded in the previous chapter. People read into them mostly what they wanted to read—politicians saw in them traces of the double dose of original sin which previously figured so conspicuously in Irish politics ; trade unionists found in them the mark of the capitalist beast who is ever ready to make holocausts of the suffering workers for the advancement of his personal ends ; while a third section, with truer insight, fully realised that what had happened was merely the natural effect of a revolutionary propaganda upon an excitable population poor in pocket and prone to turbulence.   Out of the welter of conflicting opinion emanated an uneasy impression, commonly entertained, that the police had shown undue violence in the affair of Sunday, in Sackville Street in particular. This view was strengthened by the narratives of several eye-witnesses of the occurrences, the most conspicuous of them being Mr. Handel Booth, the Liberal Member for Pontefract.   Mr. Booth is not a particularly discreet person, or one whose opinions carry much weight outside his own political circle.   But his assertions made after the rioting that the police acted with unnecessary brutality, even going to the length of kicking men lying on the ground, were not to be lightly set aside. They received, perhaps, the more credence in England because, at the meeting of the Dublin Corporation on September 1, a fierce and sustained attack was made on the police.   One of the members of the body declared that, while in Sackville Street in Mr. Booth's company, he had seen members of the Royal Irish Constabulary ' wantonly beating not only men but women and children ' ; another member asserted that the police in some instances entered houses and ' smashed every stick of furniture ' ; while a third described how unoffending spectators standing on the pavement were kicked.   In spite of a palpable element of exaggeration in these and other narratives which were made public at the time, the cumulative effect of the stories was to produce the conviction that the police had got out of hand on the occasion.   What, perhaps, was not so fully understood was the tremendous strain which had been put upon these men by the experiences they had already passed through.   Many of them had been on duty continuously for two days, conducting an unequal fight against a vicious rabble, which not only assailed them with the vilest insults, but lost no opportunity of maiming them with the deadly weapons of the slum.   Harassed and fatigued, with minds still fresh with the vivid impressions of the previous night's savage onslaughts of the mob, it is not wonderful that some of them temporarily lost their tempers.   Their conduct, of course, was inexcusable if judged by strict principles of duty ; but they were, after all, only men, and history abounds with proofs that the disciplined human machine, even at the best, is liable to breakdowns under excessive work or worry, or, as in this case, both combined.

L

Labour found an appropriate conduit for the stream of criticism which it was ready to pour out on the events of Sunday in the Trade Union Congress which, by a coincidence, opened its first session in Manchester on the following morning. Restraint is rarely a feature of the discussions of this body, and the highly flavoured reports of the events in Sackville Street, which had come through from partial sources, served to work the assembly up to a high pitch of excitement and indignation. Heated speeches were made condemning the action of the police and of the executive ; and, after a resolution had been passed demanding an official inquiry, a deputation, consisting of Messrs. W. Brace, M.P., J. Ward, M.P., J. Jones, H. Gosling, J. Hill, and J. A. Seddon, was appointed to proceed to Dublin to assist the local labour forces in their defence of what was regarded as the right of combination and of free speech. Prior to this Mr. Keir Hardie, M.P., had gone to Dublin on his own account, fired with a holy zeal for the same cause.

A circumstance which somewhat discounted the effect of the noisy preparations made in labour circles in England for the backing up of Larkinism, was a further outbreak of rioting on Monday night in and about Redmond's Hill, a thoroughfare which is on the southern side of the city, not a great distance from St. Stephen's Green. The disturbances here were of a deliberate and violent character—an outcome of sheer lawlessness. They began in the now familiar fashion, by an attack on the tramways. A car, which was passing from Terenure to the Nelson Pillar, was furiously stoned about six o'clock by a crowd of about 200 people. Recognising the storm signal the police authorities took measures to cope with the rioters. But though they struggled gallantly by repeated baton charges to clear the streets, they were unable for a long time to make any material headway. The mob was one of the worst with which the authorities had yet had to deal. ' The police,' says the *Independent* reporter, ' were attacked from all sides. Stones were hurled at them from the side streets, bottles and utensils containing filthy refuse were poured down from the windows, and pickaxes were requisitioned by the mob, who attempted to pull up the tramway setts. In a number of places the paving in the street was uprooted, and the mob, arming themselves with the large stones, retreated down side streets, firing them at the police as they ran. Every second window in the neighbourhood of Bishop Street and Kevin Street seemed to have been broken. Licensed premises were closed at eight o'clock, and the mob extinguished the gas-lamps in the side streets and hurled defiance at authority.' Another writer, the representative of the *Irish Times,* says : ' The determined spirit shown by some of the rioters was remarkable. At the corner of Strand Street a rough-looking man stood grasping what appeared to be a heavy leather belt with pieces of metal at the end, which he intended to use. Around him was a group of boys whom he exhorted not to run from the police, but to face them when they charged.' It was a perfect saturnalia of violence ; and that the mob were as ready for pillage as they were for attacks on the police was shown by a raid which they made upon the contents of a boot shop whose windows had been broken by the rioters' missiles. Fortunately the police found it possible to nip this phase of the activities of the rabble in the bud. They were, however, unable to prevent the wanton damage done by the would-be marauders to any and every form of property which was open to their vicious attack— damage which gave to the district the appearance of a city which had been subjected to a bombardment. Not until nearly midnight was complete control obtained of the streets. It was afterwards found that in the course of the evening considerably over a hundred people had been treated at the hospitals for injuries received in the conflict.   Some pitched battles have not had a larger list of casualties.

This affair of Redmond's Hill had a salutary effect in bringing home to the minds of people at a distance the character of the forces with which the Dublin police had to deal.   Even the most purblind of partisans could not help seeing that there was inherent in the local situation a danger of the enthronement of anarchy which could not lightly be regarded in any civilised community.   The time was clearly one not to weaken the hands of the law but to strengthen them as far as possible.   An inquiry, which the Government had promised into the whole question of the conduct of the police during the rioting, also tended to remove the issue to a serener atmosphere.   Nevertheless, a strong feeling of resentment against the guardians of law and order burned in the minds of the members of the Transport Workers' Union.   It was kept alive by the proceedings at the inquest of James Nolan, the victim of the Saturday night's rioting, and by the public funeral which was given his remains on September 3.   The evidence tendered at the inquiry was very conflicting ; and the jury in their verdict expressed their inability to decide who struck the fatal blow, but they held that death had been caused by a baton wound and not by a bottle thrown from the vicinity of Liberty Hall as the police alleged.   Their finding, though given at an adjourned sitting after the funeral, had been generally anticipated, and the conferment of the honours of martyrdom upon Nolan by his labour associates was widely regarded as a natural and inevitable outcome of the excited feeling that prevailed at the time.

Nothing was wanting to give impressiveness to the final tribute paid to the dead striker.   Liberty Hall, with its doors and windows heavily draped in black, and with a large placard on the front of the building bearing the inscription ' In memory of one murdered brother,' gave the note of sullen grief that was deemed appropriate to the occasion.   Thousands of strikers in motley mourning and wearing, in conspicuous places on their coats, the red hand—the badge of the Union—marched in the procession.   A considerable contingent of tramway men on strike and in uniform in the line of the mourners attracted much attention, as did also many individuals whose bandaged heads and generally battered appearance marked them out as the wounded soldiers of the campaign.   The Lord Mayor attended, thus emphasising the view expressed so strikingly in the corporation as to the conduct of the police ; and the labour leaders, with Mr. Keir Hardie conspicuously in their midst, were also prominent at the head of the cortège.   Stewards, with staves tipped with crape, marshalled the mourners and kept order in their ranks.   Their duties were not onerous, as it was a silent and depressed crowd that tramped steadily along to the mournful strains of the music supplied by two bands in the procession.   Only one incident occurred to break the sombre monotony of this funeral march of the workers.   As the procession entered Sackville Street a sudden panic seized the crowd.   A restive horse in the background, creating some little stir, gave the impression that the police were breaking up the procession.   In anticipation of a baton charge the mourners fled wildly in all directions, leaving the hearse in dreary isolation in the centre of the thoroughfare. When it was discovered that the fear of police aggression was groundless—that in fact there was scarcely a constable visible anywhere—the processionists crept shamefacedly back to their places in the ranks and the march was resumed, not again to be interrupted until the gates of Glasnevin Cemetery were reached.   The entire proceedings were brought to a characteristic close by the delivery, outside the cemetery gates, by Mr. Keir Hardie of a highly spiced demagogic oration, in which a rabid denunciation of ' Murphyism ' mingled with an almost hysterical eulogy of the 'martyr' whose remains had just been laid to rest.

A few hours before the funeral an episode occurred in Dublin which added a touch of horror to an already over-charged situation. On Tuesday night, September 2, two tenement houses collapsed in Church Street, causing the immediate death of seven persons and serious injury to a number of others. The catastrophe occurred with such appalling suddenness that escape was a matter of difficulty for anyone in the doomed houses at the time of their fall. Most assuredly, if the accident had taken place a few hours later, when the inmates were asleep, scarcely one of the fifty or sixty people inhabiting the building would have lived to tell the tale. The incident brought into dramatic prominence the conditions under which a large proportion of the inhabitants of Dublin live. Nothing hardly was wanting to complete the dark shadows of the sordid picture which was presented in the accounts of the calamity to a shocked public. Church Street is a typical slum area, the tenement houses which collapsed were characteristic specimens of their class, and the people who inhabited them were drawn for the most part from the submerged strata of the population. As if to heighten the sombre effect, facts were brought out in evidence tending to show that there had been a lament-able slackness on the part of the municipal authorities in dealing with the doomed tenements. Although adjacent houses were demolished a few years previously because of their dangerous character, and the buildings which actually fell had been reported upon as late as the previous July because of defects, they were passed by the sanitary department of the corporation as habitable in August, after an inspection had been made of the altera-tions that had been effected in response to the official demand. Sinister rumours were in circulation at the time as to the reason for the certifying of these death-traps so short a period before their collapse. But though pointed questions were put at the coroner's inquiry on the matters on which the popular voice was making itself heard, nothing was elicited to show that any undue influence had been at work. What the investigation did undoubtedly prove, however, was that the inspection of these tenement houses is more or less perfunctory, and that, while a considerable number of them ought to be swept off the face of the earth as morally and physically dangerous to the community, they have to be tolerated to a certain extent because of the enormous practical difficulties in the way of housing the dispossessed inhabitants.

Labour advocates were not slow to see in this Church Street calamity a splendid object-lesson of the evils of Dublin capitalism. Miserable wage-slaves are doomed by the greed of soulless employers to inhabit these horrible and dangerous hovels, and their revolt against the conditions in the shape of Larkinism is a natural and inevitable outcome of the system—so ran the argument which was repeated on a hundred platforms and was the theme of countless editorial pronouncements in the British Press at this period. Indeed, it is not too much to say that the episode did more to spread abroad a distorted view of the actual situation than any other event in these anxious weeks. Mr. Larkin's associates did not fail to fan the flames to the best of their ability. The fact that one of the victims was an employee of Messrs. Jacob was seized upon with avidity to enforce the lesson which they were anxious to inculcate—that low wages were the causes of the slums as well as of the discontent which pervaded the working population. It might just as well have happened, of course, that the victim had been an attendant at Liberty Hall or an employee of some of the few firms who were regarded by the Larkinites as ' fair.' But the stick was good enough to use to beat the hated employers with, and with it blows were dealt about with a lusty vigour born of prejudice and the feeling that the firm especially marked out for attention was getting the better of the Union.

It needs, perhaps, hardly to be urged here, after what has been said in an earlier chapter on the slum question, that the tenement-house evil in Dublin is not to be laid at the doors of the employers. A product of historic and economic causes which go deep into the national life of Ireland, it has, according to the best authorities, been ameliorated by the growth of Dublin industries and not heightened by them as the critics of the employers have represented. Furthermore, it is the opinion of all who have given thought to the Dublin social question that the only certain means by which this tenement-house cancer can be eliminated from the body politic is by the extension of manufacturing and trading enterprise and the consequent widening of the avenues of employment.

CHAPTER XV

ORGANISED REVOLT AGAINST LARKINISM

The Industrial Struggle Widened—Meeting of Members of the Employers' Federation to concert Measures to deal with Larkinism—Further Meeting of Employers—Coal Merchants' Manifesto locking out Members of the Irish Transport Workers' Union—Messrs. Jacob publicly announce their Intention to close their Works—Closing of the Tramway Works at Inchicore—Lord Mayor's Unsuccessful Intervention—Great Gathering of Dublin Employers—Decision taken not to employ Members of the Irish Transport Workers' Union—Mr. Keir Hardie's Opinion of Mr. Larkin—Distorted Views in England as to the Dispute—*Daily Mail* and Mr. Murphy—Conference between the Employers' Representatives and the Labour Delegates at the Shelbourne Hotel—Breakdown of the Conference—Labour Delegates' Views on the Situation—Baseless Allegations of Bad Faith brought against the Employers.

WHILE the stirring events recorded in the two preceding chapters were being enacted, the industrial struggle was proceeding swiftly onwards to an inevitable crisis. As had been widely anticipated, the area of trouble rapidly widened day by day, almost hour by hour, when the issue was really joined. It is the essence of Larkinism, as of the Syndicalism of which it is the child, that there shall be no isolation of a quarrel. ' Those who are not with us are against us ' is the principle which, in the view of the representatives of the new labour, must be carried out to the letter if there is to be success in a conflict. In Dublin, in these memorable days of the late summer period, the doctrine was acted upon to its fullest extent. From Liberty Hall in quick succession were issued edicts which struck heavy blows at one after another of the commercial and industrial activities of the city until it became evident that, by a ruthless process of elimination, there would soon be scarcely an enterprise that was not affected. Inaction or supineness in the face of attack was a policy which past events had discredited. Employers, by the inexorable logic of events, had been driven to the conviction that they would have to make a stand if they did not wish to see their businesses ruined. Like good Irishmen they accepted without flinching the responsibility which they knew to be theirs, and went into the fight with a courageous determination not to put down their arms until they had routed the enemy and reasserted their right to manage their own affairs without constant and irritating outside interference.

The organised movement of revolt against Larkinism had its inception in a meeting of certain members of the Employers' Federation which was held on August 29. Up to this period the Employers' Federation had lacked the driving force which is indispensable to an organisation charged with the duty of defending industry against aggressive interference. Now it was realised that the time had come when, if ever it was to do so, the Federation must completely justify its existence. The initial gathering was quite a small affair, but those who comprised it were all men known and respected in Dublin ; and what, perhaps, was more to the point of the business they had in hand, they were employers who knew what they wanted and how they intended to get it. In the chair was Mr. Sibthorpe, and the others present were : Messrs. Wallis, Parsons, Kennan, Crowe, Murphy, Martin, Frame, Boydell, and Coghlan (secretary). The meeting came to the sensible conclusion that the first need of the time was a general meeting of the Dublin employers so that concerted action could be taken under the most impressive conditions and with the greatest assurance of unity and continuity of policy. From the general trend of opinion in commercial circles, it was clear to the minds of those present that such a step as that contemplated would be strongly supported.

Before the general meeting was called it was decided to invite the representatives of the leading trades and industrial organisations and of several of the large firms employing labour to consult with the committee of the Federation. At this gathering the employers present made up a very representative body, the names of the new adherents to the movement reflecting in striking fashion the growth of sentiment in favour of uncompromising resistance to Larkinism. There were in attendance on the occasion : Messrs. Sibthorpe (in the chair), Dixon, Gamble, Wallis, Kennan, J. Brown, McCullagh, Frame, Crowe, Booth, Sir William Goulding, Messrs. Murphy, Watkinson, W. Brown, Thompson, Richardson, Boydell, Kellett, John Good, H. McLaughlin, P. J. O'Neill, C. Eason, J. Shackleton, J. Mooney, H. Cooper, G. Jacob, T. Buchanan, W. Dalton, W. Hewat, and Coghlan (secretary).

This joint meeting met twice and confirmed the opinion of the council, already referred to, as to the advisability of calling a general meeting of the Dublin employers. Invitations were, therefore, issued to all the leading trade and industrial organisations and the principal firms employing labour to send representatives to a meeting at the Hall, 35 Dawson Street, on September 3. In the meantime the lines which the rejuvenated movement should take were discussed and practically settled.

From the outset there was no hesitation about the proper course to be taken to rescue the community from the anarchaicl tyranny from which it was so sorely suffering. It was this consistency of thought, combined with promptitude of action, that ensured the remarkable triumph which was ultimately achieved over the forces of disorder.

Before the decisive gathering was held the members

of the Coal Merchants' Association gave an indication of the course that would be adopted by issuing, on the evening of September 2, a manifesto announcing that they had decided to lock out such of their employees as belonged to the Irish Transport Workers' Union because of the intolerable character of the interference of that organisation in the business. It was intimated in this pronouncement that the members of the association had no objection to their employees ' being members of any union acting in a lawful and reasonable manner, but that, as the union would not allow their members to deliver coal to certain firms, the merchants were compelled to decline to employ men belonging to the union.' ' The issue,' the manifesto said, ' is simply the right of employers to conduct their business on ordinary trade lines and to supply their customers.' The union officials had declared that they would not allow deliveries to be made to any persons or firms having a dispute with them—in other words, they compelled a boycott. The coal merchants very much regretted any inconvenience that might be caused to the public, but the position created had become so impossible that they had no option but to adopt the course they had decided upon. Practically all the leading coal merchants in Dublin subscribed to the document, whose uncompromising terms left no doubt as to the determination with which the contest would be conducted.

Simultaneously with the publication of the coal merchants' manifesto, Messrs. Jacob issued a letter to the Press intimating that they had decided to close down their works owing to the obstacles put in the way of the transaction of their business by the Union. They gave in the communication a recital of the events which had led them to adopt this drastic course. So far as they were concerned, they said, there was no objection to their men belonging to any union ; but of late, it having come to their knowledge that undue pressure was being brought to bear upon some of their employees to become members of the Irish Transport Workers' Union, they prohibited the canvassing for membership within the factory, or the display of any badge while on the premises which indicated membership of any special union. This action on the part of the firm, in conjunction with the dismissal of men who refused to handle flour tendered to them under contract by a firm (Messrs. Shackleton of Lucan), led to the strike. But, proceeded Messrs. Jacob, ' what we most desire to bring before the public notice is the very serious question which was emphasised to us yesterday (September 1), when we tendered to three of the shipping companies of Dublin goods for dispatch to England, which in two cases were refused acceptance, and in the other, we understand, have not been forwarded.' ' If this state of affairs is to continue,' they went on, ' it appears to us to be a matter of the utmost importance to all the traders of Dublin, and it seems to threaten the very existence of the shipping business of the port, if goods could only be delivered to firms in the city or country, or transhipped to England at the will of the Irish Transport Workers' Union.'

The closing of the tramway works at Inchicore, which had taken place on Monday, September 1, at the same time as Messrs. Jacob were coping with the crisis in their factory, added to the general sense of insecurity that prevailed. At this establishment the company carry out the building and repair of their cars and employ there, in normal times, a good many men. When certain members of the staff were called upon to repair some of the cars damaged in the streets they flatly refused to touch the ' tainted goods,' a development of the doctrine as impudent as it was whimsical. They were promptly given their marching orders. Then men in other departments took up their cause, and, as the work could not be carried on with advantage, the directors decided to make a virtue of necessity and send off the whole of the staff. Though the step caused inconvenience, it was to some extent advantageous to the company to temporarily suspend operations in this establishment, the work of which was not essential to the continuous running of the system.

A belated attempt was made by the Lord Mayor to avert the rapidly impending calamity of the closing of the port. Invitations were issued by him to both parties to send delegates to a conference at the Mansion House to put into effect the conciliation scheme which, so far, had been left in the proposal stage. It is, perhaps, not surprising in the circumstances of the moment that no response was made from either camp to the suggestion. While the Larkinites had never ceased to pour contempt upon the corporation and to hold its head up to ridicule, the employers, even if they had been disposed to permit interference at this juncture—and they decidedly were not—would not have gone to the Mansion House for the adjustment of their differences.

As far as the employers were concerned, the desire at the moment was to come to close grips with the monster which had so long tyrannised over them and played havoc with their vital interests. Their spirit was impressively shown at the great meeting of September 3 in the hall in Dawson Street. The gathering brought together the largest and most representative body of Dublin merchants, manufacturers, and traders ever held in the city. Not an important organisation, and scarcely a leading individual firm was unrepresented. With a keen sense of the value of a strong fighting leader at a time of crisis, the meeting selected Mr. William Martin Murphy to occupy the chair. The choice, unanimously approved at the time, was abundantly vindicated, as the sequel will show, by the firm, consistent line which was given to the policy formulated at the meeting. That policy, as may be surmised from the circumstances which led to the calling of the employers together, was one of unyielding resistance to the Larkinite domination—

a fight to a finish with every legitimate weapon that could
be called in aid. The first resolution, which was moved
by Mr. H. McLaughlin, seconded by Mr. George Shackleton, and supported by Mr. John Sibthorpe, gave the key-
note to the proceedings. It was to this effect : ' That
this meeting of employers, while asserting its friendly
feelings to Trade Unionism, hereby declares that the
position created by the Irish Transport and General
Workers' Union (a union in name only) is a menace to
all trade organisations and has become intolerable.' The
next resolution, which was proposed by Mr. George
Jacob, seconded by Mr. Orr, and supported by Mr.
Eason, gave practical effect to the simple declaration
of war which had already been ratified with enthusiasm.
It ran as follows : ' That in order to deal effectively with
the present situation all employers should bind themselves to adopt a common line of action by signing the
agreement presented herewith :

[AGREEMENT.]

' We hereby pledge ourselves in future not to employ
any persons who continue to be members of the Irish
Transport and General Workers' Union, and any person
refusing to carry out our lawful and reasonable instructions
or the instructions of those placed over them will be
instantly dismissed, no matter to what union they belong.'

Unanimous approval was given to this far-reaching
undertaking, and it was decided that the pledge should
take effect from September 6, 1913. After the customary
complimentary vote to the chairman, the assemblage
separated with the consciousness that they had at last
taken an effective step to win back the industrial freedom
of the city, which had been so gravely imperilled in the
previous three years by the Larkinite movement.

The glove had indeed been thrown down to the
forces of Syndicalism. That it would be picked up was
inevitable ; but it was momentarily doubtful whether

the strength of the older and staider Trade Unionism of Great Britain would be placed at the disposal of the Larkinites. Though an influential deputation had been sent across the Channel from the Trade Union Congress, there was no special love for Mr. Larkin amongst the leaders of labour in England. Many of them had had only too painful experience of his methods and of his defects of temperament to be ready to rush with enthusiasm to his aid. Even Mr. Keir Hardie, extremist as he is, in one of his first speeches in Dublin,[1] felt constrained to mingle with his eulogy of Mr. Larkin some frank comments on his shortcomings. ' They who knew Jim,' he said, ' liked Jim. They didn't like some of his faults, and that was the point he wanted to emphasise. That was not the occasion to think of his faults, but the virtues of the man and what he stood for. They knew the old saying, that " The man who never said a foolish thing never did a wise thing," and that was especially true of a man of Larkin's temperament.' Of course, the trouble with the English Labour leaders, as with other people who had come in contact with Mr. Larkin, was that he had said so many foolish things and done so few wise ones. His policy had ever been one of personal ascendancy, and, as Mr. Keir Hardie put it in the speech from which I have already quoted, ' he had trodden heavily on some of their corns.'

There was the less reason for the English unions to be in a hurry to assist the Larkinite movement, as it had been built up on rigidly sectional lines. ' Ireland for the Irish ' was the text from which Mr. Larkin and his lieutenants were never tired of preaching ; and there is little question that he gained his first hold on the Dublin working class by his denunciations of the National Dock Labourers' Union as a ' foreign ' organisation which had sold the pass to the enemy in the crisis of

[1] Address to the Irish workers at the Trades Council, reported in the *Irish Worker*, September 6, 1913.

1911.   Still, the circumstances of the dispute were
such that it was a practical certainty from the outset
that, whether they liked it or not, the English Trade
Unionists would have to take their place in the breach
by the side of Mr. Larkin.   Public opinion in England
had been very much moved by the exaggerated stories
of police brutality sent over by Mr. Handel Booth and
other excited partisans.   Moreover, an entirely distorted
view of the real character of the struggle had got about
owing to the curious attitude assumed by the *Daily Mail*,
which, in its news columns, represented the dispute as
a sort of duel for personal ascendancy between Mr.
Murphy and Mr. Larkin, and which, in the thick of the
crisis, published an article solemnly warning the employers
of Dublin that their resistance to Trade Unionism was
out of date, utterly ignoring the fact that what had
precipitated the crisis was not dislike of Trade Unionism
but a revolt against Syndicalism.   Some influence, too,
had been exercised by a statement made by a special
correspondent of the *Daily Mail* to the effect that Mr.
Murphy knew that he ' carried his life in his hands.'
' This cruel and dangerous suggestion,' as Mr. Murphy
with just indignation properly stigmatised it at the time,
conveyed an absolutely false impression that the population were fired to the extreme pitch of animosity against
that gentleman.   Up to this period Mr. Murphy had gone
about his business in Dublin without the slightest molesta-
tion or insult.   His personal character stood too high
to have been affected in the least by the ravings of the
Larkinite organ, and he was respected, even by many
of his Labour opponents, as the resolute man often is.
But after the appearance of the invidious statement
in the *Daily Mail*, which organ, it should be stated,
circulates largely in Dublin in the form of a special
edition, the police insisted on extending protection to
Mr. Murphy, an attention which he resented, but could
not resist in view of their opinion that there was a

M

real risk of the idea of personal outrage being acted upon.

All the circumstances combined to create in England a sympathetic atmosphere for the Larkinites. In exclusively working-class circles the feeling in favour of the strikers was particularly strong, and there were calls made for action which it was clear the executives of the different unions would find it difficult if not impossible to resist. At the same time the leaders, who had still a lively recollection of the tremendous strain put upon their funds by the great railway and mining strikes, from which they were only slowly recovering, had no mind to allow their organisations to be bled white for Mr. Larkin's personal advantage. Though profuse in their expressions of sympathy, they were at the outset markedly chary in accepting any financial obligation in connection with the struggle.

The employers understood too well the character of the conflict upon which they had entered to be under any misapprehension as to the possibility of terminating it speedily. They realised, however, that they had nothing to lose and everything to gain by accepting a suggestion that was made early in the crisis, that they should meet the delegates of the Trade Union Congress in conference. Reasonableness has usually been a distinguishing feature of British Trade Unionism, and they hoped that if no other end was served they would be able to carry home to the minds of the visitors the impossibility of their working under the conditions imposed upon industry by Larkinism.

On the afternoon of Thursday, September 4, Mr. Murphy received a telephonic communication from the Castle that the members of the congress representatives would be willing to confer with the employers. Mr. Murphy was placed in a considerable difficulty, as he had no opportunity of consulting the temporary committee on the advisability of meeting the delegates, and it was requested that the meeting should be arranged for the following morning. An informal consultation held with several employers showed that the feeling was that it would be unreasonable to refuse, and it was thought the best deputation that could go would be representatives of those firms who were at the time engaged in the struggle. In the result a meeting was quickly arranged for Friday, September 5, at the Shelbourne Hotel, Mr. Murphy being accompanied by Messrs. Jacob, McCormick, Barry, McLaughlin, Eason, and Hewat.

The conference between the two parties, which lasted seven hours, brought into strong relief the serious character of the difficulties which existed in the way of a settlement, and the delegates separated with very slender hopes of being able to find a way of peace. One of the greatest obstacles—it may be said the main obstacle—was the question of guarantees. The congress delegates were neither willing nor able to undertake any responsibility, and on their part the employers' representatives were not prepared to consider any settlement which did not carry with it, as an essential part, an arrangement for making agreements effective. The question of the authority of the visitors was also a stumbling-block of no inconsiderable kind. They themselves emphatically disclaimed any desire or intention to take action without the concurrence of the local men, and this attitude, though natural and even inevitable in the circumstances, was considered by the employers to confirm their view of the hopelessness of negotiations, seeing what the Larkinite pretensions were, and how, judging from past experience, any arrangement that they might enter into would be kept.

At the second sitting on Monday, September 8, the conference was enlarged by the inclusion of a representative delegation from the Dublin Trades Council as well as the following employers—Messrs. O'Reilly, Martin, Dawson, and Wallis ; and very much the same ground was covered as at the previous meeting with equally barren results.

M 2

The masters resolutely declined to entertain any proposal which would leave them as before at the mercy of the irresponsible autocracy of Liberty Hall, and the Labour delegates could not entertain any suggestion which, in their view, would give employers the right to dictate to a man as to what union he should belong.   When the meeting separated it was with the consciousness, on the employers' side at least, that the prospects of a settlement were hopeless.

The light in which the Labour representatives regarded the discussions was indicated in the speeches made at Liberty Hall a few hours after the conclusion of the proceedings by some of their members.   For example, Mr. George Burke, of the National Sailors' and Firemen's Union, stated that the meeting ' arrived at no conclusion whatever ' and that ' the fight was to go on.'   ' We never receded from one position we took up when we entered the Shelbourne Hotel to-day until we came out of it,' he added.   He went on : ' If it should happen in the course of the week that we should have recourse to some other methods in the shape of a settlement or to approach the employers, you will be well advised by us on any matter that may happen in the interim. At the same time, to-morrow morning probably the employers of Dublin, who have already shown a desire to act in unanimity, may lock out their men.'   Mr. David Campbell, of the Belfast Trades Council, another member of the conference, said that the conference ' broke up not because the Trades Union representatives were not anxious for a settlement, but because the other side were not inclined to concede the demands that they felt justified in making.'   ' They would,' he further stated, ' never concede to any employer or combination of employers the right to dictate to the workers what trades union they should or should not join.'   He dropped a significant hint that before the week was out the employers would be inclined to listen to their demands, because within that period they would have able assistance ' from one who is in jail at the present time,' obviously meaning Mr. Larkin.

These expressions of opinion were of some importance because of what followed. Nominally the conference had been adjourned until Monday, September 15, but in view of the attitude assumed by the delegates—an attitude reflected in the public speeches just quoted— the Employers' Federation proceeded to perfect an organisation for the struggle which they saw was imminent. They again called a meeting of the general body of employers (whether members of the Federation or not) for September 12, in the Ancient Concert Rooms, Great Brunswick Street, and, as on the previous occasion, the gathering was very largely attended by the most influential employers in the city. Under Mr. Murphy's presidency it was decided to appoint an executive committee to act for all these employers during the continuance of the dispute. The meeting immediately selected the gentlemen who had already acted at the conference at the Shelbourne Hotel, namely, Messrs. Murphy, Hewat, M'Cormick, John Wallis, R. Dawson, C. Eason, G. Jacob, D. Barry, M. O'Reilly, F. V. Martin, H. McLaughlin, and added the names of Messrs. John Good and W. Spence. The committee had power to add to its number a representative of any important trade, and eventually co-opted Mr. F. Hall, representing the corn trade. A further decision was come to, to take measures to give effect to the decision arrived at at the previous meeting of employers in Dawson Street to employ no man who was a member of the Irish Transport Union. In order to save the congress delegates a fruitless journey from England, the secretary was instructed to write to the Trades Union delegates and inform them that the employers could not see that any good would be achieved by sending representatives to the adjourned sitting of the conference.

The Labour leaders, who before were pluming themselves on their unyielding attitude and proclaiming with a great flourish of trumpets that ' the fight was to go on,' now made it a subject of strong complaint that the employers had taken them at their word and declined to continue what had become little better than a farce. It was the first time within their knowledge, they said in a joint communication to the Federation, in which ' negotiations of such a serious and far-reaching character have been deliberately broken off by one side when there has been a joint agreement between the parties to continue the discussion.' The action of the Federation, the signatories declared, was ' a serious, wilful, and indefensible breach of a common understanding arrived at after a long and anxious debate,' and was the more extraordinary because the lock-out decided upon by the Federation was due, among other things, to their inability to secure the proper and rigid observance of agreements.

The committee of employers, through their secretary, replied that the conference was none of their seeking ; that they had entered it as they ' did not wish to appear stiff-necked,' though they had little hope of practical result ; that the meeting of September 8, though adjourned, was not necessarily so concluded with a view of the continuance of the discussion ; and that, if the employers' representatives had met the Labour delegates again on September 15, it would only have been to convey the unanimous decision of the employers of Dublin held on the previous Friday, and so they deemed it more courteous to let them know in advance not only the opinions of the employers' executive committee but those of the employers of the city.

No question of bad faith, of course, entered into the matter. The negotiations, if such they can be called, really broke down at the first meeting. It was then obvious to everyone, the Labour delegates amongst the number, that there was no basis for an understanding, and could be none so long as the Larkinite organisation was an active force and the British trade unions declined either to act independently of it or to guarantee its *bona fides*. The complaint probably may be regarded as a characteristic specimen of Labour tactics. The delegates were in a difficult position. They knew Mr. Larkin too well to accept any responsibility for him. On the other hand, they could not confess their impotence before the world by admitting that the situation was beyond them. They therefore fastened with avidity upon the refusal of the employers to be parties to the continuance of a palpably barren discussion, in order to show to the world what an unreasonable type of men they had to deal with and how eager they themselves were to seek peace and ensue it. It was a performance which, perhaps, served its immediate purpose of diverting attention from the fundamental points at issue and creating an appropriate atmosphere of prejudice in which the delegates could obscure their lack of influence. But it deceived no one on the spot who had watched the development of the dispute and understood the character of the forces which were arrayed against each other in circumstances which differed widely from the conditions which govern an ordinary conflict between Capital and Labour.

CHAPTER XVI

THE CONFLICT PROCEEDS

A Fight to a Finish—Release of Mr. Larkin—Action of Authorities criticised—Unsympathetic Attitude of English Trade Unionists towards Larkinism—Denunciation of Sympathetic Strike by the National Union of Railwaymen—Mr. Larkin at Manchester— His ' Divine Mission '—Renewed Rioting—Result of Official Inquiry into the Conduct of the Police—Police Action vindicated.

THE issue had now been fully and finally joined. It was to be a fight to a finish, as the Labour leaders declared, with, it may be supposed, considerable misgiving. Events had really been too much for employers and employed alike. The syndicalistic fever was in the city's bones and, until it had been eliminated by drastic measures, there could be no peace. Almost every hour brought its proof of the lengths to which the virus of the new labour creed had been absorbed. One day the London and North Western Company's employees declined to unload a dray of biscuits intended for shipment because they emanated from Messrs. Jacob's factory and were ' tainted goods.' On another occasion the dockers declined, for similar reasons, or lack of reasons, to load up a consignment from Messrs. Dixon's Soap and Candle Works. Then floated in from the country districts stories of the operations of Larkinite emissaries on farms, with the object of dragging yet another interest into the web of discontent that was being woven about the business activities of the Dublin district. Anon came across the Channel an account of how the unfortunate consignment of biscuits had been held up, temporarily as it proved, in Liverpool because the local railwaymen declined, on Larkinite principles, to handle the objectionable goods. These episodes had a hardening effect on both parties—on the employers because they went to strengthen the opinion, already firmly held, that they had to cope with a far-reaching conspiracy and not an ordinary labour difficulty, and on the workers because they added to the prevalent excitement and helped to stimulate the aggressive instincts of the fighting section embraced in the membership of the Irish Transport Workers' Union.

It was at this moment that Mr. Larkin was let loose once more upon the community. He was released on bail on September 12 through the action of the Courts; but the Government were benevolently concerned in the business, if they did not actually secure the opening of the prison doors. The freeing of the Labour leader was probably inevitable in the circumstances of the time, and especially of the dependence of Ministers upon the Labour vote in Parliament. Where the authorities blundered was in prosecuting Mr. Larkin when they did and on the charge they did. At that juncture he plainly sought the attentions of the authorities as a means of diverting attention from his failure to bring out the tramway men, and in order to obtain a much-needed advertisement of a kind which is never wanting in effectiveness in Ireland. The time to have moved against the arch-agitator was a good deal earlier, when his paper was publishing the scandalous incitements to outrage which have been cited. These villainous compositions ought never to have been allowed to pass without the attention of the prosecuting authorities. Their appearance in a newspaper reflected a stain on the community which should have been wiped out by the most drastic measures possible. If action had been promptly taken it would not then have been possible, as it was later, to represent the prosecutions as an attack on the principle of Trade Unionism. Even Mr. Keir

Hardie would not have had the hardihood to declare that the suppression of the advocacy of murder was an interference with the rights of combination and of legitimate freedom of speech.   But the whole conduct of the Government in dealing with Larkinism was characterised by lamentable weakness and inconsistency.   At one moment they were deferentially placing motor cars at the disposal of the Labour leader and listening anxiously and eagerly to the pearls of wisdom that he let fall from his lips, and at the next they were harrying his steps as a criminal and treating him as a most desperate and dangerous character whose presence within prison walls was a matter of State necessity.   One attitude was as foolish as the other.   It was not at all necessary to flatter Mr. Larkin's colossal vanity either by fawning upon him or by falling upon him.   He ought to have been left severely alone if it was deemed inexpedient to bring him to book for the offences to which we have referred.

When Mr. Larkin emerged from seclusion he was confronted with the painful necessity that existed of financing the workers in the crisis which had been brought about by his policy.   The situation was about as black as it could possibly be.   The Transport Workers' Union, which always lived from hand to mouth, had an almost empty exchequer, local sympathisers were few and unable or unwilling to do much and although the English Trade Unions had been profuse in their expressions of sympathy, they displayed a marked disinclination to convert those warm sentiments into solid cash.   On the other hand there was a daily increasing list of members rendered idle by the dispute who would have to be satisfied if the whole movement was not to collapse. Surveying the position and recalling, doubtless from his experience, how extremely exigent a body of hungry strikers is, it is not surprising that Mr. Larkin thought that it would be altogether more comfortable for himself and more profitable for his cause if he crossed the Channel and sought to raise the sinews of war for the conduct of his campaign. It must have struck the Labour leader as somewhat ill-omened for his enterprise that, almost simultaneously with his landing in England, there was issued from the head quarters of the National Union of Railwaymen a circular signed by its secretary explaining at length the reasons why the English railwaymen could not support the Irish movement by declining to handle 'tainted goods.' The writer, in the course of a well-reasoned argument, pointed out that railway companies are compelled by statute to accept any goods tendered to them, and that a refusal on their part to deal with them would involve the management in serious consequences. He showed, moreover, with great cogency that, if the doctrine of the sympathetic strike were accepted, the railwaymen would be continually involved in labour troubles, owing to the intimate connection that existed between the railways and all classes of industry. Finally, he warned the members of the Union that any departure from the sound principles of Unionism, based on the strict observance of agreements, would inevitably lead to 'anarchy and disruption.' A more reasonable and sensible manifesto had never been issued from a trade union, but it was the very last thing Mr. Larkin wanted. Shrewd judge as he is of human nature, he could not have failed to understand the depressing effect that the pronouncement would have on his dupes in Dublin.

To Manchester Mr. Larkin devoted his earliest attention on entering upon his campaign. He probably recalled the old saw which asserts that what Manchester and Lancashire think to-day the rest of England think to-morrow. He may also have been drawn to the place by old associations, for he told his hearers at the open-air demonstration which he addressed in the northern city on September 14, that there was not a roadway between Manchester and London that he had not tramped nor a hedge under which he had not slept as a boy. He had, he proceeded to say, hungered in Manchester, slept in railway trucks there, and also worked on the Manchester quays. Whatever the motives may have been which dictated the selection, Mr. Larkin appears to have entertained no doubt as to the sympathy which he would receive there from the working classes. His discourse was in a familiar, full-blooded vein which seemed to convey the implication that the speaker felt that he was amongst close friends. He was out, he said,[1] to save William Martin Murphy and those associated with him from eternal damnation. ' I care for no man or men,' Mr. Larkin went on. ' I have got a divine mission, I believe, to make men and women discontented. I am out to do it, and no Murphy nor Aberdeen, nor other creatures of that type can stop me carrying on the work I was born for. Some men will say, you should not start to arouse men's minds until they get Home Rule. Home Rule ! You have got it in England, and you are making a damn bad job of it. A question of Home Rule ? No. It is an economic question—a bread-and-butter question. Our whole Trade Union movement is absolutely rotten. If we were the men we think we are, the employing classes would be wiped out in an hour and we should become the employing class.'

Another characteristic outburst was in a passage dealing with the attitude of the Church towards labour questions. ' I knelt down,' he said, ' in Sligo Cathedral at the feet of a bishop, when he said " Anti-Christ is come to town : it is Larkin." Thank God, for his soul's sake and my own, before he died he understood the problem better. I do not blame him. Better men than I in Ireland have been cursed. I prefer to go to the seventh pit of Dante than to go to heaven with William Martin Murphy. Hell has no terrors for me. I have lived there. Thirty-six years of hunger and

[1] The extracts are from a lively report of the speech in the *Manchester Guardian*.

poverty have been my portion. The mother who bore me had to starve and work, and my father had to fight for a living. I knew what it was to work when I was nine years old. They cannot terrify me with hell. Better to be in hell with Dante and Davitt than to be in heaven with Carson and Murphy, not forgetting our good friend the Earl of Aberdeen.' A significant reference to the Labour delegates' visit to Dublin was contained in the speech. The speaker said that ' when the delegates came over Larkin was in jail ; and one of them told him, in the presence of the Governor of Mountjoy prison, that he had come rather in a judicial capacity, and was not concerned which came out on top : he only wanted to see what the facts were so that he could make his report. If it did not matter to them who came out on top, they were going to sell the pass.' In a final outburst Mr. Larkin said : ' I am out for revolution or anything. What do I care ? They can only kill me, and there are thousands to come after me.'

This Manchester speech, with its blatant egotism and its nauseous mingling of blasphemy and scurrility, did more to open the eyes of people in England to the true inwardness of the Larkinite propaganda than the many articles that were daily appearing in the papers explanatory of the causes of the Dublin industrial up- heaval. It caused, as it was well calculated to do, great offence in leading Trade Union circles, and was even scoffed at by so devoted a champion of Labour as the *Daily News and Leader*. ' If Mr. Larkin really has a divine mission to improve the lot of the working man by per- suading him to demand a rise of 5s. a week, which he will get for the asking, why does he stick at 5s. ? ' asked the editor sarcastically. ' Why should he not make his mission diviner still by raising the demands to 10s. ? There seems no more practical reason why one demand should be refused than the other.'

Mr. Larkin did not remain to face the storm of

criticism that this harangue raised in England.   On
September 15 he was back again in Dublin attempting
to grapple with the difficulties which were accumulating
there to an alarming extent.   The Builders' Association,
after an unsuccessful attempt to induce their labourers to
accept the rule that no employee should be a member
of the Irish Transport Workers' Union, that day locked
out 3000 of their men ; and the Farmers' Association
of the county of Dublin, for similar reasons, had the same
day dispensed with the services of their labourers, who
numbered about 1000.   By this time there were, it
was estimated, no fewer than 15,000 men idle in and
about Dublin owing to the dispute.   The fact that the
movement in support of Larkinism in Liverpool had
extended to the dockers and was threatening to bring
about a general strike, added to the uncertainty of the
situation.   With several of the shipping services suspended and others working intermittently, it was every
day becoming clearer that complete paralysis of the
trade of the port was rapidly impending.

As the position of the port became more desperate,
a fresh disposition to violence manifested itself in the
Dublin streets.   Matters came to a head on Sunday,
September 21, when the city experienced what was
afterwards described by the Commissioners appointed
to inquire into the disturbances as ' the most determined
and disgraceful riot ' of the whole series.   At 5.30 P.M.
on that day one of the now familiar processions was
formed up in Beresford Place for a march through the
streets.   It was composed of several thousand persons,
and we have the authority of the official record for the
fact that it was led by a ' crowd of roughs, many of
whom were under the influence of drink.'   Some sixty
sergeants and constables, under the orders of Chief
Superintendent Dunne, accompanied the procession.
Before the demonstrators had gone very far, the more
violent of them commenced to stone the tram cars which

were passing at the time. A number of the vehicles were seriously damaged, the police being powerless to prevent the mischief. The march continued in disorderly fashion until Townsend Street was reached, when an organised attempt was made to overwhelm the small force of police that accompanied the procession. 'Showers of stones and bottles were thrown in many instances from the houses,' observed the Commissioners in their report, 'and a hand-to-hand struggle went on here for twenty minutes between the police and the rioters. Some of the horses belonging to the troopers were knocked down; the men themselves received severe injuries, and in many instances their lives were only saved by their helmets, which were broken by the stones and missiles. Pieces of concrete, iron nuts, and bricks were freely thrown. Batons were drawn and used at several points in the street, but for some time even this measure had not the effect of dispersing the crowd or restoring order. Some of the constables were knocked down and rendered unconscious, and in one instance a member of the Dublin Metropolitan Police was wounded by a knife.' Altogether thirty-six constables were injured in the riot, or more than half the force engaged. For more than half an hour the street was a veritable pandemonium.

Mr. Larkin was in Glasgow continuing his campaign amongst the British Trade Unionists at the time of this outbreak, but that he was present in spirit was shown by a reference in his speech in the Clyde city to 'the Dublin Cossack—that dirty brute in blue clothes whom they paid and kept up,' and who was 'the tool of the oppressing classes.' Quite as significant in its way as this scurrility was a speech made in Beresford Place a few hours after the riot by Mr. James Connolly, one of the Larkinites involved in the conspiracy charge who, after arrest, had distinguished himself by a hunger strike, the upshot of which was that he was released at the end of seven days' incarceration. 'The employers,' remarked this worthy, 'said the men could not be trusted to keep their agreements. If that were so, why ask the men to sign agreements now? His advice was, if the employers had brought the people to the verge of starvation, let the men sign any agreement asked of them, go into work for a week, and then leave off for a fortnight.' This recommendation was in complete harmony with the policy expounded by the *Irish Worker* in regard to agreements on an earlier occasion, to which reference has been made in a previous chapter. It expressed in fact a common principle of Syndicalism. But it is important as an indication of the spirit prevailing at Liberty Hall at this time. Nothing hardly could have brought into stronger relief the fatuity of the efforts of well-meaning conciliators to build up a peace on the basis of an understanding with the Larkinite leaders.

As the rioting of Sunday, September 21, was the last serious disturbance of the peace that occurred during the strike, it may be convenient here to make reference to the official inquiry which, in response to the popular demand, was held into the conduct of the police.[1] The Commission, which was composed of Mr. Denis S. Henry and Mr. Samuel Lombard Brown, two well-known Dublin King's Counsel, with Mr. Thomas Patton, B.L., as secretary, sat during the greater part of January at the Four Courts, exhaustively inquiring into the circumstances of the riots. At the eighteen sittings that were held, 281 witnesses were called, no fewer than 202 of them being members either of the Dublin Metropolitan Police or of the Royal Irish Constabulary. The proceedings were at one point enlivened by a series of personal incidents, in which Mr. J. B. Powell, K.C., who represented the police, and Mr. Handel Booth, M.P., were the principal actors. Considerable heat was engendered in the course of one of these altercations by a remark applied by the

[1] See Appendix for Report.

counsel to the legislator. Mr. Handel Booth so keenly resented this treatment that he could not persuade himself to continue at the inquiry, and, as the Commissioners say in their report, they ' had not the advantage of hearing his evidence or receiving further assistance from him.' The omission of the testimony probably was not important, as Mr. Booth had shown himself too much of a partisan to be in a position to make any really helpful contribution to the inquiry. The Commissioners had no difficulty in coming to the conclusion, from the mass of evidence which was placed before them, that the stories of gross brutality on the part of the police, in the case of the rioting of August 31 in O'Connell Street, were either untrue or grossly exaggerated versions of incidents that happened owing to a misunderstanding by the police stationed in Prince's Street as to the object of the rush of a crowd of people who were flying before a charge made by the police in Sackville Street. To the police, observe the Commissioners in their report, 'this movement very naturally appeared to be a renewed and determined effort by a suddenly and greatly increased crowd to force a passage through Prince's Street, and they dealt with it accordingly.' ' Any unnecessary or excessive force used by the police during the suppression of the riot was due to this misunderstanding,' add the Commissioners.

In regard to the general conduct of the police during the disturbances, the Commissioners had no hesitation in finding that they ' discharged their duties throughout this trying period with conspicuous courage and patience.' ' They were exposed,' says the report, ' to great dangers and treated with great brutality, and in many instances we were satisfied that, though suffering from injuries which would have fully justified their absence from duty, they remained at their posts under great difficulties until peace had been restored. The total number of constables injured during these riots exceeded 200.

N

Notwithstanding the extent and violence of the disturbances, in no case save one, and then only for the purpose of protecting two tram cars, was the assistance of the military called for. The riots were dealt with and suppressed by the police, and the police alone ; and, had it not been for their zeal and determination, the outbreak of lawlessness which took place in the months of August and September would have assumed more serious proportions, and been attended by far more evil results.'

With this final judgment every impartial person who studies the history of these eventful weeks in Dublin must concur. The most casual examination of facts shows that the police were not the brutal ruffians, nor were the strikers the innocent lambs, that they were represented to be by the Larkinite apologists. Against isolated cases of excessive zeal on the part of the police may be set a hundred cases in which, under the most intolerable provocation, they acted with remarkable patience and tact. As to the other party, we have only to read the records of the men [1] who were charged with offences arising out of the riots to understand what a desperate criminal band the police had to contend with in these anxious days of August and September.

[1] See table in Appendix.

CHAPTER XVII

THE GOVERNMENT INTERVENES

Breakdown of the Sympathetic Strike Movement in England—Report of Trade Union Delegates on the Dublin Situation—Misrepresentations of the Delegates—English Trade Unionists vote £5000 for Food for the Dublin Strikers—British Employers support their Dublin Confrères—Government appoint a Commission, with Sir George Askwith as President, to visit Dublin—Sir George Askwith's Reputation as a Conciliator—Violent Speeches by Larkinite Leaders—Increase of Distress in Dublin—First Food Ship for the Strikers arrives in Dublin from England—Mr. Larkin publicly repudiates the Binding Character of Agreements.

IN the third week of September the Larkinite combination received a heavy blow in the breakdown of the sympathetic strike on the English railways. Responding to the Dublin call for aid, men had come out in Liverpool, Manchester, and Birmingham ; but they received no support from their union, and in the end had to go back after the useless sacrifice of several days' pay. This collapse of the railway movement was conclusive evidence that the Dublin strikers' cause was not to be taken up whole-heartedly by English Trade Unionism. As much might have been anticipated from the very gingerly way in which the congress delegates handled the question of financial aid in their public utterances, and the general attitude of detachment which they assumed, greatly to Mr. Larkin's disgust, as we have seen. But all the same, the stroke was a deadly one, and the Transport Workers' Union visibly reeled under it. There were not wanting at the moment candid friends to emphasise the unpleasant truth that the prop, which alone could have saved the crazy structure of Larkinism, had fallen. 'There is no such practical enthusiasm for the " tainted goods " doctrine as would justify any hopes for the future in this direction,' wrote the *Daily News and Leader*, and the journal went on to express a hope that ' it will not be long before the significance of these facts is realised and the example of the English unions taken to heart and followed in Dublin.'

Simultaneously with the return of the English railway strikers to duty, the report of the Trade Union delegates to Dublin was made public. It was a long and laboured document drafted, it would seem, on the Talleyrand principle that language is given to conceal thoughts. Much of it was occupied with a self-laudatory account of the brilliant manner in which the delegates had ' vindicated the rights of free speech ' by forcing a practically open door at Dublin Castle and holding a meeting in Sackville Street on Sunday, September 14. The references made to the actual circumstances of the dispute were meagre and unimpressive to a degree quite remarkable, having regard to the fact that the delegates were men of some experience of public life. The Irish Transport Workers' Union was blessed because it had ' considerably raised the wages of the various sections of industry which it had organised,' and ' brought hope to thousands of the lower paid workers of Ireland.' It was noted that Mr. Larkin had adopted a ' very aggressive policy,' identified with the enforcement of the ' tainted goods ' theory, and that the employers had met this ' with an equally aggressive policy of a sympathetic lock-out.' But the delegates were so blind to the far-reaching issues that were involved that they brought themselves to write that, at the time of their arrival, the dispute had degenerated into a personal quarrel between Mr. Murphy and Mr. Larkin. ' Quarrel ' is an absurd phrase to use in such a connection. Mr. Murphy never quarrelled with Mr.

Larkin, nor was the latter's vilification of him, as appears to be insinuated in a sentence in the report, the result of an attack made on the Labour leader by one of Mr. Murphy's papers.   He simply declined to allow himself to be made a sacrifice on the altar of Syndicalism, and took measures accordingly, most of which, no doubt, were extremely distasteful to Mr. Larkin.   In that sense he quarrelled with that gentleman ; but then, so al ,o did the four hundred or more employers associated with him. The simple fact is that there has rarely been an instance in which a great principle more dominated a movement than this Dublin rising against Larkinism.   Mr. Murphy headed it, greatly to his honour, but probably no man ever entered a fight of the kind with less feeling of personal animosity.

Misrepresentations of this character may have been necessary in order to cover up the ugly tracks of the monster which had been gnawing at the vitals of Dublin trade until the whole community were stung to revolt. But the same excuse cannot be found for a deliberate untruth contained in a passage of the report dealing with the futile peace efforts.   ' From information obtained since the negotiations broke down,' wrote the delegates, ' we are thoroughly convinced that the Dublin Employers' Federation Committee are not prepared to make any kind of agreement with responsible Trade Union representatives, and are determined to crush out Trade Unionism in Dublin.'   A more monstrous travesty of the facts could scarcely have been penned.   So far from there being any desire to crush Trade Unionism in Dublin, all the leading men in the Employers' Federation are warm supporters of it, as they realise that in these days collective bargaining is an advantage to the employers as well as to the employed, and that the best interests of Capital as well as of Labour are involved in the maintenance of a well-balanced system under responsible management. What they undoubtedly did intend to crush if they could was the anarchical system which found its embodiment in the Irish Transport Workers' Union. They had had their fill of Mr. Larkin and were not disposed again to place themselves in a position which would permit him or his Union to tyrannise over them. If the delegates had been perfectly frank they would probably have expressed entire sympathy with the employers now that agreements based on Mr. Larkin's word were an impossibility. The man, whose most conspicuous comment about them when they were doing their best within the restrictions imposed upon them to aid the movement was that they were ' going to sell the pass,' was not one whom they could have honestly recommended the employers to take to their arms.

We shall, perhaps, not be far wrong if we assume that the peculiar tone imparted by the delegates to their report was due to the exigencies of the English rather than of the Irish situation. English Trade Unionists were greatly agitated by the lurid reports which had been sent over relative to police ' brutality,' and the spirit of Larkinism, with its defiance of authority, its abuse of capitalists, and its strident assertion of the majesty of labour, had captured many of the younger minds. Generally, there was a strong feeling, confined to no particular class or district, that something ought to be done on behalf of the gallant strugglers for freedom in Dublin. The leaders probably would have gladly evaded the financial action altogether, for they did not love Mr. Larkin and, quite apart from personal reasons, they did not care to deplete the union coffers for a cause which had so little in it to justify expenditure from the English standpoint. But the pressure from the ranks was too strong to be resisted with safety. The most that the Trade Union executives could do was to see that the assistance should be given in such a form that the control of the administration of the funds was absolutely retained in their hands. Voting in the first instance a lump sum of £5000, they spent the money on food products with the intention that their disbursements should, in the directest possible way, go towards the relief of the strikers. They were actuated, no doubt, by motives of pure humanity in thus intervening ; but the whole business, there can be little doubt now, was a blunder of a very bad kind. Not only was the support accorded absolutely useless as a solvent of the employers' opposition, but it had a positively mischievous effect by prolonging a hopeless struggle for many weary weeks, during which the degradation of the working classes was accentuated to an appalling extent. Trade Union honour, however, was satisfied by this plunge into the dispute, and for the time being that was all that was considered to matter.

On the employers' side the need of outside assistance had also engaged attention. Early in the struggle it was realised that Dublin's industry could not bear upon its shoulders the entire burden of what, even then, was foreseen must be a long and costly business. An appeal to the general body of British industrialists was the natural means by which the Federation could seek to strengthen its position. The fight that the Dublin employers was waging was no ordinary local affair. It was a conflict which touched the very springs of British industry and involved a common responsibility which could not be evaded without serious detriment to the interests of all associated with it. Some members of the employers' committee were dispatched across the Channel as the representatives of the Federation to conduct a mission to the great industrial centres of England and Scotland. They found that the distorted views of the dispute which had been circulated in the English papers had created a certain amount of prejudice. But they were easily able to show how unfairly the employers had been treated, and, when the mists of doubt had been cleared away and the true position brought out in its full significance, the British confrères of the Dublin employers were not merely willing but eager to help. After an exhaustive tour of the manufacturing districts, the delegates returned to Dublin with such a measure of assistance as to place beyond doubt the financial capacity of the Employers' Federation to conduct the fight to the bitter end, if such it should prove to be.

That the dispute was not to have an early termination was only too apparent as the shortening of the days brought with them the chill of autumn as a reminder that a sterner feature must soon be added to the conflict. The idea of a peaceful settlement still had a foremost place in the public mind, or at all events in that section of it which did not fully comprehend the character of the principles involved. The Lord Mayor, with praise-worthy industry, still worked at his project for the setting up of a conciliation board, and he even went so far as to get together a list of Labour men who were to represent the side of the workers. But as these representatives included, necessarily so perhaps from his standpoint, the Larkinite leaders, the employers declined to have any-thing to say to the scheme. They knew the futility of any composition that might be made under such auspices, and they resolutely refused to be diverted from their purpose of winning their freedom by any specious argu-ments as to the advantages of conciliation based on the totally different conditions which prevail across the Channel. Meanwhile, the Government, properly anxious for the termination of a conflict which was having such a serious effect on the peace of Dublin as well as its commercial interests, decided to send over to the city a Commission, with Sir George Askwith as its head, with instructions to inquire into the situation and report upon it with a view to a settlement.

Sir George Askwith enjoys a deserved reputation as a mediator in industrial disputes. His qualities are those which make for success in the adjustment of differences. A well-balanced, judicial habit of mind is associated in him with a marked capacity for that form of diplomatic finesse that tells in such difficult and complicated negotiations as those affecting the relations of employers and employed, in which strong passions and prejudices oftentimes constitute the most serious obstacles to peace.   At the time of his Dublin appointment he was at the height of a brilliant career.   One successful achievement had followed another in his official service, until it seemed that he had but to appear upon a scene of trouble for the mists of difficulty to dissolve, leaving an atmosphere of peace and sweet reasonableness.   In the circumstances the decision to dispatch him to Dublin to try his gifts of conciliation on the opposing elements there is easily to be understood.   But the public, not less than the Government, had overlooked the peculiar conditions of the dispute there and the limitations they imposed to the exercise of the skill even of the most able exponent of the arts of compromise.

Even while the echoes of the chorus of congratulations on Sir George Askwith's appointment were reverberating through England, the course of events in Dublin was showing how hopeless his mission was.   On the one side were the employers declining with polite emphasis to be led into any discussion in regard to a settlement unless the preliminary conditions offered an absolute guarantee that any agreement arrived at should be respected.   A suggestion had been made that the merging of the Irish Transport Workers' Union in the English organisation might meet the difficulty, but there was no evidence that Mr. Larkin would be content to efface himself, and, in any event, the Employers' Federation were not disposed to consider this solution until it had been shown that Mr. Larkin's influence and personality would be entirely eliminated.   In the Larkinite camp there was, at the period, a revival of incendiary oratory as if to emphasise on that side the utter impossibility of carrying through any scheme of conciliation.   Speaking at a meeting at

Beresford Square on September 25, Mr. James Connolly stated, in reference to a rumour that the Shipping Federation were bringing free labourers to Dublin, that ' if they bring that scab ship here, unload and distribute their goods, I know, you know, and God knows that the streets of Dublin will run red with the blood of the working classes.' At the same gathering Mr. Partridge, another prominent Larkinite, said that if the present fight went on they might have to do some things they did not like to do. ' We will,' he added, pointing to the public street lamps, ' put out these gas lamps and leave them out.' A number of fresh attacks on the police, which occurred about the time that these outrageous speeches were made, further indicated the extent to which the spirit of lawlessness permeated the movement. And that the authorities were apprehensive of serious outbreaks, owing to the temper of the strikers, was shown by their action in calling out a detachment of 100 soldiers to provide guards for the tramway depôts. This measure was taken primarily because the police were inadequate for the heavy duties imposed upon them, but that a grave feeling of danger prompted the action is self-evident from the great restraint that the authorities had previously shown in resorting to military aid.

The presence of a hungry multitude in the city daily becoming hungrier and more desperate was a sufficient source of anxiety to account for much of the official perturbation. Harrowing stories were published in the press of the terrible privations of the poor in the slum districts, but to the sojourner in Dublin there was no need of testimony of this kind to the acuteness of the situation. One could not walk through the streets without being confronted at almost every step with miserable victims of the dispute in the persons of forlorn women and tattered children, whose pinched features, even more eloquently than their fervid pleas for charity, bespoke the fierceness of the crisis which they were passing through   Local funds were opened for the relief of the distress, but the amounts contributed were utterly inadequate to provide for a tithe of the cases of extreme destitution that existed.

It was at this juncture that the English Trade Unionists gave effect to their vote in support of the strikers by sending to Dublin the first of a series of food ships which were afterwards to play a prominent and historic part in the dispute. This method of intervention did not fail to evoke criticism. Comment was excited at the curious spectacle of cargoes of food being forwarded from England to Ireland, and the suggestion was forthcoming that golden sovereigns would have occupied much less bulk and would have purchased probably more in Ireland than they would in England. More cogent was the line taken by another class of critics, who warned the English Trade Unionists that they were entering upon a course which would degrade and pauperise the community and probably be ineffective from their standpoint. One local organ was so struck with the ' strange spectacle ' of this English food ship entering the port that it was reduced to moralising. ' What a sad commentary,' said the writer, ' it all is upon the conditions that, in these modern days of highly developed industrialism, rule the relations of man with man, that these things should be.' Generally, perhaps, the local feeling may be said to have been one of curiosity as to the effect that the novel procedure of the English Trade Unionists would have on the dispute.

Wise or unwise, the English Trade Unionists' action unquestionably had a fine dramatic effect at the moment. There was something inspiring to the mind of the man who took short views in this gallant effort for the ' Relief of Dublin,' as it was termed, with due regard to the belligerent atmosphere in which the operations were conducted. The *Hare,* the vessel which took the cargo of food from Manchester, was, in the eyes of some enthusiasts,

likely to go down to history with the *Mayflower* and other
craft which have been associated with struggles for the
rights of man.   On their part the Trade Union delegates
who accompanied the *Hare* took pains that the episode
should lose nothing in spectacular effectiveness in their
hands.   As the ship came up the river on the afternoon
of Saturday, September 27, they stood on the upper deck
and acknowledged with effusion the shouts of joy that went
up from the serried masses of strikers on the quays.
When at length the *Hare* had been tied up at Sir John
Rogerson's Quay, speeches were made appropriate to
the occasion.   The note sounded in them, it is worthy
of mention in view of the subsequent course of events,
was one of strong encouragement and even defiance.
' Should this dispute unfortunately be continued,' said
Mr. Seddon, ' rest assured that this, the first ship, will
not be the last.'   ' We recognise, as Trade Unionists and
workers, that your fight is our fight, and we are going to
stand by you until that fight is won.'   Mr. Gosling, who
also spoke, was even more emphatic as to the backing
that would be given the strikers from the other side.
' I hope you are all going to stick together to the finish,'
he said.   ' If you stick together we will stick to you.'
' There is plenty more help if you want it,' he added.
    Whether the delegates intended it or not, the impres-
sion conveyed by their speeches was that the English
Trade Unionists had completely and absolutely cast in
their lot with the strikers.   The immediate effect of
their intervention was a stiffening of the attitude of the
Larkinites.   In his speech at Beresford Place the same
evening Mr. Larkin referred triumphantly to the breaking
of the ' starvation boom,' and said that he and those
associated with him would make the employers ' eat dirt '
before they were done with them.   He repeated, almost
in the same words, the threat about agreements which
had been made by Mr. Connolly a few days previously.
' They would, he was sure,' he said, ' go back to-morrow

for a week, sign the agreements, and then come out again if they were told to do so ; and that was the spirit which should animate them if they were to achieve victory.' He added in conclusion : ' For victory they were heading, for the toiling masses of Ireland were the classes which were most certain to win a triumph, and it was the marvel of most people that the strike had lasted so long ; but, if it were to be prolonged, they could hold out for a year and a day with the support which they could command from all quarters of the world.' With such an utterance as this on record—an unabashed exposition of the doctrine that agreements might be repudiated by the men—the prospect for the success of the then rapidly impending inquiry was remote. Obviously employers were not going to allow themselves to be inveigled into an under-standing based on the word of a man who openly professed principles of this character.

CHAPTER XVIII

THE GOVERNMENT INQUIRY

SIR GEORGE ASKWITH was not required to deal single-
handed with the knotty problem of finding a way out of
the industrial tangle in Dublin. Associated with him in
the work of the inquiry were Sir Thomas Ratcliffe Ellis
and Mr. Clyne, M.P., the former a well-known and able
expert in mining matters, who had come conspicuously
to the front in the great labour upheaval of 1911, and
the latter a labour representative of the best type. They
brought to their work a good store of experience acquired
in dealing with labour matters in England, but none of
the trio had ever had any previous acquaintance with
Irish industrial questions. The drawback was a serious
one, as they were unable to appreciate to the full extent
necessary the peculiar conditions which had created the
dispute and the exceptional difficulties which stood in the
way of a settlement. There was, however, no disposition
in any quarter in Dublin to criticise the appointments.

Employers welcomed the opportunity that the inquiry appeared to offer of putting themselves right with the public, whose mind had been prejudiced to some extent against them by biassed newspaper reports and flagrant labour misrepresentations ; and the strikers and their friends were hopeful that the Commissioners would be able by their influence to force a settlement which would leave them with, at any rate, the nominal fruits of victory. Outside these directly interested quarters, amongst the great mass of Dublin people, there was an earnest desire for the ending of the strike, which was causing such havoc in trade quarters and disturbing the harmony of the city's life in many ways.

At the time that the members of the Commission of Inquiry arrived in Dublin, towards the end of September, the situation had reached a point of greatly increased gravity. A rough estimate of the number of workers out of employment, directly or indirectly, through the disputes put the total at over sixteen thousand, and fresh additions were constantly being made. On the very day that Sir George Askwith arrived in the city, a number of men employed by the Grand Canal Co. came out because they would not agree to handle ' tainted goods ' which the company as common carriers were compelled to accept. Though a certain amount of trade was being done in the face of great obstacles, and notably by the coal merchants with the use of motor lorries run under police escort, the deadlock was practically complete.

On Monday, September 29, in the historic precincts of Dublin Castle, the inquiry was opened in circumstances which did not augur very happily for an amicable discussion of the points at issue. A considerable part of the proceedings was occupied with a wrangle between Mr. Gosling, who was the spokesman for the Trade Union delegates, and Mr. James Brady (a solicitor), who appeared to represent the United Builders' Labourers and General Workers of Dublin Trade Union, as to whether the latter

should have a *locus standi* at the inquiry.   There was also
shown a sharp cleavage of opinion between the two
principal parties to the dispute as to whether the inquiry
should be held in public or not.   Mr. W. M. Murphy, who
with Mr. George Jacob, Mr. W. Hewat, and Mr. Coghlan,
represented the employers, urged strongly that the proceedings should be in the full light of day.   Mr. Gosling,
on the other hand, held that the interests of peace would
best be served by private deliberations where the points
at issue could be thrashed out with business-like expedition
without the aid of lawyers.   No decision was given by
the Commissioners at the opening sitting upon the point,
but it was clear that the demand for publicity which was
made by the employers was one which could not be
resisted.   They had been made the objects of virulent
attack for weeks past, their motives had been impugned
and their actions had been misrepresented, and they had
been generally held up to public opprobrium as a body of
merciless capitalists who were deaf to the dictates of
reason and of humanity.   Now that the subject was to
be investigated before an impartial tribunal, they could
not reasonably be denied the right to place their case
before the public in circumstances which would allow of
a proper judgment being formed upon their policy.

When the inquiry was resumed on October 1, it
was in circumstances which showed that the question of
publicity had been decided in favour of the employers'
view.   For the first time counsel appeared to assist
in the deliberations—a token by itself that the investigation was to be of a thoroughgoing kind.   The employers
had to represent them a notable array of forensic talent.
The Employers' Federation had retained the services of
Mr. T. M. Healy, K.C., M.P., Mr. Hanna, K.C., and Mr.
E. A. Collins, while Serjeant Sullivan appeared to look
after the interest of the County Dublin employers.   Upon
Mr. Healy devolved the important duty of presenting
the employers' case as a whole.   No better choice could

have been made of a spokesman in such an emergency.
Mr. Healy has a remarkable grasp of facts and a happy
capacity for stating a case with lucidity and force. A
gift of pungent humour, which is his in no common degree,
adds piquancy to his discourse and ensures for his utterances a wider circle of readers than is possessed probably
by any Irishman to-day. A large and lucrative practice
at both the English and the Irish Bar has not staled the
infinite variety of his wit. He enlivens many a dull case
by his quaint conceits and whimsical turns of expression,
and yet he is no mere chartered jester. Few counsel are
more skilful in getting directly to the heart of a subject
and laying bare the points which are really essential to a
true understanding of the position.

Mr. Healy's speech at the Dublin Labour Inquiry will
live amongst his happiest efforts of forensic oratory. It
was a clear, convincing statement in which, by the cumulative force of facts set out in proper sequence with many
flashes of wit and a wealth of apt illustration, he demonstrated that the Larkinite movement was a purely
anarchical one, in which the most subversive principles
were backed by an insidious system of moral and physical
intimidation. In his address, which extended over two
days, the eminent counsel touched all the salient points
in the history of the movement from its inception in the
circumstances narrated to the final cataclysm in which all
Dublin trade had been involved. As the ground has
already been covered in these pages, it is unnecessary to
follow him in detail through his able survey. Some of his
leading points, however, must not be missed, as they
help very materially to a full appreciation of the extraordinary organisation against which the employers were
compelled to fight.

In his preliminary remarks Mr. Healy made the
striking declaration that within the past five years
Dublin had been subjected to more strikes than during
its entire existence as a capital. He went on to say that

probably no more serious condition of affairs had ever affected the city. It had been brought about by action taken in the name of Trade Unionism, which was sufficient 'to make every honest trade unionist throughout the three kingdoms ashamed of the abuse of the name.' What had gone on was in defiance of every trade union principle. The principle of collective bargaining had been attacked, employers had been called upon to pay dues to this so-called trade union, and, wherever an attempt had been made to bargain with this organisation, the agreements made had been scandalously and shamelessly broken.

Mr. Healy gave the history of the various arrangements entered into, accompanying his narrative with a lively comment on the subjects with which he was dealing. He caustically criticised the irresponsible manner in which strikes were called. 'Was there,' he asked, 'even the poorest and the humblest organisation of men in England in which the men were not consulted before a strike was declared ? Was it ever done by one man ? It was done in every case in Dublin, but not at all in England. They heard Trade Unionism appealed to. Trade Unionism in the mouths of these people was a mockery ; it exists only in name. The men were mere puppets in the hands of three or four of their leaders. Mr. Larkin acts the part of a Napoleon : he orders this or that and the men obey him ; and that was what had brought about the strikes.' Describing the case of the holding up of the British and Irish Company's steamers in defiance of an agreement, Mr. Healy remarked, 'and yet the masters who resent this system are told by the English Trade Union Congress that they are out to smash Trade Unionism. 'Why,' he added scornfully, 'these haughty masters have worn out their marrow bones in kneeling at the shrine of Larkin.' An allusion to Mr. Larkin's arrest in Horse Show Week drew from the counsel the comment : ' In this great country, whenever any agitator, labour or political, is in trouble, the Government always comes to his assistance by locking him up.' The scandalous character of the *Irish Worker* was expatiated on in some searching sentences. Mr. Healy selected one passage for special notice. In this a man was described as ' a lodging-house keeper and brother-in-law of a beer shark,' and the notice went on to say, ' He is one of the good men and true who sat in the jury box and found Jim Larkin guilty.' ' In the old days,' observed Mr. Healy significantly, ' a person who ventured to publish such a statement would certainly have been closely attended to by the authorities.'

Coming to the *Independent* and tramway disputes, Mr. Healy said that Mr. Larkin, ' like a skilful general, in order to inflame his troops, had for some years been engaged in abusing Mr. Murphy.' Mr. Larkin described Mr. Murphy ' as the greatest ogre, as a monster in human shape, a sweater, and wound up with the statement that he would break his heart.' This went on for two years and Mr. Murphy took no notice of it, but when he saw that Mr. Larkin was determined to have a strike on his paper and to disorganise the trams, he thought it time to intervene. Mr. Murphy differed from other employers in one important respect. ' Nearly all the others met Mr. Larkin, dealt with Mr. Larkin and yielded to him. Mr. Murphy never dealt with Mr. Larkin ; he would not meet him. In fact, Larkin knew that Mr. Murphy was of that stamp that he would not see him, and he never even applied to see him. There was one man in the city who would not deal with Larkin and with whom Larkin could not deal.'

As to the actual circumstances of the tramway strikes, Mr. Healy pointed out that the majority of the men employed in the service were opposed to a strike when the attempt was made to paralyse the system. ' Would,' he asked, ' any colliery in England—leaving out the question of a sympathetic strike—be " struck " when the majority of the men were opposed to a strike ? And if the minority of the men struck, would they have a right, according to the common sense of the country, to describe the majority who remained in as " scabs," to have their houses boycotted, and to be publicly stoned in the streets ? '

Mr. Healy made some striking points about the cruelty of the tramway strike. He showed that if Mr. Larkin's promise to the strikers, that there would be no tramways running on the streets for twelve months, had been carried out, the end sought by the strikers would have been no nearer. ' Some one foolishly said,' he proceeded, ' that the freedom of the world was not worth a single drop of blood. I do not hold that ; but if you put on one side any gain Mr. Larkin may have won, and on the other the enormous loss he has caused to business and the sufferings he has caused the poor, the benefit that he has done to any man or body of men in the city is but a drop in the ocean to the mischief, misery, tumult, and ruin of which he is the author.' Mr. Larkin professed to have a ' divine mission.' ' If,' remarked Mr. Healy with cutting irony, ' you go into the country for ten miles you will not find a single labouring man in employment. The very harvest is rotting, and farmers are going about with revolvers, and all in the name of the divine mission to create discontent.' The last words, said with inimitable effect, elicited, as the reporters faithfully recorded, ' loud laughter, in which Mr. Larkin joined.' In the final passages of his address Mr. Healy said that the action of the employers was brought about by the attacks made on them. ' They saw no way by which they could have any guarantee that the sympathetic strike which had been put down and crushed in England would be stopped in Ireland.'

It was an extremely able and, as the Labour leaders afterwards acknowledged, moderate presentation of the employers' case that Mr. Healy submitted to the Court.

For most purposes it was amply sufficient as a statement of the history of the dispute ; but, in order that no opening should be given for any accusations that the employers were withholding information, several prominent employers were called into the witness box. Mr. David Barry, Secretary and Manager of the British and Irish Steam Packet Co., and Mr. Samuel McCormick, of Tedcastle, McCormick & Co., gave evidence as to the breaking of the agreements of 1908 and 1911. Mr. Thomas McCormick, also of the firm of Tedcastle, McCormick & Co., and Mr. John Wallis, who represented the Master Carriers' Association, spoke to the irritating interference of Mr. Larkin's union with the coal trade, while Mr. George Jacob and Mr. W. M. Murphy testified to the facts with which they were familiar. Other witnesses called were Mr. Charles Eason, Mr. A. W. Spence, Mr. T. E. Booth, Mr. Matthew McMurtry, the Right Hon. L. A. Waldron (Chairman of the Grand Canal Co.), Mr. P. J. O'Neill, Mr. Jolly, and Mr. Dixon.

Nearly all the witnesses were subjected to rather severe cross-examination by Mr. Larkin. His desire appeared to be to discredit the statements made by attempts to prove inaccuracies in matters of detail. To Mr. Jacob he was deliberately offensive. ' You don't pretend to carry on your business as a philanthropist ? ' was the first question he addressed to the witness. Mr. Jacob treated the attack with silent contempt. Afterwards, to smooth over matters, the chairman himself put the question, and then the witness gave the sensible reply : ' You cannot carry on any business at all if you are not to make money. The more successful you make your business, the more you can do for your workers.'

A number of questions were put as to wages which Messrs. Jacob paid. To one of these inquiries relative to the carpenters in the firm's employ (a very small body) the witness replied he did not know, whereupon Mr.

Larkin broke out : ' Don't know what you pay ! Don't care what you pay ! And you are here asking for the protection of this Court ? ' Shortly afterwards there was another outburst. ' This man is ashamed of himself and his position,' shouted the Labour leader. ' The conditions of work at his factory are damnable slavery. I have asked questions and he has refused to answer them. He has refused to say what wages he pays or what overtime he pays. It is these people who are causing all the turmoil.'

There was less of this studied offensiveness when Mr. Larkin came to examine Mr. Murphy. The witness stood up to receive the attack : not to be outdone, Mr. Larkin also rose. The two had, as Mr. Murphy stated in his evidence, never met until they were brought together at the inquiry. The circumstance gave an element of piquancy to the encounter. Mr. Larkin's main line of attack appeared to be directed against an assertion Mr. Murphy had made, that until the present episode he had never in all his long experience as an employer had any difficulties with any of his employees. Although the business relations of the witness during the previous thirty-five years were searchingly brought under review, nothing was elicited to discredit the statement. Mr. Murphy's cool and collected manner was occasionally disconcerting to the Labour leader. ' You complain bitterly I have been attacking you in the columns of a paper called the *Irish Worker* ? ' asked Mr. Larkin. ' I did not complain,' replied the witness quietly. ' You stated yesterday that I suggested that you should be murdered ? ' was the next question. ' I stated that what appeared in the paper was an incitement to murder,' answered the witness, and he added with emphasis, ' and so it was.' Later on the question was put : ' Did you ever see any official of the Transport Union intimidating any man, or did you see myself doing it ? ' ' No ; you are generally in a safe place,' came the reply swiftly. 'Did I ever make a statement that I didn't make good ?' inquired the cross-examiner. 'You said you would paralyse the trams, and you did not make it good,' responded the witness. There was a good deal more of this cut and thrust, but Mr. Larkin never succeeded in breaking down the imperturbable demeanour of his antagonist. He once, however, severely upset Mr. Healy's equanimity by asking a witness (not Mr. Murphy) whether a particular employers' representative was not a freemason, and whether on that account he did not object to the men going to mass. As 'a strong Catholic' Mr. Healy stigmatised it as 'an abominable statement.' On the occasion of another interruption by Mr. Healy, Mr. Larkin told him angrily : 'I am not going to submit to you or anybody else bull-dozing me.' 'I am only a wage-slave,' responded the counsel meekly. With this comic relief the proceedings went on to the close of the third day, October 3, by which time the employers had exhausted their evidence and the way was cleared for the Transport Workers' Union to present their case.

A surprise awaited the employers, and also, it may be added, the general public who had intelligently followed the proceedings. The natural supposition was that some attempt would be made to meet the very serious allegations of broken faith and systematic industrial lawlessness which had been put forward on the employers' behalf. Indeed, Mr. Larkin himself gave support to this view by a statement made in the course of the examination of one of the witnesses, that he intended to call evidence to rebut a particular charge. Instead, however, of taking the expected course, Mr. Larkin confined himself to delivering an address, which not merely was no answer to the case he was called upon to meet, but added fresh fuel to the flames of discord. It was in the main a highly pitched, rhetorical plea of justification based on the social conditions prevailing in Dublin for which the employers were held to be responsible. Christ, he added, would not be crucified any longer in Dublin by these men. The majority of employers of the city had no association with Dublin by birth and had no feeling or respect for Dublin or Ireland's development. They came there to grind down the body and soul of poor unfortunate workmen and their wives and children. In some of the factories they saw the poor married men and women not only with their bodies seared but their souls. When they were no longer useful they were flung out on the human scrap-heap. At every corner they would find places of degradation—the public-houses—controlled by these men. Driven to the verge of death, so to speak, the workmen made their way to the bastille owned by these men, and they came out with a kind of stimulation. He was out to lift the class he belonged to from social shame in which they existed, and he would do so ; and, what was more, he believed he would also lift those opposed to him. Mr. Murphy had called his union an anarchist union. Would Mr. Murphy define what anarchy was ? Anarchy meant the highest form of love.

A strain of exaggerated egoism ran through the whole of the speech. In a great many cases, he said at one point, he had come out on top. Why ? Because he had never been faced with men who were able to deal with him, he was never faced with a social conscience such as they had now aroused, and he was never faced with a combine of workmen who were bound to win, come weal or woe. Mr. Murphy had stated that he would drive Larkinism headlong into the sea. A very able theologian of his own Church had also assailed him, and somebody had said that it would require to build a wall round the country so that the thought of modern Europe could not come in. Well, no matter how high the wall was built, thought could not be kept out even by the theologians, or the police, or the politicans, corrupt as they were.

Turning from his introspection, Mr. Larkin went on to deal in characteristic way with his chief antagonist. He described Mr. Murphy as ' an able man who was backed up by able men,' but, he said, he used his power relentlessly. In his present action he was backed by the people who were choking the life of Dublin and who had given him privileges he had no right to possess. Then followed a lengthy reference to the conditions of the tramway employees, which Mr. Larkin represented were infinitely worse than those of their Belfast confrères. He was soon back again on his favourite theme—himself and his ' divine mission.' It was because of his love for the working classes that he was working for them. He had tried to make peace, and he was called Anti-Christ and an Atheist. If he were an Atheist he would not deny it. A Socialist he was, and always claimed to be one. He believed in a co-operative commonwealth, which was a long way ahead in Ireland. In another passage Mr. Larkin alluded again to his services to the cause of social regeneration. He had, he said, closed more public-houses than were ever closed before. He had given the men stimulation, hope, and heart. He had changed jail-birds and wastrels and made men of them. Then, dropping into a vein of menace, he warned employers not to drive the workers too far. The employer might make them recognise their power by starving them out, but they could only compel them to go back for a time. ' By the Creator that made them they would break the bonds, and they would go back to the old position and give back blow for blow, for they would not be beaten though various agencies might be employed against them.'

Occasionally, in the course of his harangue, Mr. Larkin condescended to deal with facts. Referring to the 1908 agreement, he denied that he had ever had any act or part in the final clauses. He came to the Castle on a Saturday and arranged to go back on the following Monday, and when he arrived he was told that he would not be allowed to go in. After that he went down to a public meeting and said that, as this was a fight against him, he would withdraw. The speaker indignantly denied that he had ever signed an agreement in favour of free labour as this one was. A passing allusion to Mr. Jacob was accompanied by the expression of a hope that that gentleman would not take anything he said in a personal sense. The remark brought into sharp relief that curious kink in Mr. Larkin's understanding which prevents him from appreciating the consequences of his language and of his acts. He had vilified Mr. Jacob in terms of unparalleled scurrility, and had done his best to ruin the operations of his firm, and yet he hoped that Mr. Jacob would not mind it ! Mr. Jacob might well have responded in the language of J. P. Kemble :

> Perhaps it was right to dissemble your love,
> But—why did you kick me downstairs ?

The speech throughout was characteristic of the man, and not least so in the expression it gave of his colossal vanity. What he really meant by it was well expressed in the concluding sentences: ' I would suggest to the employers,' he said, ' if they want peace, they can have peace ; and if they want war, let it be war.'

As far as Mr. Larkin himself was concerned it was plain that nothing would be done which would prevent the conflict from going on. Nor did the subsequent proceedings at the sitting tend to relieve the gloom which was now settling over the inquiry. Mr. J. H. Havelock Wilson, of the Seamen's and Firemen's Union, made a not unconciliatory speech suggesting that, though it would be difficult to arrange monetary guarantees as the employers suggested, there might be supplied other guarantees, first by the Dublin Trades Council and secondly by the English trade unions. Mr. Wilson was followed by Mr. Harry Gosling, who scarcely poured oil on troubled waters by reiterating the libel that there was a deliberate attempt on the part of the Dublin employers to destroy Trade Unionism, by declaring that he did not believe that ' any other weapon but the sympathetic strike would have done the least bit of good ' in the circumstances in which the Dublin workers were placed, and by asserting that the English trade unions were going to back up the Irish Transport Workers' Union with their funds as long as it was necessary. A still more threatening speech was made by Mr. Robert Williams, general secretary to the National Transport Workers' Association, who intimated that the men of the federation to which he belonged might stop coal from being shipped to Ireland. He described the attitude of the employing classes as ' obsolete if not obsolescent,' and truculently observed that the union for which he spoke could not see the men in Dublin humiliated. Mr. Healy quickly took up the challenge implied in the last utterance. He said that the employers could well stand abuse from Larkin, but they could not in any sense yield to threats.

Afterwards, in the course of some conversation, Mr. Larkin said that the English, Scotch, and Welsh unions would not help the employers to deport him from Ireland. ' Let them understand, that,' he added significantly. On the other side, Mr. Healy made an emphatic statement that the employers would never consent to the dismissal of the men they had taken into their employment during the dispute where these men were found to be suitable and honest. It was with these uncompromising notes re-echoing in the room that the inquiry was adjourned until the following Monday, October 6. Before the end was reached the President announced that the case on both sides was considered to be closed. Upon this Mr. Healy raised a protest, pointing out that damaging statements had been made against certain employers and that he had had no opportunity of cross-examining in regard to these. No satisfaction was given upon the point at the time, and it was afterwards apparent that none was to be given. The course adopted was distinctly unfair to the employers, who were compelled to submit to attack on matters connected with the conduct of their business without being given the right to demonstrate the absolute falsity of some of the charges. It was especially unjust to a firm like Messrs. Jacob, whose conduct had been maligned to an extraordinary extent and whose representative had been made a special target for abuse in the witness box.

CHAPTER XIX

FAILURE OF THE INQUIRY

Presentation of the Commissioners' Report—Its One-sided Character—Views on the Sympathetic Strike and the Employers' Agreement—Criticism of the Commissioners' View that the latter is ' Contrary to Individual Liberty '—An American Case cited in Disproof of the View—The Report a Dead Letter as soon as issued—Bitter Criticism of Employers by Mr. Geo. Russell—Mr. Larkin's English Campaign—' To Hell with Contracts '—English Public Opinion alienated from the Larkinite Cause by his Violent Utterances—Dublin Industrial Peace Committee's Abortive Efforts to arrange a Settlement—Employers' Formal Reply to the Report of the Commission.

IF the Dublin industrial inquiry had no other merit, it was expeditious in its procedure—too expeditious for perfect fairness, as has already been demonstrated. Apparently the idea of the Government was that the Commissioners should come, and see, and conquer ; and in ordinary trade disputes there is a good deal to be said for a policy of the kind. By pushing the business rapidly along, differences have no time to develop, personal ambitions have no wide scope, and the utmost is made of the latent desire for peace which is never absent in these cases. But the Dublin conflict—to emphasise a point previously demonstrated—was a thing apart in the region of labour disputes. It was not a question so much of hours of work or rates of wages as of a system. If that system could be changed, all well and good ; if it could not, all the arbitrating talent in the empire was useless to find a solution. As we have seen, the attempts that had been made to suggest a new arrangement which would effectually depose the order of things which the employers found so intolerable were outwardly unproductive.   To all intents and purposes the sitting of the inquiry on October 4 ended in a deadlock.   The only open question was whether the Commissioners, by the exercise of some almost superhuman intelligence, were able to point to a way out of the *impasse*. The answer was soon forthcoming in the report of the Commissioners, which was read at the opening of the adjourned sitting of the inquiry on October 6.

The report is a long document surveying the history of the labour troubles from the period of Mr. Larkin's first appearance on the scene in 1908 until the present day, and concluding with an elaborate series of proposals for the setting up of a Conciliation Court.   In the historical summary the Commissioners deal very sketchily with the events which marked the progress of the various disputes. Without possibly intending it, they gloss over the facts which tell against the Larkinite organisation.   A conspicuous example of this partial method is to be found in the paragraph dealing with the failure to establish a Conciliation Board as recommended by the conference of 1911.   It will be recalled that it was a strong part of the employers' case that they were prepared to adopt this suggestion, and that the proposal failed to be made effective because the Larkinites sent in no names of representatives to accompany the list of delegates which had been promptly supplied on behalf of the employers.   The report dismisses the matter in a few sentences, which almost seem to be designed to conceal the neglect of the Labour party.   After mentioning the scheme which was put forward by the Viceroy's conference, the Commissioners say : ' These proposals appear to have received support from certain sections of the employers, and it is stated that the names of the employers' representatives on the board were sent to the Under Secretary.   The Conciliation Board was not, in fact, established.'   Not content, it would appear, with the suppression of the important circumstance that the Larkinites treated the proposals with contempt, the Commissioners proceed immediately to refer to a suggestion, made nearly two years later in Mr. Larkin's paper, the *Irish Worker*, in regard to the establishment of a Wages' Board to deal with disputes, as if to give the impression that the opposition to conciliation machinery did not come from his side.

More serious even than this unhappy handling of the question of the Conciliation Board is the omission of the report to deal in any shape or form with the malignant system of moral intimidation persistently followed in the columns of the *Irish Worker*. That system was an essential part of the Larkinite movement, and it should certainly have been treated in any survey of events which emanated from a quasi-judicial authority essaying to apportion responsibility for the trouble.

When the Commissioners approach the question of the sympathetic strike they recover, to some extent at least, their sense of fairness. They point out how the ramifications of this method of industrial warfare involve loss and suffering to large numbers of innocent persons, how the system leads to the breach of agreements solemnly entered into, and how by its action reprisals on one side are met by reprisals on the other ' in such rapid succession as to confuse the real issues.' ' No community could exist,' the report affirms with satisfactory emphasis, ' if resort to the sympathetic strike became the general policy of Trade Unionism, as, owing to the interdependence of different branches of industry, disputes affecting even a single individual would spread indefinitely.' The effect of these sensible words is appreciably weakened by the remark that follows, that ' in our experience of the better organised employers and workmen the sympathetic strike or the sympathetic lock-out is not recognised as a reasonable way of dealing with disputes.' The Commissioners' experience, which, of course, was

entirely with English labour troubles, had little relevance
to the crisis with which they were dealing.   If they had
studied the pages of the *Irish Worker* attentively they
would have discovered that the Larkinite movement was
founded on principles diametrically opposed to those of
the great mass of English trade unions.   It was hampered
by no scruple and bound by no law other than the fiat
of its autocratic leader.   As late as September 21
previously, as we have seen, Mr. Connolly, Mr. Larkin's
lieutenant, was asking the members of the Irish Transport
Workers' Union to sign agreements merely afterwards to
break them.   This was no isolated utterance, but one of a
series of declarations showing that the Larkinite code
of morality regarded repudiation not as a crime but as
a distinct virtue.

The incapacity revealed here for realising the true
character of the forces that had been called into being
in Dublin, is further strikingly shown in the unsparing
condemnation of the document which the employers
required their workpeople to sign as a condition of
employment.   'Whatever may have been the intention
of the employers,' observe the Commissioners, 'this
document imposes upon the signatories conditions which
are contrary to individual liberty, and which no workman
or body of workmen could reasonably be expected to
accept.'

'Contrary to individual liberty' is a very sweeping
phrase to use in this connection.   It is difficult to understand precisely what Sir George Askwith means by
it.   Is it his view that an employer must engage an
employee without reference to his or her association with
a particular organisation, however objectionable that
organisation may be to him ?   Would it, for example, be
'contrary to individual liberty' if Mr. Asquith and
the members of the Cabinet made it a condition of
employment in the case of their domestic servants that
they should not belong to the militant Suffragette

organisations ? Assuredly they would be well within their rights in enforcing a condition so necessary to the peaceful ordering of their lives, and if that is so, equally are the Dublin employers entitled to say that they will engage no one who belongs to an organisation which has shown itself capable of grievous wrongdoing.

The theory of the limitation of the liberty of the employer to enforce conditions upon the men he engages, which underlies Sir George Askwith's report, is one which probably could not be justified by a reference to the statute law of England. Curiously enough, it has been distinctly repudiated in a judgment of the Supreme Court of the United States, which was cited in some arbitration proceedings held at the end of 1913 in the State of Indiana in connection with a tramway strike. In discussing the legal relations of union labour and employers, the Public Service Commissioners, who were the arbitration tribunal in this instance, in their report said that, while it was manifestly right of the employees to join a labour union to promote their own interests ' to secure the highest wages, shortest hours, and the best conditions that they can peaceably compel,' it was equally right that the employers should, if they pleased, refuse to employ union labour in the operation of their cars and in the conduct of their business. They relied upon the judgment referred to to support their view of the respective rights of employer and employed. This judgment was given in the well-known case of Adair v. United States, which arose in Kentucky, where a State law had been passed making it illegal to dismiss a man because he belonged to a trade union. Adair was fined $50 under the law, and the State Court of Appeal confirmed the conviction. The Supreme Court of the United States declared that no State had power to make such a law and reversed the judgment of the inferior tribunal, holding that it is ' not within the functions of Government, at least in the absence of a contract between parties, to

P

compel any person in the course of his business and against his will to retain the personal services of another.' ' So,' adds the judgment, ' the right of the employee to quit the service of the employer, for whatever reason, is the same as the right of the employer, for whatever reason, to dispense with the services of such employees.' Clearly from this, in ' the land of freedom ' at all events, there is considered to be no question of the infringement of individual liberty when a man is refused employment because he belongs to a particular union.

If the Larkinite organisation is revolutionary and lawless, as the employers insist and as all the records of the movement go to show, Sir George Askwith's comment is quite beside the point. An exceptionally outrageous method of attack had to be met by an exceptionally direct style of defence. The conditions of the pledge exacted by the employers were not nearly so ' contrary to individual liberty ' as the iniquitous system of moral intimidation and organised ruffianism that the employers were by their action seeking to break down. Let me make the point clear by a citation from the prolific pages of the *Irish Worker*. In the issue of the paper following the presentation of the Commissioners' report appeared upwards of a column of notices of free labourers with names, addresses, and other particulars. The most infamous personal attacks were made upon these individuals, whose crime was that they had preferred not to remain idle. Concerning two girls, who are mentioned by name, the writer of the precious effusion says : ' Now I am giving these girls timely warning that if they persist in scabbing it on the men that are locked out it will not be well for them.' What could be more contrary to individual liberty than this shameful system of intimidation ?

Additional proof seems to be furnished in the paragraph in the report following the one commenting on the pledge of the inadequate attention that the Commissioners gave to the characteristics of the Larkinite movement. Here we have almost a condonation of the sympathetic strike and inferentially of the other features of the Irish Transport Workers' plan of campaign. ' Without attributing undue blame ' to those who considered that the conditions of Dublin necessitated a resort to these tactics, the Commissioners think that ' the time has now come when a continuance of the same methods will be fraught with disastrous results to all concerned.' In these mild terms the report refers to the prolonged orgy of Syndicalism in which the Larkinites had indulged from 1911 onwards. It is not remarkable that the Larkinites and their sympathisers seized upon this passage in the report and circulated it with embellishments as a sort of certificate of character to the justice of the movement. Thus the report, in a very real degree, contributed to the unfair impression which afterwards prevailed in England as to the inadequacy of the employers' grounds of objection to the Irish Transport Workers' Union.

The proposals relative to the establishment of a Conciliation Court do not call for lengthened comment. They are very well suited to a state of affairs in which parties are reasonable and there is a wholesome sense of responsibility on the labour side, but they were quite out of place in Dublin, owing to the abnormal methods adopted by the labour leaders and the pernicious principles upon which their organisation is based. The fatal weakness of the scheme is that it makes no adequate provision for guarantees that agreements entered into will be observed. The proposal that complaints as to breaches of understandings shall be referred to the Conciliation Court, and that in the event of the complaints being substantiated no support whatever shall be given by the respective associations by any affiliated association to the parties responsible for the breach, is almost farcical, having regard to the tenets of the Larkinites

and their contempt for any form of moral restraint.
Nothing is more certain from Mr. Larkin's antecedents
than that, if the scheme had been put into execution, he
would have snapped his fingers at those who attempted
to restrain him from irregular action under the authority
of these clauses.

Regarding it as a whole, the report is a rather poor
specimen of that type of mental balancing which is common
form in the findings of industrial arbitrators.   A point
conceded here, a dose of censure administered there, a
general splitting of the difference in assigning moral
responsibility as well as in settling the lines of future
action—such are the characteristics which stamp this
class of document.   In the case of the Dublin inquiry
the Commissioners appear to have thought that if they
could make sure of Mr. Larkin they might leave events
to take their course.   However that may have been, their
exercise has a more lop-sided appearance than is customary
with the semi-judicial pronouncements of an industrial
tribunal.   Too little was said in some places and too
much in others, and both restraint and excess were at
the expense of the employers.   It looks now almost
as if there had been an idea of forcing a settlement by
the weight of public sentiment aroused strongly on the
men's side.   If a design of the kind was actually contemplated it failed miserably.   The public sentiment was
not lacking in volume, but it was confronted with the
quiet determination of the employers not to be deflected
from the course they had marked out for themselves,
which falsified all the confident predictions of the so-called
conciliators.

Although Sir George Askwith, by adjourning the
sitting of the Commission, gave the two parties to the
dispute several hours in which to consider their attitude
in regard to the report, the decision upon it might have
been given at once, as far as the employers were concerned.
They intimated through Mr. Healy, when the Commission

reassembled, that they were deeply disappointed at the method in which the inquiry had been conducted. They had called their witnesses and submitted them to cross-examination, naturally expecting that evidence would be called on the other side. But not only was this not done, but Mr. Larkin was allowed to deliver a speech, making fresh allegations which the employers were given no opportunity of answering. As to the proposals for a Court of Conciliation, it was stated that the employers were much more concerned ' to put an end to present difficulties than to consider problems relating to future unrest.' They felt that the failure of the report to touch upon the question of guarantees for preventing further outbreaks afforded proof that the Court had found itself unable to devise a remedy for the difficulty which led to the breakdown of the negotiations with the members of the English Trade Union Congress.

On the labour side the intimation was given by Mr. Gosling that the report was accepted as a basis of discussion. Manifestly the intention was to make as much as possible of the tactical advantages of an apparent acquiescence in the findings in contrast with the stern, unyielding attitude of the masters. But events soon made it apparent to how limited an extent the Larkinites really agreed with the terms of the report.

As soon as the failure of the Government intervention had become evident, the employers were assailed with bitter criticism from many quarters. In the pages of the *Irish Times*, Mr. Geo. Russell, a well-known publicist interested in the economic development of Ireland, published, under the familiar initials ' A.E.,' a column of violent abuse of the masters, who he represented had rejected a reasonable offer of peace and fallen back on the ' devilish policy of starvation.' In less hysterical but equally unfair terms the London *Times* solemnly called the Dublin employers to account for their obduracy, and warned them that, in acting as they were doing, they were playing into the hands of agitators.　These censures were taken up by journals in sympathy with the labour movement with zest, and for a brief space the Dublin merchant was the best-abused man in the three kingdoms.　The scene then suddenly changed.　Mr. Larkin, who had gone off to London at an early moment after the conclusion of the inquiry, very considerately put matters right with the public for the employers by making one of those frank speeches of his which tell with convincing force what manner of man he is and what is the true character of the movement which he directs.　In addressing a meeting at the Memorial Hall, Farringdon Street, on October 10, he made some strong comments on the action of the Railway Men's Union in condemning the sympathetic strike.　Carried away by excitement in referring to the argument that agreements stood in the way of the execution of the policy, he shouted ' To hell with contracts ! ' He could not have given a terser description of his policy than is contained in these four words.　The significance of the declaration, following as it did immediately after the breakdown of the Dublin inquiry, was fully grasped by the public.　The London correspondent of the *Birmingham Post*, Mr. Alfred F. Robbins, who is one of the ablest and most experienced judges of the drift of public opinion, in writing of the episode said that if Mr. Larkin had been the accredited agent of the Dublin employers instead of their avowed enemy, he could not have done them better service, as far as London popular opinion was concerned, than by his utterance.　' As long as London only read of Larkinism,' Mr. Robbins wrote, ' it was apt to consider it a chimera of the Dublin employers' imagination, but now it has heard the doctrine publicly proclaimed in its midst by its inventor, it knows just how to regard the man and his mission.'　The *Westminster Gazette*, another important authority conspicuously friendly to the labour movement, observed that if Mr. Larkin's attitude was that of any considerable body of the organised working classes,

' the position taken up by the Dublin employers would be justified.'

Mr. Larkin's indiscretions were not confined to this timely exposition of his policy. In his London speech he was equally candid about his English labour friends, who had done and were doing their best, within the limitations imposed upon them by his recklessness, to keep the Irish Transport Workers' flag flying in Dublin. There was a biting reference to Mr. Snowdon, a working-man representative, ' who had never done a day's manual work in his life.' This was a preface to an attack on the Labour party, who, he said, ' could wrap themselves up in cloth to-morrow and they would be just as useful as the mummies in the museum.' ' You have only got to look at them, that's enough,' he added. These courtesies, as may be imagined, did not tend to strengthen the feeling of regard entertained for Mr. Larkin in the ranks of the official Labour party in England. Still, his cause was one which appealed too insistently to the workers in Great Britain for support to be ignored or even slighted. In this period arrangements were made by the English labour organisations for financing the strike for ten weeks to the extent of a minimum of £5000 per week, the total amount to be disbursed on food supplies for the families of those who were out of work by the dispute.

Meanwhile, an attempt had been made in Dublin by a number of well-meaning persons, banded together as the Dublin Industrial Peace Committee, to arrange a truce with the view of procuring a settlement of the dispute. Under Professor Kettle's presidency a largely attended meeting was held at the Mansion House, and earnest speeches were delivered in support of resolutions in furtherance of the objects of the meeting. The movement at no time had any very great promise of success ; but even if the prospects of arranging an armistice had been brighter than they were, they would have been irremediably injured by the Larkinite declarations.

These showed beyond all cavil that the movement was what it had always been—a purely anarchical crusade directed against industry. While contracts were consigned to the nether regions by the Labour leader, all whom it might concern were told by him in unequivocal language that the sympathetic strike was the most effective weapon in the armoury of the organisation and could not be abandoned. 'This is war to the knife—a fight to the death,' Mr. Larkin also assured an English audience. Reluctantly the Dublin peacemakers were driven to the conclusion which the employers had all along held, that there was no sure basis on which to build an edifice of reconciliation.

The uncompromising profession of the syndicalistic creed which was heard at the meetings addressed by Mr. Larkin and his leading supporters in the period following the close of the inquiry gave additional point to the employers' formal reply to the Commissioners' report which was issued on October 14. This document, which was drafted after the opinions of the members of the Employers' Executive Committee had been definitely ascertained, confirmed the action taken by the committee on the day of the conclusion of the inquiry. It was intimated that, in spite of misrepresentations, the employers adhered to the attitude they had defined in their letter to the Trade Union delegates of September 12—that they favoured trade unionism and collective bargaining, and were prepared to negotiate as soon as the workers provided trustworthy machinery and trusty men to end the system of sympathetic strikes. The communication went on to say that while they did not wish to appear to dictate as to the internal management of trade unions, in the face of the conclusions come to by the Commission, and in view of the subsequent declarations of Mr. Larkin in regard to contracts, they were compelled again to refuse to recognise the Union until it had been reorganised on proper lines, with new officials who had met the approval

of the British Joint Labour Board.   Pending the conclusion of such an arrangement, the Executive Committee
declined to recommend the withdrawal of the undertaking
as to non-membership of the Irish Transport Workers'
Union which the Commissioners criticised.   Finally, in a
reference to agreements, the committee declared that the
question of guarantees would, apart from any settlement
that might be now arrived at, have to be the subject of
legislation, ' as it has become of universal importance to
the whole trading community.'

In the light of this matured view of the Employers'
Committee of the report, no further misconception was
possible of the attitude of the employers towards Larkinism.   ' War to the knife—a fight to the death '—if Mr.
Larkin chose to put matters that way they were not
disposed to contradict him.

CHAPTER XX

THE CHURCH AND LARKINISM

Politics and Religion introduced into the Controversy by the Larkinites
—Mr. Larkin's Insolent Attitude towards the Roman Catholic
Authorities—Scheme for Deportation of Children to England—
Archbishop Walsh's Denunciation of the Scheme—Organised
Resistance to the Deportation—Mr. Larkin's Violent Attack on the
Priests—Great Public Protest—Criminal Proceedings instituted
against the English Managers of the Deportation Scheme—Further
Public Protest—Abandonment of Deportation Scheme—Arch-
bishop Walsh's Efforts to secure a settlement of the Industrial
Dispute—Proposed New Conference.

POLITICS and religion are so closely woven into the
fabric of Irish social life that they touch every movement
with their influence. The Dublin industrial upheaval
was no exception to the rule. Though a purely economic
issue involving apparently no question of faith or political
conviction, it gave rise to furious controversy in both
these directions. This, it must be stated at once, was
entirely through the action of the Larkinites. The
employers, to their infinite credit, from the very first
declined to allow either influence to enter into their
calculations. Unionist co-operated with Nationalist and
Catholic with Protestant in the heartiest fashion. A
Nationalist chairman had the unanimous and enthusiastic
support of the entire body of members, and sturdy
Unionists sat amicably on the executive with thorough-
going Nationalists. If it had been left to the employers
nothing would have been heard throughout the dispute
either of political or religious differences. But they

were only one of the parties to the issue, and in this particular matter they were, perhaps, the least important. The Larkinites, at all events, counted most in their capacity for mischief. Not only did they include the elements of the population which are most prone to political and religious excitement, but they were led by chiefs who were given to running amok in a moral sense.

Long before the conflict reached an acute stage Mr. Larkin, in his paper, girded at both the politicians and the priests. Of the former he spoke with withering contempt as mere creatures who, in the municipal sphere, made their professions of Home Rule principles a cover for every sort of jobbery and corruption, and who, in the higher domain of Parliament, were invertebrate opportunists reduced to inactivity by £400 a year. That the parliamentary party had studiously avoided mixing themselves up with his 'divine mission' was a standing cause of offence. Mr. Larkin could tolerate much, but he could not readily sit down under that form of contemptuous treatment which consists in leaving the subject of it severely alone. The policy of the parliamentary representatives was possibly at one point carried to an extreme of reticence. The country looked to them for light and guidance at a difficult juncture, and it looked for the most part in vain. Too much, however, ought not to be made of the reserve shown. If the politicians were indisposed to talk, they had excellent reason for avoiding entrance into a quarrel which was outside their proper sphere of action. The truth is that far more injury was done by intervention than by abstention from interference in this crisis. It is probably not too much to say that if well-meaning people, both in Dublin and at a distance, had kept outside the arena and allowed the combatants to have their trial of strength unmolested, there would not have been a tithe of the suffering and loss inflicted on the community that there was.

As for the Church—and here the word is used to indicate the Roman Catholic Church—Mr. Larkin maintained towards it an attitude of insolent dictation and censure amazing to all who knew how much ecclesiastical authority counts for in Ireland. One worthy priest, who had ventured to warn his flock against the dangers of Larkinism, was railed at in the most offensive way; and, not content with the effect of this general vituperation, the *Irish Worker*, following its usual practice, attempted to assail the private character of the cleric who had thus dared to speak the truth in the pulpit. Even the institutions of the Church were not immune from the vicious attentions of the Union. At one stage in the conflict there was interference with a community of nuns who managed a laundry, and who had got themselves into the black books of the Larkinites by offending against the ' tainted goods ' edict. The Church dignitaries did their best by quiet action to reprobate these manifestations of disloyalty on the part of men who professed to be Catholics. But their influence had little apparent effect in inducing a change of policy at Liberty Hall. A crisis was eventually reached in the relations of the Church to the Larkinite movement over a question which touches Catholicism in one of its tenderest spots—the training of the children of the faithful. Amongst the schemes hatched in the fertile minds of the labour leaders and their British sympathisers to relieve the pressure of the industrial situation, was the transfer of a number of the children of the strikers to England for maintenance there in artisan homes until the trouble had ended. It was a project conceived no doubt to a large extent in a genuine spirit of charity and kindliness, but the practical difficulties in the way of the very considerable deportation that would have been necessary to influence events were enormous, and beyond them lay the invincible repugnance which the Roman Catholic hierarchy everywhere, and in Ireland more particularly, have to the withdrawal of the young from Catholic supervision. The scheme had barely got to work before its futility was demonstrated by a series of events of almost dramatic significance. On October 21 appeared in the Dublin papers a letter from Archbishop Walsh, condemning unsparingly the whole procedure. Assuming that the mothers of the children to be deported were mainly Catholics, his Grace asked, ' Have they abandoned their faith ? Surely not. Well, if they have not they should need no words of mine to remind them of the plain duty of every Catholic mother in such a case.' ' I can only put it to them,' went on his Grace with significant emphasis, ' that they can no longer be held worthy of the name of Catholic mothers if they so far forget that duty as to send away their children to be cared for in a strange land without security of any kind that those to whom the poor children are to be handed over are Catholics, or, indeed, are persons of any faith at all.' The letter concluded with an appeal to the disputing parties to come together again in order to find some peaceful means of settling the conflict which was having such disastrous effects on the community.

At the moment the Archbishop's admonitions on the subject of the children carried a great deal more weight than his peace proposal. Religious feeling caught fire at the suggestion from the highest Catholic quarter in Ireland that the faith of the young was being imperilled by the deportation measures. In vain did Mrs. Montefiore, the English lady who was responsible for the initiation of the scheme, and who was superintending its carrying out, explain that the utmost care was taken to see that the children were placed in good hands in England, and that their religious instruction would, if possible, be in Roman Catholic hands. People were not at the moment in a frame of mind to listen to representations of this character. Even if the serious ecclesiastical warning had not been given, there was the evidence that the pages of the daily press afforded that the deportation scheme was being conducted on lines which called for strong reprobation. One writer, from his personal experience, described how he had ' met a group of girls, between fourteen and sixteen, walking in a kind of disorderly procession.' ' They were,' he said, ' decorated with Larkinite mottoes and were singing some kind of doggerel in praise of this person. But every now and then they gave utterances to most shockingly obscene language about the Catholic priests.' Elsewhere stories were published of coercive measures used to secure recruits for these bands of children. The position appeared in a more sinister light because an offer from Countess Plunkett, a wealthy Dublin lady, to place a large number of children in Irish homes was contumeliously rejected by the Larkinites.

In view of all the circumstances it is not remarkable that the deportation scheme met with organised resistance from a large body of people who were genuinely and, on the whole, not unnaturally alarmed at this strange new development of Larkinism. On October 22, the day after the appearance of Archbishop's Walsh's letter, arrangements were in progress for the despatch of a contingent of about fifty children to follow in the wake of parties that had already been sent forward on two previous days. The youngsters were being washed, preparatory to the voyage, at the Corporation Baths, under the supervision of Mrs. Montefiore and the other ladies associated with her, when a body of priests appeared on the scene prepared to contest with the strangers for the possession of their charges. Mrs. Montefiore declined to be moved from her purpose by the representations made to her by the clerics, but she could not prevent them from taking out of her custody a considerable number of the children. Undaunted by this rebuff, the intrepid lady sent off the remnant of the band— nineteen in number—to Kingstown for embarkation on the outgoing mail steamer. The priests, following in the track of the little voyagers, captured ten of the party before the landing stage was reached, and ultimately induced the remaining nine, after they had gone on board, to come ashore.

The ecclesiastical victory stung Mr. Larkin to the quick. The same evening, speaking from his forum at Liberty Hall, he made a bellicose speech assailing the priests in strong terms. He denounced the clergymen who had been actively concerned in preventing the deportation of Mrs. Montefiore's charges as 'a disgrace to their cloth.' 'Some of the priests,' he said, 'were afraid of these children going to England for a short stay; they were fearful lest their faith would be interfered with ; but the religion which could not stand a fortnight's holiday in England had not very much bottom or very much support behind it. Of course he knew that many of these clergy had shares in the Tramway Company, but while soul-destroying agencies were at work in Dublin for many years there was no protest made against them.' 'Those clergymen and the employers,' he added in a final outburst, 'had lighted a fire which it would take more than an hour to extinguish.'

These insulting words, applied to a class held in the highest respect by the great mass of the people of Dublin, had the effect of stimulating the opposition to the deportation scheme to an extraordinary extent. It was no longer a question of priests against Liberty Hall, but of a concerted movement of the whole of the Catholic forces in Dublin against what they regarded as an insidious Socialist attack on the faith. On Thursday, October 23, as the hour approached for the departure of the cross-Channel steamers, immense crowds gathered about the quays at North Wall with the declared intention of preventing the embarkation of any more children. A large number of priests were conspicuous in the throng and took an active part in directing what was in reality a picketing of ships. Cabs which drove up were detained until the excited Catholics had made sure that they contained no juveniles of the class marked out for deportation. In one instance a family party, including children, were detained until one of the attendant priests had assured the crowd that they had nothing to do with the Larkinites' scheme, when they were permitted to resume their journey. Eventually, after the last boat had cast off from the wharf and there was no further possibility of deporting children that night, the great crowd, now numbering many thousands, formed in processional order and marched along the quays bareheaded, singing ' Faith of our Fathers,' ' Hail, glorious St. Patrick,' and other sacred melodies. Thus they proceeded until they reached College Green, where a halt was called and the assembled multitude were addressed by Father Farrell, of Donnybrook, a priest who had taken a conspicuous part in the evening's operations. ' Remember,' he said, ' that this great demonstration was unorganised and unprepared. It shows the love you have for the Catholic children of this city. It is a magnificent protest against the proselytising of our children in the Socialistic homes of England.' The crowd cheered these sentiments with enthusiasm, and then dispersed to their homes with cries of ' Away with the Socialists,' and ' Down with Larkin.' By general consent it was one of the most remarkable and significant uprisings of Catholics that Dublin had witnessed for many a long day.

Apart from the weight of the popular protest, a heavy blow had been dealt at the deportation movement by the institution of criminal proceedings, associated with charges of abduction against Mrs. Montefiore and Mrs. Rand, an American lady who had been prominently identified with the scheme for the removal of the children. Nevertheless, the Larkinites declined to abandon their project without a further struggle. On Friday, October 24, an attempt was made under the direction of Mr.

Larkin's sister, Miss Delia Larkin, to despatch a party of juveniles to Belfast by rail. They were to have travelled by the six o'clock train in the evening from Amiens Street Station, and their tickets had actually been taken for the journey, when a number of priests, with an escort of youths, appeared upon the scene with the evident determination of preventing the execution of the plan. Miss Larkin stood her ground for a time, but the persistency of the clerics, reinforced by the action of a hostile crowd who blocked the approach to the train, compelled her eventually to retrace her steps to Liberty Hall with her charges. Flushed with their fresh victory over the forces of Larkinism, the priests and the other demonstrators marched down to the quays to picket the evening boats. There was, however, no further attempt made to get the children out of the country. After the departure of the last boat there was a repetition of the demonstration of the previous evening. A huge procession, numbering in its ranks thousands of earnest sons of the Church, marched off towards O'Connell Bridge, singing appropriate hymns. As the processionists passed Liberty Hall a crowd of strikers vigorously hooted the procession and cheered for Larkin. The compliment was returned with interest by the demonstrators, who varied their cheering for the Pope, the Archbishop, and the Priests, with cries of 'Down with Socialism,' 'Larkin must go,' and 'Kidnapper Larkin.' At one point it appeared as if the two opposing crowds would come to blows. But the large force of police present kept the rival forces apart and the evening closed without any untoward incident.

This demonstration of Friday, October 23, virtually closed the history of the deportation project. There were echoes of it afterwards in the law courts and in the press, but Dublin was spared any repetition of the humiliating scenes which had marked the development of this the most tactless of all the manœuvres of Larkinism.

If Mr. Larkin is ever given to counting the cost of his blunders, it must be with a very rueful countenance that he reckons up the bill of damages of this particular move.   It is certainly not too much to say that, as far as Dublin opinion is concerned, it did more to alienate public sympathy from him than any other action of his during the strike.   Previously there had been in many quarters merely a colourless prejudice against his Socialistic views, mixed perhaps in many cases with a certain sympathy with his labour ideals.   But his open defiance of ecclesiastical authority in a sphere where it is considered to be supreme, his vulgar abuse of the priests, and the association of his project with the propaganda of the extremest section of the English Socialists, shocked and alarmed that large section of the Dublin community which is swayed by Catholic tradition and which puts before everything else the maintenance of the principles underlying it.

The Archbishop of Dublin, as has been noted in his letter in regard to the deportation of children, threw out a suggestion for the renewal of the peace negotiations. His Grace had been prompted to undertake this effort as conciliator by a statement made by Mr. Gosling to a press interviewer to the effect that ' if the parties would come together ample guarantees would be forthcoming to ensure the carrying out of agreements.'   Recalling the circumstances under which the previous efforts to secure a settlement had failed, and especially the employers' disinclination to accept any arrangement which was not accompanied by a proper system of guarantees, Dr. Walsh asked, ' Why in the face of this explicit statement the parties should not come together.'   The Archbishop's proposal was amplified in a further letter, dated October 24, in which the names of Lord MacDonnell and Sir A. H. Porter were mentioned as ' men of rare capacity ' whose services might be utilised in connection with a new conference.   Mr. J. A. Seddon, the President of the

British Trades Union Congress, who happened to be in Dublin at the time, gave his support to the Archbishop's proposal, stating that the Congress had already ' offered its good offices towards a settlement based upon adequate guarantees, and that no one would be more delighted than himself and his colleagues if his Grace's suggestion should lead to a speedy and happy consummation of this most unhappy dispute.' Subsequently a meeting held at the Mansion House, under the presidency of the Lord Mayor, carried the scheme a stage further by appointing a committee to wait upon the representatives of the workers and the Employers' Federation to secure their assent to a conference. The labour party raised no difficulty to a meeting, but the employers objected to joining in a general conference such as was proposed, though they intimated that they were prepared to meet three of the English Trade Union leaders then on a visit to Dublin (Messrs. Bowerman, M.P., Seddon, and Gosling) to discuss the situation. Before a meeting could be arranged, the three representatives named had returned to England, and it was announced that they would not again visit Dublin until they were advised that their presence was necessary for the direct opening up of negotiations. It was given out at the time that the British Trade Union leaders were endeavouring to induce the Irish Transport Workers' Union representatives to stand aside and allow them to conduct the negotiations, but that Liberty Hall declined to relinquish its prerogatives. Thus, the old difficulty still barred the way even to an approach to a settlement. While the employers never wavered in their determination to have nothing to say to Larkinism, Larkinism was equally emphatic in declining to allow anything to be said without it. So as the days slipped by the prospects of peace became more remote and the gaunt realities of the struggle were more depressingly apparent.

CHAPTER XXI

A MARTYR AND HIS FIERY CROSS

Waning Influence of Larkinism—Trial of Mr. Larkin—Attorney-
General's Indictment of Movement—The Defence—Sentence—
Agitation for Mr. Larkin's Release—Government succumbs to
the Clamour—Violent Speeches of Mr. Larkin on his Release—
Calling out of the Dock Labourers—' Fiery Cross' Crusade checked
—Mr. Larkin's Intemperate Oratory—Mr. Thomas, M.P.'s,
Repudiation of Larkinism—Counterblast to the Larkinite Pro-
paganda in England.

AT the period of Archbishop Walsh's well-intentioned
effort to bring about peace at the end of October, there
were many indications that the long-drawn-out dispute
was reaching its inevitable end. The tramways, which
had been the cockpit of the struggle, were running
smoothly with their full complement of hands, not a few
of whom were disillusioned strikers. In other directions
industries, though hampered by the difficulty of getting
supplies and removing goods, were working with some
regularity. The strikers, too, were not responding with
the alacrity they once did to the calls from Liberty Hall.
What was to have been a great mass demonstration in
Phœnix Park on Sunday, October 26, resolved itself into
a meeting of quite ordinary proportions, to which the usual
Sunday crowd in the Park contributed in large degree.
Generally speaking, there was at the time a marked
absence of the enthusiasm which a few weeks earlier had
been so conspicuous in the ranks of Mr. Larkin's adherents.
It seemed almost that, with the damaging failure of the

project for deporting the children, Larkinism had run its course. Unfortunately, it was at this juncture that the law once more stepped in to give the strike the new lease of life it so sadly needed. Probably the placing of Mr. Larkin upon his trial on the charge of using seditious language, on which he had been committed, was inevitable in view of all the circumstances, but the fact remains that the proceedings were the starting-point of a new phase of the strike movement which did not terminate until the lapse of many weeks and after much additional suffering and loss had been inflicted upon the sorely tried community.

Mr. Larkin's trial took place on October 27, before Mr. Justice Madden, in circumstances which heightened the effect of the advertisement it gave his cause. A court crowded with spectators, many of whom the reporters recorded ' were clergymen and ladies,' a great array of Counsel, with the Attorney-General leading for the prosecution, and a small army of journalists and press photographers ready to deal with the business as with a new sensation—all these gave *éclat* to proceedings which were the veriest farce if they were not intended by the Government to run to their logical conclusion. At the outset there was, as is often the case in Ireland, a good deal of trouble in empannelling the jury. One gentleman, a prominent employer, asked to be excused on the ground that he was an interested party, but was told that the prosecution was not for the labour dispute and that he must serve. Afterwards several challenges were made by the prisoner's Counsel (Mr. Hanna, K.C.), and the spectators in the court witnessed the curious ceremony of specially sworn jurors trying the issue whether individuals summoned could act impartially. In two instances the decision was against the gentlemen named serving, and in a third case the jurors disagreed. Eventually the full jury was sworn and the trial entered upon.

As the facts embodied in the case for the prosecution

were identical with those adduced in the evidence given in the police court, it is unnecessary to deal with them here. The only point in the Attorney-General's opening speech which calls for notice is his defence of the prosecution. 'Some well-meaning people,' he said, 'thought that Mr. Larkin should not have been prosecuted at all, but that was not his view. He thought that, under the circumstances that would be detailed to the jury in evidence, it was imperative that the law should be vindicated, and that the offences with which the prisoner was charged should be suppressed and punished.' 'There was,' he went on, 'nothing at all novel in the situation in which they found themselves at present. Mr. Larkin and his friends were doing nothing but committing the oldest kind of sins in the newest kind of way, and as in the past the firm and courageous and impartial administration of the law had been found certain to put down matters of the kind with which the prisoner was charged, so in the future it would be found efficacious. If it did not, anarchy must prevail. There would be an end to society—to the bonds of society—and in a short time Mr. Larkin, or somebody in his position, would be at the head of affairs, and that, then, would be followed by a military despotism.' 'Mr. Larkin,' he added, 'was not being prosecuted as a demagogue, but as a wicked and dangerous criminal.'

These remarks of the Attorney-General set out with the utmost plainness the view of the authorities who were responsible for the government of Ireland and the peace of Dublin at the time. There could not have been stronger grounds urged for the prosecution, and in the event of a conviction more powerful reasons could not have been adduced for non-interference with the course of justice. Yet, as we shall see, the prisoner was let loose upon society before he had served more than a tithe of his sentence.

Mr. Hanna made out as good a defence of Mr. Larkin

as was possible in the circumstances.   He scored a point
by securing the acquiescence of the judge in his declaration in regard to the proclamation of the Sackville
Street meeting, that no proclamation of a magistrate could
make a legal meeting an illegal meeting.   In another part
of his speech he drew a skilful parallel between the position of Mr. John Burns, the hero of the Trafalgar Square
episode of 1888 and the then President of the Local
Government Board and Privy Councillor, and Mr. Larkin,
the leading actor in the O'Connell Street affair of 1913.   As
to the suggestion contained in Mr. Larkin's speech relative
to looting, Mr. Hanna said that as a matter of fact not
one shop had been looted, nor had one piece of coal been
stolen in the city.   Mr. Hanna either forgot or con-
veniently overlooked here the looting of the shops in the
Redmond's Hill quarter on the night of September 1.
The will to give effect to the Liberty Hall injunction of
August 28 was certainly not wanting.

The judge in his summing-up pointed out that no
attempt had been made to dispute the words used in the
speech.   Any speech used in the furtherance of a strike
which was calculated to arouse bad passions or to lead
to violence, he laid down, was an offence against the law.
What construction, he asked, could reasonably be put on
the expression, ' for every one of our men who falls, two
must fall on the other side.'   Again, was it a mere platitude
to say to hungry men, ' There is food in the shops and
clothes in the shops and coal on the banks ' ?   The summing-up pointed to the inevitability of the conviction.
After half an hour's private deliberation, the jury returned
a verdict of guilty on the first count of using seditious
language, and not guilty on the two other counts of
inciting to riot and inciting to steal.

Claiming his right to address the court before sentence
was passed, Mr. Larkin raised the question of the accuracy
of the report of his speech, but was stopped in the middle
of his argument by the judge, who told him that he must

confine himself in his remarks to the question of the sentence.   Thereupon Mr. Larkin said that he was sorry he had not been tried by his peers—the working men. He was not, he added, satisfied with ' a verdict from a packed jury composed of Jews and Gentiles.'   In passing a sentence of seven months' imprisonment upon the prisoner, Mr. Justice Madden said that Mr. Larkin, with his knowledge of labour questions, must have known the consequences likely to follow from a speech such as that which formed the subject of the indictment in the midst of a great labour dispute.   ' He ought to have known— and I must attribute it to him,' observed the judge, ' that crime and violence would follow, and would result in the sending to gaol of a great many men who followed his advice.'

With an imposing escort Mr. Larkin, at the close of the trial, was removed to Mountjoy Gaol to undergo his term of imprisonment, which, as was made clear in the court, was ' simple imprisonment,' carrying with it the privileges of a first-class misdemeanant.   Thereafter for a brief space he was a martyr languishing in a prison cell, but there were not wanting inconvenient commentators to point out that while he was enjoying all the luxuries which are possible to a first-class misdemeanant—the wearing of his own clothes, the eating of his own meals supplied from outside, and, possibly, even the smoking of his own fragrant cigars—his poor dupes who had followed his advice were undergoing the ordinary hard labour treatment.

From the very outset, as has been noted, the prosecution of Mr. Larkin was considered by many people who were utterly opposed to his views to be a mistake.   They did not and could not then foresee that the Government, after incurring themselves all the odium of proceedings and giving Mr. Larkin all the advertisement that they carried with them, would weakly stultify themselves in the face of the world by interfering with the execution of the sentence. But great is the power of Demos when expressed through

the ballot boxes. Ministers stood firm while they were
being told in peremptory language by their press organs
that ' Larkin must be released ' ; they faced steadily the
fire of countless resolutions couched in the strongest
language from labour organisations ; they regarded un-
concernedly a great Albert Hall meeting at which Mr.
George Bernard Shaw and other personages of light and
leading in the Socialist world hurled their anathemas at
them with all the concocted fury of men who see a magnificent opportunity for self-advertisement. But directly
the Larkinite influence appeared to their discomfiture,
apparent or real, at by-elections, their stoic resolution
broke down. The loss of a seat at Reading and a heavy
reduction in the Ministerial majority at Linlithgow were
arguments which appealed irresistibly in favour of the
enlargement of the Dublin labour leader. With one
consent the principal Government organs declared that
the factor which was working against the Ministerial
Party at the by-elections was the continued imprisonment
of Mr. Larkin, and that this cause of offence to British
labour must be removed. Mr. Lloyd George lent official
support to the Press campaign by declaring, in a speech
made on November 11, that there were explanations of the
electoral rebuffs that had been administered to the
Government, ' the most prominent of which is Jim Larkin.'
When the Chancellor of the Exchequer made that speech
he had only a short time previously left a Cabinet Council,
at which, according to rumour, the release of the prisoner
of Mountjoy had been decided upon. However that
may have been, on November 13, not many hours after
this high Ministerial authority had testified to the damaging political effect of the agitator's incarceration, Mr.
Larkin was free. Some feeble attempts were made by
Ministerial apologists, and notably by Mr. Birrell at Bristol
on November 13, to show that the interference with the
operation of the law was not due to any form of political
pressure. But the facts were too patent to be denied,

and when a leading London paper (*The Standard*) denounced the step that had been taken as ' a shameless
prostitution of the prerogative of mercy,' there was a
widespread disposition to endorse the criticism.

If Ministers anticipated—and after Lord Aberdeen's
experience they probably did not—any gratitude from
the object of the Crown's ' clemency ' they were grievously
disappointed.   The first use made by Mr. Larkin of his
release was to deliver in Beresford Place a violent speech
denunciatory of the Government.   ' The fight,' he said,
' was only starting.   The Government made a mistake
in sending me to prison, and they have made a greater
mistake in letting me out.'   ' I am going in a few hours
to raise a fiery cross in England, Scotland, and Wales.'
Further on in the speech he declared that ' Lord Aberdeen
must go.'   In sentences full of sound and fury he girded
at the employers.   He promised them that they were
going ' to sup sorrow with a long spoon.'   Descending to
particulars, he forecasted a general strike ' not only in
Dublin but in England, Scotland, and Wales.'   Out-
Heroding Herod, Mr. Connolly, Mr. Larkin's lieutenant,
declared ' that they were now in a state of war, and
possessed a power which made government impossible.
No vessel would be allowed to leave the port until all
their demands were conceded.'

These speeches strikingly indicated the spirit in which
the ill-advised Ministerial action was received.   But
even before Mr. Larkin's actual release, a foretaste of the
new conditions that would be created by the surrender of
the Government had been given to Dublin by an attempt
to paralyse the trade of the port.   On November 12,
at midday, delegates from the Transport Workers'
Union visited the quays and called out on strike all the
dock labourers to the number of about a thousand.   The
effect of the action was a complete cessation of work on
the quays.   Many of the men, probably the majority,
left their work reluctantly, but such was the intimidatory

influence exercised from Liberty Hall that none dared openly to resist the orders of the delegates.   The step was taken avowedly as a reply to the action of the employers, who a few days previously had imported a number of free labourers, the last detachment of whom had arrived in the river in the steamer *Ella* the same morning.   It is certain, however, that the desire was to create a sensation as an appropriate accompaniment to Mr. Larkin's release, which it was generally understood at that time was impending.   A sensation unquestionably was created, whether intended or not.   The menace to the trade of the port was too direct for anyone closely interested in commercial operations to be otherwise than seriously alarmed.

A characteristic Larkinite feature of the struggle was the way in which Liberty Hall had struck at everybody, including even those who had made terms with them. Thus, the City of Dublin Steam Packet Company, which had gone to the extreme length of withholding ' tainted goods ' from delivery to placate the Union,[1] were involved with the rest of the employers in the withdrawal of labour.   In this case, as in others, an agreement made was treated as so much waste paper, although it had been ratified with all proper formalities as the outcome of a conference between employers and employed held under the presidency of the Recorder of Dublin.   This shameless renunciation of a contract entered into only a short time previously in circumstances which one might suppose would have made the Larkinite executive especially scrupulous about the observance of the conditions set

[1] On September 23, 1913, an application was made at the Northern Police Court, Dublin, on behalf of Messrs. S. N. Robinson & Co., for an order for the delivery of 40 bags of molasses which the City of Dublin Steam Packet Co. had brought from Liverpool, and which, it was alleged, were withheld from delivery owing to the influence of the Irish Transport Workers' Union.   The Magistrate (Mr. Mahony) made an order for the delivery of the goods, or, in the alternative, for the payment of £8 15s., their value.   In a somewhat similar case heard at the same Court about a month later an order was made for the delivery of the goods.

out in the document, convinced many who had hitherto held aloof from the employers' organisation that it was hopeless to seek peace through any arrangement to which the Larkinite executive was a party.

Mr. Larkin's fiery cross crusade did not proceed with the lightning rapidity that he and his friends had evidently anticipated. He met with a serious rebuff at the very beginning of his campaign at Liverpool where the local representatives ignored him, and he found himself so isolated that he had to abandon the demonstration that he had intended holding in the city. Proceeding to Manchester, the same studied coldness was shown by the Trade Union leaders, but, with the aid of the extreme socialists, the pseudo-martyr was able to arrange a meeting in the Free Trade Hall, which to some extent was a salve to his wounded vanity. A crowded audience, bubbling over with enthusiasm for 'the cause,' gave him an uproarious welcome. His moving stories of capitalistic tyranny, garnished as they were with lurid descriptions of slum horrors, for which, of course, the employers were held responsible, excited alternate shouts of rage and groans of pity. Under the influence of the hysterical oratory of the hero of the evening, women wept and strong men were compelled to find vent for their feelings in audible curses and execrations. It was a veritable feast of unreason as well as a flow of soul.

Even some characteristic Larkinisms were not wanting to give completeness to the demonstration. The phrase ' Damn the Empire ' was sent to keep company with ' To hell with contracts ' and other refined gems of Larkinite oratory of an earlier period. Quite as typical of the man was his repudiation of the statement that he would bring about a general strike. All the Dublin papers had reported his explicit declaration on this point, but this did not deter him from telling his hearers that those who ' used the word general strike trippingly on the tongue were a general nuisance.' This and other little inconsistencies, however, passed unnoticed by the meeting, which, as was said at the time, was 'a cross between a Welsh Revivalist gathering and a Continental Anarchist Conference.' The demonstrators had, most of them, paid handsomely for admission in the expectation of what in the music halls would be called 'a star turn,' and they were not disappointed in the performer or his performance.

Even while the shouts of the Manchester socialists and the tunes of their revolutionary songs were ringing in his ears, Mr. Larkin was conscious that, so far as effective English support in his fight was concerned, the game was up. At this time the British labour leaders had had more than enough of the intrusive Irish agitator, who kept popping up at such inconvenient moments. They resented his abuse and his dictatorial airs, and they feared the effect of his propaganda on the more explosive elements of their own following. Mr. J. H. Thomas, M.P., doubtless voiced the general opinion of the Trade Union leaders when, in addressing a meeting of railwaymen at Swindon on November 17, in obvious allusion to Mr. Larkin, he enunciated the doctrine that 'no trade union official, no matter how able or influential he may be, ought to have the sole power of telling men when they shall cease work.' 'Such responsibility,' he declared, 'rested upon the elected representatives of the rank and file, and it was neither honourable nor true on the men's part to stop work at the dictates of Tom, Dick, or Harry.'

Still, Mr. Larkin bulked too largely in the popular imagination in England to be safely ignored by the representatives of the English unions. They summoned him to a meeting of the Parliamentary Committee of the Trade Union Congress in London on November 18, nominally to discuss the question of the ways and means of helping Dublin movement, but in reality to convey to him pretty plainly that there would be no sympathetic strike on the English side. After the conference it was publicly intimated that the question of the method to be adopted in dealing with the situation was adjourned to a special meeting to be held on December 9, and that in the meantime the food supplies to Dublin would be continued.

A wholesome counterblast to the Larkinite propaganda in England was at this juncture given by the holding in London of an influential meeting of the employers of Great Britain to devise measures to resist the encroachments of Syndicalism. Messrs. H. McLaughlin and John Good attended as a deputation from the Dublin Employers' Federation and put the case for the employers in powerful and convincing speeches. Subsequently a resolution was passed declaring that the Dublin employers were acting in the interests of freedom and pledging the meeting to extend to them material support. Almost simultaneously with the holding of this gathering, Mr. Murphy contributed to the English Press a letter in which he set himself the difficult task of dispelling the misconception which prevailed in England as to the character of the Larkinite movement and the attitude assumed by the employers in regard to it. A certain amount of success attended these efforts to keep public opinion right, but now as ever Mr. Larkin constituted the best missioner that the employers could possibly have. He seldom opened his mouth on an English platform without being guilty of some extravagance which went a very long way to justify in the minds of all reasonable men the determination of the Dublin employers to have nothing to say to any arrangement in which he had a part.

CHAPTER XXII

THE ROUT OF LARKINISM

THE month of December opened in Dublin without any indication, even the faintest, that the end of the protracted struggle was near. Mr. Larkin was away in England continuing his ' tearing, raging propaganda ' with equal damage to his personal reputation and the cause that he championed. In Dublin itself business at the port was proceeding with some semblance of activity through the agency of free labourers, who, under police protection, were engaged in loading and unloading vessels which were banned by the strikers. At Liberty Hall energies were mainly centred in the drilling, under the general supervision of Captain White, D.S.O., the son of the hero of Ladysmith, of the ragged levies of the Irish Transport Workers' Union, in imitation of the Ulstermen, whose example was deemed to be worthy of adoption by the ' wage slaves ' of Dublin in the prosecution of their war against capital. The general public were deeply interested in the proceedings of the Housing Inquiry, where an attempt was being made to evolve a practical solution of the terrible slum problem and its sequelæ of social evils. Peace had disappeared from the thoughts of the citzens with the admitted failure of the Dublin Peace Committee, whose organisation had been broken up a short time previously. Ahead loomed, none too promisingly, the special sitting of the Trade Union Congress at which the vital question of the continued support of Larkinism by the British Trade Unionists was to be settled. Generally, local opinion was settling down to the belief that nothing could prevent the fighting out of the issue until one or both parties had reached the state of exhaustion.

At this juncture, when England was ringing with the Larkinite denunciations of the Dublin capitalist, and when even usually fair-minded publicists were showing a disposition to accept the grossly distorted view of the struggle which was presented by the Irish labour leader in his wild harangues, the Executive Committee of the Dublin Employers' Federation issued a statement explanatory of their attitude. It was a temperate and well-reasoned document, showing with convincing force that, whatever might be the result of inquiries then pending, the Dublin employer would not ' be found blameworthy or neglectful of his responsibilities to his City and Country.' Once more, and with added emphasis, the Committee denied that they were out to ' smash trades unionism.' It was absurd, they said, that a large body of employers representing varied interests, who had everything to lose and nothing to gain by a strike, would band themselves together to destroy trades unionism, with which they had always worked in harmony. They maintained, however, that a trade union had its obligations as well as its rights, and that it was no part of its business to ' smash ' capital or to make the business of traders unworkable. This, they maintained, was the policy that had been adopted by the Irish Transport Workers' Union, and in return, they observed, ' the employers are surely entitled to say that if they are to be smashed, they may lawfully elect to die fighting rather than suffer extinction by being smothered.'

An able review of the history of the Irish Transport Workers' Union followed this general statement of the employers' case. Stress was laid upon the malign influence exercised by the Union's organ, *The Irish Worker*, ' which spared neither man, woman or child in pursuance of the official policy which aimed at making Mr. James Larkin Dictator of the City of Dublin.' The charge of sweating brought against Dublin employers, it was asserted, had as little foundation as the statement that out of the whole of the Dublin employers there were only two Roman Catholics. Summarising the policy of the Transport Workers' Union, the Committee declared that the organisation sought to establish a universal domination of the community, that, having made agreements, the Union declined to be bound by them, that it adopted as a favourite weapon the sympathetic ' strike,' whereby no man, woman, or firm, no matter how far removed from the original dispute, is safe from being forced into the vortex, that it pursued a villainous campaign of abuse through the medium of *The Irish Worker*, and that it followed an ' avowed policy of destruction without any effort at construction.' Finally, the Committee announced that they were prepared to fight to a finish or to confer with those whom they could trust to see agreements carried out. ' Peace,' observed the Committee, ' suits employers best, war being wasteful. Peace with honour we welcome, but freedom in the management of our business we fight for to the finish, if necessary.'

This manifesto, revealing as it did the fixed determination of the employers to adhere to the principle for which they had tenaciously fought from the

R

first—freedom from the thraldom of Larkinism—served
to dispel any illusions that might still have lingered as to
the possibility of an arrangement which left any door
open for the continuance of the despotism against which
the employers were fighting. By a curious coincidence
the statement appeared side by side in the Dublin papers
with a letter from Archbishop Walsh pleading for a renewal
of the peace negotiations.   His Grace based his action on a
statement made in a letter written by Mr. W. M. Murphy
on November 17, in the course of which that gentleman
stated that there were not five per cent. of the men out
of employment ' who may not return before their places
are filled up, without any sacrifice of principle, or without
any undertaking except to do the work they are paid
for doing.' As was afterwards pointed out, the reference
in the letter was to members of the Irish Transport
Workers' Union and not to the general body of those out
of employment.   But Dr. Walsh, construing the statement
in the wider sense, argued ingenuously that the declaration
opened the door to the establishment of peace conditions,
more especially as Mr. Connolly in a public utterance
had affirmed that though he would never consent to
abandon the sympathetic strike he would agree ' to
check its operation to the extent that the sympathetic
strike would not be used recklessly and indiscriminately.'
The foundation which Dr. Walsh indicated for a possible
accommodation was a very insecure one.   Indeed, to
those who were more intimately in touch with the
realities of the situation than his Grace could possibly be,
the basis which he discovered did not exist at all, for while
there was no evidence in Mr. Murphy's statement that
the employers had receded from their original determination to have nothing to do with the Irish Transport
Workers' Union in its existing condition, there was
abundant proof in the declaration made by Mr. Connolly
that the weapon of the sympathetic strike was still a
part of the Larkinite policy. Nevertheless, his Grace's

letter received, as it was bound to do, a respectful hearing, and his suggestion bore the fruit that he desired in a renewed attempt to reach a settlement.

The response to the Archbishop's proposal came in the first instance from the Joint Board of Trade Union organisations in England, which, as a preliminary to the special sitting of the Trade Union Congress arranged for December 9 to deal with the Dublin dispute, decided to despatch to Dublin a delegation to initiate a new peace conference. The deputation assigned for the important duty was a strong one, consisting of Messrs. J. A. Seddon, H. Gosling, and C. W. Bowerman, M.P., representing the Trades Union Congress, Mr. Arthur Henderson, M.P., Chairman of the Joint Board, Mr. Tom Fox, Chairman of the Labour Party, and Mr. James O'Grady, M.P., Chairman of the General Federation of Trades Unions. Mr. Larkin was reported to have been present at the meeting, at which it was decided to send the delegation to Dublin to re-open negotiations with the employers, but the public had not long to wait for evidence that he and his friends were out of harmony with the move. Speaking in Beresford Place on December 2, Mr. Wm. Partridge, one of Mr. Larkin's principal lieutenants, assured 'those men,' referring to the deputation, that Liberty Hall would show them what a strike that was 'fizzling out' was like, and he told them that the one thing certain about the position was that 'whenever the strike was settled it would be settled by Jim Larkin and nobody else.' That Mr. Partridge rightly read the mind of his chief was shown in the next issue of the *Irish Worker*, published on December 6, in which a manifesto appeared from Mr. Larkin warning his supporters against the machinations of the peace-makers. 'Certain well-disposed gentlemen that you and I have a bitter experience of,' he wrote, 'are prepared to settle the present difficulty by hook or crook—mostly crook. The lines upon which they are working is to get the blood-suckers to withdraw the ban against our Union ; they will then go their way—the victimisation of men and women they will minimise, the questions of the future ignore. . . . Be not confounded with the tactics of our false friends in the Trade Union movement. They have burnt their boats. . . . The saying " Fools rush in where angels fear to tread " holds good.' Manifestly the view was that the English delegates might amuse themselves with negotiations, but that nothing would come of them until the autocrat of Liberty Hall had deigned to extend to them his gracious approval.

A more unpromising beginning for a peace campaign can scarcely be imagined. But no doubt the delegation was despatched with a two-fold purpose. It was to settle the dispute if it could, and if it could not it was to build up a suitable line of retreat along which the English Trade Union forces might retire from the difficult and even impossible position they had rashly taken up in defence of Larkinism. The fact is that the English Trade Unions were tired of paying the piper without having any effective voice in calling the tune. Their position was very clearly defined at the period by Mr. T. Shaw, of the Northern Counties Textile Trades Federation, a leading Lancashire Trade Unionist. ' If the workers of Dublin really wish that Larkin should be the sole determining factor in the matter, and that he should have the power he claims to have,' he wrote in a letter to the *Daily Citizen*, ' then I am not prepared to pay the price. . . . I am not the only one who thinks that with Larkin in supreme control all the money that we can subscribe will be thrown into a bottomless bog.'

In spite of rebuffs and warnings, the deputation devoted themselves whole-heartedly to the task which had been allotted to them. The moment they arrived in Dublin they got into communication with the employers, and a preliminary meeting was held on December 4 at which the visitors conferred with Messrs. G. Jacob, C. Eason, and Martin in reference to the conditions which might be defined as the basis of a settlement. On the following day a formal conference was held in Commercial Buildings, at which the Executive of the Employers' Federation and the Trade Unionist deputation thrashed out the points at issue.

Eventually six clauses were agreed upon as a basis for discussion. They were (1) Abandonment of the sympathetic strike and the refusal to handle ' tainted goods,' the employers undertaking to confer with the labour representatives with a view of framing a scheme or schemes for the settlement of future disputes ; (2) Every employer to conduct his business in any way he might consider advantageous, not infringing the individual liberty of the workers ; (3) No strike or lock-out to be entered upon without a month's notice on either side, and no strike to take place without a preliminary ballot of the men and the carrying of the resolution by a majority of the workers affected ; (4) That the representatives of the Joint Labour Board and of the Dublin Trades Union should undertake that their policy and methods should be conducted on proper and recognised trade lines, and that agreements made with the employers should be kept by the unions and their officials ; and, further, that any union or official failing to observe these conditions should be repudiated and should receive no assistance, financial or otherwise, from them ; (5) That while employers would not undertake to dismiss men who had been employed during the strike, they would re-employ ' such men as are required as soon as possible,' it being understood that owing to the disorganisation of trade many firms would be unable to employ a full staff immediately ; (6) That the agreement should apply to all workers, skilled and unskilled, affected by the dispute in the City and County of Dublin.

A certain measure of agreement having thus been

reached, it was deemed advisable to broaden the Trade Union representation by calling in eight delegates from the Dublin Trades Council and the Irish Transport Workers' Union.   In this enlarged form the conference held a third sitting, commencing on Saturday morning, December 6, and lasting, with an interval on Saturday afternoon, until five o'clock Sunday morning.   In spite of the sincere desire manifested on both sides to reach an agreement, the word ' failure ' had finally to be written over the deliberations of the conference.

Now, as before, re-instatement was the rock upon which the conference split.   The English labour leaders were willing to devise measures for putting an end to the sympathetic strike, and to agree to a revision of the method of calling a strike, but they resolutely declined to recede from the demand that the employers should agree to take back all men thrown out of employment by the dispute.   The condition, which was no doubt put forward at the dictation of the Larkinite leaders, was an impossible one from the employers' standpoint.   As one of their members explained publicly at the time, the strike had so injured trade in many directions that it would be years probably before employment could be found for the full number of men who were at work before the dispute occurred.   Moreover, the Dublin industries were of such a varied character that what might be practicable in one quarter would be absolutely impossible in another. In the circumstances the farthest that employers could be expected to go—the farthest in which they could safely go with any prospect of carrying out their pledges—was to agree to re-instate as many of the displaced workers as they could make provision for.   As the members of the deputation were not permitted by Liberty Hall to accept any solution short of the full demand for re-instatement, the negotiations came to an end before the whole of the points at issue had been discussed.

British Trade Unionists were at this time chafing

with daily increasing impatience under the goads of Larkinism. The Irish Trade Labour leader did not even take the trouble to cultivate the friendship of the men whose support was so important to him. His 'fiery cross' crusade had become largely a campaign of abuse directed against the English Trade Union leaders. The fact that in most cases they were unable to retaliate, owing to considerations of prudence, added to the irritation that was excited by the attacks. Thus on the eve of the momentous gathering of the Congress, at which the future policy of dealing with the strike was to be settled, the whole atmosphere of English Trade Unionism was as unfavourable to Larkinism as it could possibly be.

The actual proceedings of the gathering bore out to the full the early premonitions of Larkinite defeat. A resolution proposed by the extremists in the body for the further prosecution of the strike by a blockade of Dublin was rejected by 2,280,000 votes to 203,000. Mr. Larkin himself was practically howled down by a thoroughly hostile assembly. In the few peaceful interludes permitted him, he contrived to hurl defiance at the Congress. 'Neither you nor these gentlemen on the platform can settle this Dublin dispute,' he shouted to the chairman. 'I defy you to try it,' he added. Another characteristic outburst was : 'The men of Dublin will never handle " tainted goods " as long as I am an official.' 'The scene was as painful as it was purposeless,' wrote a correspondent of a labour paper. Nor did the Congress confine its manifestations of dislike to vocal demonstrations while Mr. Larkin was speaking. In continuance of a feud which had already been carried a long way by pamphlet and speech, Mr. J. Havelock Wilson fiercely attacked the Irish labour leader for his conduct of the strike, affirming that the state of affairs in Dublin would not have existed twenty-four hours if Mr. Larkin had shown a little more common sense. Notwithstanding the passing of resolutions pledging the Congress to a continuance of the support of the strike and protesting against the importation of strike breakers, it was only too palpable at the close of the gathering that the final kick had been given to Larkinism by the Congress.

Even before the decision of the Congress was reached the unmistakable shadows of defeat began to gather over Liberty Hall. Some days previously the traffic on the Grand Canal had been resumed, and the day after the gathering in London the men of the London and North Western Railway Company returned to work, their action making possible the opening of the port after a closure extending over many weeks. The disposition everywhere was to consider that the trouble was virtually at an end, and probably it would have ended then and there if the Trades Union Congress had not deemed it necessary to again intervene with the object of procuring a formal settlement. They were possibly driven to adopt that course by the exigencies of a situation of a peculiarly perplexing kind, but whether so or not they must have realised that nothing had altered in the circumstances which led to the breakdown of the earlier negotiations. Mr. Larkin resolutely declined to be a party to 'victimisation,' as he whimsically termed the reaping by the strikers of the fruit of the seed that they had sown. On the other side the employers as determinedly declined to entertain any proposal which would compel them to really victimise men whom they had taken on to fill the places of the strikers, and which in addition would bind them to impossible conditions. Still, nothing was left undone to give *éclat* to the conference. An imposing preliminary gathering of British and Irish Trade Union delegates was held to discuss the position and make arrangements for the attendance of delegates. As Mr. Larkin, who had just previously returned from his abortive ' fiery cross ' crusade was one of those present at the gathering, the public were led to infer that the ensuing conference was to lack nothing in comprehensiveness and authoritativeness. To this extent the omens were no doubt propitious, but it was not exactly a reassuring circumstance that, in speaking at Beresford Place the same evening, Mr. Larkin utilised the opportunity presented by the re-assembling of the conference to ventilate his extreme views as to the establishment of a ' co-operative commonwealth.' ' The workers,' he said, ' had the divine right and the divine injunction and the moral law on their side. The workers were the producers of wealth and entitled to share it.' . . . ' The working classes did not want capital ; they wanted to control capital.' That, of course, was the crux of the difficulty. While the Larkinite aimed at the ' control of capital ' the employers absolutely declined to submit to such control.

When the conference assembled on December 18, it had before it as a basis of discussion a set of conditions drawn up by a sub-committee of the Joint Board of Great Britain and delegates from the local trade societies, and approved at a general meeting of the labour representatives held subsequently. The conditions were : (1) That the employers should withdraw ' the circulars, posters, and forms of agreement known as " the employers' agreement " ; (2) That the unions as a condition of such withdrawal should abstain from any form of sympathetic strike pending the establishment of a Wages Board by March 17, 1914 ; (3) That no member should be refused employment on the grounds of his or her association with the dispute, and that no stranger should be employed until all the old workers were re-engaged ; and (4) That all cases of old workers not re-employed on February 1, 1914, should be considered at a conference to be held on February 15, 1914. Outwardly there was unanimity on the labour side in regard to these proposals, but it was stated with some show of authority by the Labour Press Agency that the terms put forward were not those originally drafted by the Joint Board. 'The original draft,' the communication stated, 'was amended materially in order to meet the wishes of Mr. Larkin, who stood out for uncompromising terms but was outvoted, and the published terms represent the utmost concession the other parties interested in the dispute were willing to make to carry Larkin with them.' Mr. Larkin now as ever was thus the stumbling-block to a peaceful adjustment of the dispute.

On the very day of the sitting of the conference he had forwarded to the *Daily Herald*, the extreme labour organ, a furious manifesto addressed to 'comrades' in England, asking for their support of him in the warfare he was waging against a 'foul and black conspiracy afoot here' against 'the greater unionism.' After noting the various measures adopted by the British Trade Unionists to bring pressure to bear upon him, he said, 'This treachery must cease.' 'Are,' he asked, 'the rank and file going to allow this betrayal ? Get busy, rebels in branches and lodges, and send us help direct at once. We will not bend. We appeal to all honest men and women to make public protests at their officials' treachery. . . . Are you rebels going to allow this dirty business to succeed ? Arouse yourselves.'

When the conference actually assembled, it was speedily seen that Mr. Larkin's influence would effectually prevent any concession to the employers' views on the one point—that of re-instatement—upon which their determination was fixed. The labour leader made an ostentatiously belated appearance upon the scene, and, when he did attend, it was only to demonstrate his intention to enforce his own decided views on the all-important question at issue. Brushing aside Mr. A. Henderson, M.P., who had up to that point acted as the Labour spokesman, he dominated the situation from the standpoint of the workers, emphatically vetoing all suggestions by way of compromise. Nevertheless, the attempt to find a *via media* was persistently made throughout the whole of the day and during a good part of the forenoon of the next day. At length, when the impossibility of reconciling divergent views had been revealed to the satisfaction of the most sanguine of the delegates, the conference broke up.

So ended the last of the formal efforts made to terminate by agreement the disastrous conflict which for many weeks had raged in the Irish capital. The employers were roundly abused for their part in this collapse, but from the statements made by labour representatives as to the course of the negotiations, it is perfectly plain that they took up no unyielding attitude. Nothing indicates this better than the fact that they were willing to withdraw the ban on the Irish Transport Workers' Union to clear the way for a settlement. This was a very real concession, and if there had been in the Larkinite camp a genuine desire to make peace, the action taken would have been reciprocated in a more accommodating spirit on the question of re-instatement. But, having made up their minds to insist on full satisfaction for their dupes, Mr. Larkin and his associates were content to see the conference break up rather than give way. If they had been the victors in the dispute, or even if a reasonable prospect of final triumph had existed, their line of action might have been justifiable. Notoriously, however, they had been beaten at every point, and their only hope of retaining some shred of reputation for leadership was by rescuing as much as they could from the wreckage. That they did not do so is in itself a vindication of the attitude of profound distrust which the employers assumed towards them from the outset of the dispute.

The breakdown of the Peace Conference was in a very real sense the beginning of the end. Though the Larkinites talked loudly about continuing the struggle, and there were threats in British Trade Union circles

of assisting in this fight to a finish, the seeds of decay
were too plainly in the movement to keep it longer
alive. With the cessation of the food supplies from
England and the signs that were only too apparent to
the deluded strikers of the approaching suspension of
the exiguous doles of strike pay which they had been in
the habit of receiving at Liberty Hall, there was a marked
desire shown on the part of the men to return to work.
In some instances the strikers sought re-employment in
considerable bodies ; in others, the process of voluntary
re-instatement was gradual, the workers putting in an
appearance by twos and threes, and acting afterwards
as recruiting agents for the firm amongst the body of
employees still out.   In this way the long vacant workshops were in a comparatively brief period of time
running at full pressure.

Perhaps the most striking of the episodes which
marked the collapse of the strike movement was the return
of the Dublin builders' labourers to work, practically
en masse, at the beginning of February. The incident is
sufficiently important to deserve special notice. To
make the position clear it is necessary to give a short
preliminary explanation. For over two years prior to
the strike a feud had existed between the Irish Transport
Workers' Union and the Builders' Labourers' Union, and
the officials of the latter had made repeated requests to
the employers not to employ any Larkinites. The
builders at the outset, for various reasons—chiefly that
they did not like to bar any union—had declined to
make the distinction. But when the crisis occurred in
September they, in conformity with the action of other
employers, took measures to enforce the signature of the
well-known document adopted by the general body of
employers. The course was taken by them because they
believed that their labourers would be quite ready to
sign any agreement which would have the effect of preventing the Larkinites from getting any employment from

the builders. The Trades Council, however, used its influence on the Larkinite side to such good effect that the men declined to sign, with the result that a complete stoppage was brought about in the building trade.

From a period early in December the men had been anxious to resume work, but as they still declined, for reasons best known to themselves, to repudiate the Larkinite organisation nothing came of their overtures. Some weeks later, when the pinch of want had become more acute, their views underwent a change. They then expressed their willingness to enter into an engagement not to allow any of their members to become members of the Irish Transport Workers' Union. On January 31, at the last of two conferences that were held between the Builders' Association and the men's representatives, an undertaking was formally ratified as the basis of a settlement of the outstanding difficulty. On behalf of the Labourers' Union, Mr. John O'Toole, the President, Mr. Thomas McCullagh, the Secretary, and Messrs. Thomas Hefferman and John Doyle, delegates, undertook that none of the members of the Union would remain or become in the future members of the Irish Transport Workers' Union. They further pledged themselves that their members would not take part in or support any form of sympathetic strike, and would handle all materials no matter how delivered, would carry out all instructions given them in the course of their employment, and would work amicably with other employees, whether they were members of a union or not. Finally, on their part it was agreed that any member of the Union who broke any of the provisions of the undertaking should be instantly dismissed from membership, while the employers on their side undertook to re-employ such of the members of the Union as they might require on the terms in force prior to the previous September 13.

At the earliest moment effect was given by the employers to the agreement by admitting to work every member of the Union on the production of his card of membership. Those who were not members of the Labourers' Union were required to sign the original document issued by the Employer's Executive Committee. It speaks eloquently for the change which had come over the situation in the early days of the new year that many hundreds accepted the condition and subscribed to the much discussed declaration. This surrender to the employers in the building trade may be regarded as the final blow to Larkinism. Before the new year had far advanced there was every promise that the great strike would soon be but an evil memory.

The struggle had been a costly one for the employers : for the workers it had been disastrous. ' So far from bringing any benefit to the working men,' said Mr. Murphy, in addressing the shareholders of the Tramway Company at the general meeting early in the year, ' Larkin's campaign has brought nothing but untold misery on them and their families. I get letters every day of the most pitiable character from men whom we should readily have employed if they applied in time, but who delayed so long that their places were filled and their names can now only be put on a waiting list.' Other employers have a similar story to tell of the wretched plight to which the unfortunate dupes of Liberty Hall have been reduced. For many of the strikers, indeed, it has literally proved ' a fight to a finish.' Bankrupt in pocket and broken in spirit, they have been left by the wayside to indulge in bitter musings on the folly of Larkinism.

CHAPTER XXIII

A STUDY OF LARKINISM

Extraordinary Character of the Larkinite Movement—Influences that fed the Agitation—Mr. Larkin's Personality an Important Factor—Mr. Larkin's Views on Irish Industrialism—He favours the Adoption of Guild Principles—Can the Guild System be Adapted to Modern Conditions?—Failure of the Larkinite Movement—Conclusion.

THE rise and decline of Larkinism in Dublin constitutes one of the most extraordinary chapters in the history of modern industrial conflict. It is a phenomenon which deserves to be studied carefully by every sociologist who wishes to take accurate note of the development of modern democratic thought. The extraordinary personality of the leader of the movement, the amazing audacity of his plans, and the strangely powerful influence he exercised over the working population of Dublin and over many outside that class, all gave to the recent labour struggle in Dublin an interest peculiarly its own. Though outwardly invested with the attributes of an industrial conflict, the movement stands quite outside the ordinary category of labour disturbances. It was in essence a revolutionary rising, one in which the ultimate aims of its promoters involved the destruction of Society quite as much as the betterment of the wage conditions of the workers. Red Republicanism, Anarchism, Syndicalism, and all the extremest forms of modern revolutionary thought found expression in the literature and oratory of the movement. Even anti-clericalism of a kind was not wanting to complete the syllabus of advanced ideas to which the rising gave such blatant expression.   And this in Dublin, the centre and citadel of the most disciplined force of Roman Catholicism in Europe, and the home of perhaps the sincerest conservatism—using that phrase in its broadest sense—in the Empire !   Many strange things have happened by the banks of the Liffey, but none probably stranger than that open flouting of authority—ecclesiastical quite as much as civil—which marked the progress of Larkinism.

In the foregoing pages the causes that brought about this remarkable situation have been indicated, but it may be useful in this concluding chapter to gather together the threads of the narrative and attempt to show the picture of Disturbed Dublin as a whole.   It is beyond serious cavil that the evil social conditions of Dublin were a cause, possibly the primary cause, of the Larkinite movement obtaining the hold it did.   In the depressed and degraded population of the slums Mr. Larkin found a double source of strength.   On the one hand it supplied fertile ground for his ' divine mission of discontent ' ; on the other, he was able to draw from it in due abundance the requisite tools for the enforcement of his intimidatory decrees.   Indirectly also the social factor enormously strengthened his arm by evoking for his propaganda the sympathy of an outside public which otherwise would probably have been little concerned with the dispute. The public conscience, ever sensitive to stories of moral wrongs, was deeply shocked by the accounts, which were forthcoming in abundance from various sources, of the horrors of over-crowded tenement houses of Dublin.   Burning with zeal for reform, people only too readily accepted the Larkinite theory that the evils were due to the sweating practices of a merciless body of employers who ground the faces of the poor with unexampled callousness.   In point of fact, the Dublin employers are neither better nor worse than those in any

other part of the United Kingdom.   If there is a difference
it is in their favour, for probably as a whole they are
a more humane class than their prototypes in more
exclusively manufacturing cities than Dublin is.   The
black sheep—and of course they are not absent from this
any more than from any other flock—are of the minor
and baser sort who are to be found in every populous area
where a large indigent population offers scope for
unscrupulous exploitation by the Gadgrinds of industry.
Still, the impression having once got abroad that the heel
of the oppressor in Dublin was that of the employer, it
was difficult to eradicate it, and it was doubtless a most
potent force in keeping the movement going long beyond
the period when in the ordinary way it would have spent
itself.

Government mismanagement must also count for a
good deal in any estimate of the influences which went
to the building up of the edifice of Larkinism.   If Mr.
Larkin had been treated at first, as he should have been,
as a dangerous firebrand whose vicious incitements to
outrage and intimidatory practices were a menace to
Society, Dublin would probably have been saved the
calamity that overtook it.   But instead of pursuing this
policy, which would have been adopted as a matter of
course a few years ago, the authorities truckled to the
offender.   The result was fatal to the cause of peace.
From the moment that Mr. Larkin received official notice,
he never ceased to pour contempt on authority, and
especially on that most exalted form of it which had been
most prominently associated with him.   The effect of
this on an impressionable population was immense.   Even
Parnell, in his palmiest days, had not been ' agin' the
Government ' in so piquant and altogether alluring a
form.   The ill-timed energy afterwards shown in dealing
with the labour leader was less mischievous in its effects,
locally at all events.   It was too familiar a development
of Government activity to influence the population to

s

any lasting degree.   Not until Ministers again showed weakness by releasing Mr. Larkin unconditionally in abject fear of the further electoral consequences of his incarceration did the Dublin workers really respond again to the spur of events.   That melancholy example of political opportunism gave a vigorous fresh stir to the cauldron of strife and led, it can scarcely be doubted, to the protraction of the struggle by several weeks.

In examining the causes which have contributed to the rise of Larkinism it is impossible to avoid giving a prominent place to the personality of the founder of the movement.   Few agitators, in modern times at least, have obtained such an absolute domination over a population as Mr. Larkin did over the workers of Dublin. Probably there is none who for so long a period has commanded the implicit obedience of large bodies of his fellow men without any other authority than that of a committee of obsequious satellites.   Dublin is divided in opinion as to Mr. Larkin's sincerity ; but there are scarcely two voices as to his forceful personality. He has ever proved himself an impossible man to work with.   Dictatorial, headstrong, and vain, he goes his own way, absolutely indifferent to anything but the maintenance of his personal ascendancy.   His extreme recklessness of speech adds a final and fatal touch to his defects.   No consideration of prudence ever prevents him from making the most compromising statements.   To score a personal point over a rival he will endanger the whole future of the plans of the moment.   In order to elicit a passing cheer he will blurt out some remark which will give deadly offence to those with whom it is essential he should be on good terms.   If he had some of the statesmanlike restraint of Mr. John Burns and a little of the Northern caution which characterises Mr. Thomas Burt, he might have a successful public career before him.   As things are his future seems likely to be the barren and stormy life of an impracticable idealist who is ever seeking the bubble reputation in the devious byways of industrial strife. His failure in Dublin is so complete, his promises to the workers have been so utterly falsified, and the misery entailed on those who sacrificed their employment in following him has been so great, that he can never again hope to secure any very large following in the same field. It is only by seeking fresh fields and pastures new that he can expect to win any measure of success in adventures of the character of those which he conducted in Ireland with such disastrous results to his reputation for leadership.

During a visit to Dublin in April 1914 I sought and obtained an opportunity of hearing at first hand from Mr. Larkin the views he held upon the question of industrial regeneration in Ireland. I found him at first unwilling to discuss the question, in view of the fact that Mr. Connolly, his chief lieutenant, was bringing out a book on the subject of the strike, but eventually he opened his mind and we had a most interesting talk on the varied phases of the problem. Appropriately enough, the interview took place in Croydon Park, the recreation ground belonging to the Irish Transport Workers' Union. At the period of my call Mr. Larkin, with two assistants, was engaged in erecting a platform for a meeting to be held later in the week in the park. Standing in his shirt sleeves with his pipe in his mouth, he was directing with practised skill the joining of the planks which were the main support of the structure. A tall, loose-limbed man, with a slight stoop in the shoulders, he gave at the moment little impression of the popular idol; but we had not been speaking long before I discovered that the man was no ordinary type of agitator. His brain was full of ideas, crude and impracticable for the most part, but suggesting originality of thought and a wider outlook than that commonly attributed to him.

With the aid of some notes I made of the conversation at the time I may, perhaps, profitably reproduce here the views he expressed, as they throw an interesting

light upon the psychology of the man. In reply to a
statement of his that his movement was more advanced
than most labour agitations, I hazarded the remark
that it was on continental lines. He answered that it
was and it was not. It was being conducted on the
old Guild principle, on lines which were admirably laid
down in a series of articles in the *New Age*, written by
Mr. Orage,[1] which he recommended for my perusal. I
told him that as a writer on municipal questions I had
studied the history of guilds very closely, and had accumu-
lated a mass of material with the intention of some day
writing a book on the subject. He seemed interested,
and we discussed for some time the peculiar feature of
the ancient Guild system. The talk drifted on to the
strike. Mr. Larkin said that the Dublin employers were
different to their English prototypes. They were a
merciless lot, and did not give and take as the others
did. I suggested that a good deal of the trouble was due
to the fact that there was not enough work to go round.
He demurred to this. There was, he said, plenty of
work for all under a proper system. The mischief was
that men now worked 72 to 78 hours a week for
a pittance. I asked whether it was not a fact that
they were in Dublin badly in need of more industries.
He cordially agreed, but said that people were so unenterprising in Dublin that nothing could be done. Moreover, there were other drawbacks. One was the policy
of the banks. The Dublin banks were stuffed full of
money at the present time, but anyone who wanted
capital for their business had to pay 7 or 8 per cent.
for the accommodation—an impossible price. Then there
was the action of greedy landowners to contend with.
He mentioned the case of an owner of some land in that
very locality who declined to sell it for the purpose of a

---

[1] Since published in book form under the title *National Guilds :
An Inquiry into the Wage Question and the Way Out*. London :
G. Bell & Sons.

shipyard, though it was admirably adapted for that
purpose.   Here was a case in which a promising new
industry was choked off by the selfishness of an individual.
That was typical of Dublin and of Ireland.   He then went
on to talk of general affairs.   The priest and the politician, he stated, were the curses of Ireland.   ' Between
the Pope and King Billy the people come to the ground.'
He spoke in scathing language of the Ancient Order of
Hibernians.   He called them Catholic Orangemen, and
said they were worse than the Protestant Orangemen.
The latter, he said, were misguided but sincere, and something might be made of them with proper treatment.
The ' Catholic Orangemen,' on the other hand, were
' unscrupulous ruffians '—they stuck at nothing.   I spoke
of the slums.   That, he said, was the root fact of the
situation.   He denounced the corporation.   It was
honeycombed, he said, with corruption and jobbery.
Contractors waxed fat out of ill-gotten gains.   He spoke
of a case in which a public-house, which might at one time
have been bought for £100 or less, was acquired by the
corporation for £1000 for a public improvement.   The
registration laws were next touched upon.   The whole
system was, he said, rotten.   The party in power did
what they liked with the registers.   Names of known
Larkinites were deliberately left out.   On the other hand,
he knew of a case in which six votes were given for a
house and no one at the house knew the voters.   I
suggested that proceedings should be taken to alter such
abuses.   He replied that proceedings would cost too
much money.   It would be a High Court matter and they
could not afford the amount that would be required.
Though the party in power were supreme, he said, John
Redmond dared not hold an open meeting in Dublin.
If meetings were held they were ticket meetings.   I asked
about rural Ireland.   He said that there was great
unrest everywhere.   New ideas were penetrating the
brain of the labouring classes.   Long ago a priest told

him that they would build a high wall around Ireland
to keep out the evil influences of the outside world.
Where was that wall to-day ?   People were thinking for
themselves, and they were moving, slowly perhaps, but
they were certainly moving, and no one could stop the
movement.   But they were terribly handicapped by the
educational system.   The priests controlled the schools
and taught people only just what they pleased, with the
result that young men were turned out into the world
with very inferior equipment as compared with the
young men in England and Scotland.   He knew of youths
of seventeen or eighteen who had been through the Irish
schools who could hardly write their own names.   Educa-
tion should be under popular control.   It was useless
if it was not.   I asked if the Land Purchase Act had not
been a great boon.   He replied : Certainly not ; quite the
reverse.   It led to speculation in land.   Men sold their
rights for large sums as soon as the transaction was carried
through.   The purchase money was taken out of the
country or left lying idle in the banks.   The poor labourers
got nothing.   The half-acre of land he was entitled to
was always selected from the worst land, and the measure-
ment was made so as to include the public road.   No,
there was nothing in the new agricultural movement
that was beneficial.   The Creameries made people lazy
and more unenterprising than they were.   Why was
there such large emigration at the present time if all
was well ?   The farmer was a poor type of man.   He
had no ideas beyond his farm.   One of his sons became
a priest, a second a policeman, and a third a publican.
Drink could always be obtained in the country on a
Sunday although the public-houses were supposed to be
closed.   He mentioned a place (I think in Clare) where
there were 137 public-houses and only 150 dwelling-
houses.   Men might be seen lying drunk outside public-
houses on Sunday and policemen passing and re-passing.
There were seldom any prosecutions for breaches of the

licensing laws. Drink could always be obtained at the police barracks in the canteens, and it was cheap.

Mr. Larkin touched on Home Rule. It was the one thing, he said, which would save Ireland. If Ireland had Home Rule the power of the machine politician would be broken. People would discover what were the realities, and they would not be hoodwinked by the bosses as they were to-day. He spoke of the jerry-mandering of the constituencies in the Home Rule Bill— how rural areas had been tacked on to urban constituencies in the obvious hope that the existing domination might be maintained. But, he said, as soon as Home Rule became a certainty the scene would be changed in a way which would be unpleasant for the Redmonites. We parted after some further conversation of a discursive character on subjects of little importance.

I give these opinions without, of course, taking any responsibility for the accuracy of the statements made. Mr. Larkin's assertions on several points would, I am sure, not bear close investigation. But the talk has an interest as a reflection of the mind of a man who has filled a large place in the public eye in Ireland in the last few years. As far as this work is concerned, the most important of the declarations made were those relating to the prosecution of the Irish labour movement on Guild lines. The old Guild system was one of the glories of medieval England, in spite of its narrow oligarchical tendencies. It bound men together in bonds of real brotherhood, it strengthened authority and encouraged a spirit of reverence for the unseen, it inculcated principles of true charity and benevolence, and it instilled into the worker that pride in the productions of his labour which is the truest and highest form of industrial efficiency. Whether in our complex modern life, with its immense aggregations of labour in particular industries, its infinite sub-divisions of skilled workers, and its vast and complicated processes involving the employment of costly

machinery which must be continually replaced to keep
a business abreast of its foreign competitors, a reversion
to the old system, even to a modified extent, is feasible is
extremely doubtful.   But if there is a sincere desire on the
part of Labour to emulate the spirit of the ancient Guilds,
to give to their organisations the duties and responsibilities as well as the privileges of those bodies, there is no
reasonable man who will not wish well to the movement.
It is to be feared, however, that those, like Mr. Larkin,
who have taken up with the Guild idea as a panacea
for modern industrial evils, do not properly appreciate
the character of the instrument whose aid they invoke.
In the old Guild nothing was more strongly insisted upon
than the duty of the worker to do good work.   The
records of these institutions are full of instances of the
infliction of fines upon members for neglect of this cardinal
principle.   The Guildsmen realised that the success
of the particular industry in which they were engaged
depended on the zealous maintenance of a high standard
in the quality of the workmanship.

Quitting this highly speculative field, we are brought
face to face once more with the grim realities of a situation
like that which exists in Dublin, where a large section
of the population are unable to obtain the means of
livelihood on a scale of decency and comfort.   The
Larkinite movement, which was started to change this
state of affairs, failed, as it was bound to do, because it
attempted the impossible and attempted it in the worst
possible way.   Wages, it is true, were raised in many
directions, but the betterment of the lot of the regular
workers in the long run will probably only intensify
the struggle in the ranks of the casual labourers, whose
precarious conditions of employment are the root difficulty of the Dublin social problem.   As has been pointed
out elsewhere and cannot be too often repeated. the
pressing need of Dublin is for more avenues of lucrative
employment.   Create new industries and enlarge the

operations of those that exist, and the worst phases of Dublin poverty will disappear. In no conceivable circumstances can a violent and unscrupulous attack on capital such as that recently witnessed have any other effect than to make the general lot of the Dublin workers more wretched than it is.

The future of Dublin is one of the most interesting of the political speculations of the time. Whatever may be its lot in the years to come, it is sincerely to be hoped that it may be spared another such experience as the one it went through in the second half of 1913. Not only was trade disturbed to an unprecedented degree and grievous loss inflicted on all sections of the community, but moral evils were caused which it will take years to eradicate. The sole compensation for all this mischief is that people have been aroused to a sense of the social deficiencies of Dublin, and that minds have been set actively at work to find a solution of the housing and other problems inherent in the present conditions of the city's life. If eventually out of the evil of labour strife good should come in the form of a reconstructed Dublin, the memory of Larkinism will be a less painful one ; but nothing that may happen will deprive it of the reputation it has won as being the crudest and cruellest emanation of Labour belligerency that modern history takes count of.

APPENDICES

I

REPORT OF THE GOVERNMENT COURT OF ENQUIRY

1. The Court of Enquiry, whose appointment was announced on September 26, met the representatives of the employers and of the workpeople in the first instance on Monday, September 29, and again on Wednesday, October 1, and the three following days.

2. The terms of reference to the Court were :—' To enquire into the facts and circumstances of the disputes now in progress in Dublin, and to take such steps as may seem desirable with a view to arriving at a settlement.'

3. For the purposes of our enquiry we think it unnecessary to go further back than 1908, in which year the unrest which culminated in the present disputes may be said to have begun.

4. In that year the Docks and Quay workers, the Carters and similar classes of workmen in Dublin were being organised by Mr. Larkin, an official of the National Union of Dock Labourers, whose head quarters are in Liverpool. Difficulties arose between the local branch of this Union and certain shipowners and other employers, and on July 4 notice was given by the men to their employers that, on and after July 20, no member of that Union would work with any non-unionist. A stoppage of work ensued on the part of certain men, and as a result of negotiations conducted by Lord MacDonnell an agreement was signed by representatives of the employers and by the President and General Secretary of the National

Union of Dock Labourers, and by officials of the General Federation of Trade Unions on behalf of the men.

The terms of the agreement included the following :—

> ' If no settlement be arrived at, the question shall be referred to a Conciliation Board consisting of a representative of the employers, a representative of the employed, and an umpire. The umpire to be agreed upon by the two representatives, or, failing agreement, to be appointed by the Board of Trade.'

So far as we have ascertained no effective steps were taken to carry out this part of the agreement. No Conciliation Board was formed.

5. In November of 1908 a strike of Carters occurred, and as a result of the mediation of His Excellency the Lord Lieutenant, assisted by Sir James Dougherty, the Under Secretary, it was agreed that work should be resumed and that the matters in dispute should be referred to arbitration.
6. The Arbitrators were the Rt. Hon. Sir A. N. Porter, Bart., and Mr. P. J. O'Neill, J.P., who in their award recommended :—

(1) That both parties should agree that there should be no stoppage of work by either side without a fortnight's notice, save in case of breach of agreement or other misconduct ; and

(2) That a permanent Court of Conciliation to deal with disputes should be established.

As in the case of the earlier agreement in this year, the proposal to establish a Conciliation Board was not carried out.

7. Subsequent to this date certain differences appear to have arisen between the National Union of Dock Labourers and its Dublin members, acting with Mr. Larkin. These differences resulted in the severance of the Dublin members from the National Union and the formation of a new Union, called the ' Irish Transport and General Workers' Union,' with Mr. Larkin as General Secretary.

8. In 1911 further strikes occurred, and as a result of a conference of employers and employed, held at the invitation of the Viceroy, proposals for the establishment of a Conciliation Board were again made. These proposals appear to

have received support from certain sections of the employers, and it is stated that the names of the employers' representatives on the Board were sent to the Under Secretary. The Conciliation Board was not, in fact, established.

9. In the same year proposals for the establishment of a Board of Conciliation are stated to have been forwarded to the Irish Transport Workers' Union on behalf of certain shipowners, but the matter does not appear to have been proceeded with.

10. In the *Irish Worker* of April 26, 1913—a paper edited by Mr. Larkin—an article by Mr. Larkin appeared proposing the establishment of a Wages Board to deal with disputes, and during the present year, and up to a recent date, efforts were made with a similar object by the Chamber of Commerce and by the Lord Mayor of Dublin.

11. Disputes appear to have taken place more or less frequently between 1911 and the present date.

12. Statements have been made to us regarding the conditions of labour in the city. It is alleged by the representatives of the workpeople that in many cases wages are low and the conditions of employment unsatisfactory. The events that have occurred in the various industries indicate that grievances of considerable importance have existed.

13. One of the methods which has been adopted by the Irish Transport Workers' Union with a view to remedying grievances is that known under the name of the ' sympathetic strike.' The sympathetic strike may be described as a refusal on the part of men who may have no complaint against their own conditions of employment to continue work because in the ordinary course of their work they come in contact with goods in some way connected with firms whose employees have been locked out or are on strike. This practice has far-reaching results, as, for example, the refusal of Porters at Kingstown to handle parcels of publications consigned from England to a firm of newsagents in Dublin who had declined the request of the Union that they should refuse to distribute newspapers printed by another firm whose dispatch hands were involved in a dispute.

14. In actual practice the ramifications of this method of industrial warfare have been shown to involve loss and suffering to large numbers of both employers and workpeople who not only have no voice in the original dispute

but have no means of influencing those concerned in the original cause of difference. Even collective agreements, signed on behalf of employers' and men's organisations, a provision of which was that no stoppage of work should take place without discussion and due notice, were entirely disregarded under the influence of this ever-widening method of conducting disputes. The distinction between strike and lock-out became obscured ; attacks on one side being met with reprisals on the other side in such rapid succession as completely to confuse the real issues.

15. No community could exist if resort to the 'sympathetic' strike became the general policy of Trade Unionism, as owing to the interdependence of different branches of industry disputes affecting even a single individual would spread indefinitely. If this should be the policy of Trade Unionism it is easy to understand that it does not commend itself to the employers ; but in our experience of the better organised employers and workmen the sympathetic strike or the sympathetic lock-out is not a method which is recognised as a reasonable way of dealing with disputes.

16. Possibly it was with the hope that it might result in a termination of this method of industrial warfare that a large number of firms in the city agreed to require their workpeople to sign the following notice as a condition of employment :—

I HEREBY UNDERTAKE to carry out all instructions given to me by or on behalf of my employers, and, further, I agree to immediately resign my membership of the Irish Transport and General Workers' Union (if a member) : and I further undertake that I will not join or in any way support this Union.

Signed ....
Address ....
....
Witness ....
Date ....

Whatever may have been the intention of the employers, this document imposes upon the signatories conditions which are contrary to individual liberty, and which no workman or body of workmen could reasonably be expected to accept.

We understand that many of the workmen asked to sign this or similar documents were in no way connected with the Transport Workers' Union, and we think it was unfortunate that they should have been brought into the dispute. It will be obvious that the effort to secure signatures to such a document would be likely to create a maximum of ill-feeling.

17. We have given very careful consideration to the contention put forward that the labour conditions obtaining in Dublin required on the part of the workpeople action of the drastic character which seems to have been taken during the past few years, and, without attributing undue blame to those who considered that these conditions necessitated a resort to the methods which they adopted to remedy them, we think that the time has now come when a continuance of the same methods will be fraught with disastrous results to all concerned. Thousands of workers have now become associated with the Transport Workers' Union, and the workpeople in many of the industries of the city have shown during the past few years a determination to organise themselves under its officials. If this struggle is not adjusted by consent, rather than by resort to the extremes of force, the industries of Dublin will not, we think, be free from further serious troubles. Even if, after many weeks of suffering and loss of business, the resort to force should seem to be successful and result in a resumption of work, resentment and bitterness would remain, with a very probable recurrence of the disputes. On the other hand it cannot be expected that employers—many of whom have no grievance whatever with their employees, can continue their business if they are to be subjected, no matter what conciliatory steps they may themselves take to prevent it, to constant interruptions through the effects of the sympathetic and sudden strike.

18. All the great industries of every civilised country have long recognised that trade and manufacture can only be conducted by the practical acceptance on the part of both employers and employed of the fact that there is a mutual interest, and that such interest can only be adjusted satisfactorily by friendly discussion. Irish employers and Irish workers will find they can be no exception to this modern development.

19. We think, therefore, that this position should be frankly accepted by both sides, and while we recognise that

a uniform method of settling differences is impracticable, owing to the varying circumstances in different trades, we think that the following methods of settling differences that exist or may arise hereafter might well be accepted as a basis for discussion :—

DRAFT SCHEME

1. Conciliation Committees shall be appointed to deal with questions referred to them relating to rates of wages, hours of labour, or conditions of service, other than matters of management or discipline.
2. The grouping of the various industries for the purposes of these Committees to be such as may be agreed upon.
3. The workpeople in the various sections shall elect by ballot from among themselves representatives to hold office as members of the Conciliation Committee.
4. Members of the Conciliation Committees shall hold office for   years from the date of their election, and shall be eligible for re-election.
5. The employers' side of each Conciliation Committee shall be composed of employers selected by the employers in the section concerned.
6. Workpeople acting as representatives on the Conciliation Committees shall have leave of absence from their work, without prejudice to their employment, on such days, or portions thereof, that they may be required to attend meetings of the Committee.

SECRETARIES

7. Each side of each of the Conciliation Committees shall have a Secretary, who may take part in discussions and act as advocate, but shall have no vote unless he is a member of the Committee.
8. The Workpeople's Secretary shall be chosen by a majority of the workpeople's side of the Conciliation Committee, who may select him from any source they please.
9. The Employers' Secretary of each of the Conciliation Committees may be appointed by the employers from any source they please.

10. The length and conditions of office of the Secretary shall be determined by the side of the Committee appointing him, subject to the provisions of these Rules.

PROCEDURE

11. In the event of a dispute arising affecting one or more employees, it shall be the duty of the workpeople concerned to bring the matter in the first instance before the foreman, or other person under whose immediate supervision they are working.

12. Failing agreement within seven days of the complaint having been made, the workpeople concerned may bring the matter before their representatives on the Conciliation Committee, and such representatives, accompanied, if they desire, by the Secretary of the workpeople's side of the Committee, shall be granted an interview with the management for the discussion of the dispute.

13. If within seven days of the receipt of the deputation an agreement is not arrived at upon the matter in dispute, the Secretary of the workpeople's side of the Conciliation Committee shall give notice to the Employers' Secretary of a request for a meeting of the Conciliation Committee, and such meeting shall be held on a suitable date within fourteen days of the receipt of the application for the meeting of the Committee.

14. The Conciliation Committee shall meet under the chairmanship of an independent Chairman selected from a panel of chairmen formed by the Board of Trade. If the parties cannot agree upon a Chairman, one shall be appointed by the Board of Trade.

15. The Chairman to preside over the meeting of the Conciliation Committee, and to endeavour to secure an agreement upon the point at issue. Should he fail to secure an agreement he may either

    (a) at his discretion recommend to the parties such terms of settlement as he thinks fair and reasonable ;

T

or, if the parties previous to or at the meeting request
him to do so, and agree to be bound by his decision,
(b) give a decision upon the point in dispute.

16. Pending the reference of the matter in dispute to
the Conciliation Committee, and pending the Committee's discussion and (if necessary) the Chairman's
recommendation or decision, no strike or lock-out
shall be entered upon ; such recommendation or
decision to be given within   days from the first
meeting of the Conciliation Committee.

17. No assistance, financial or otherwise, to be given by
an Association to any of its members or to any
affiliated Association entering upon a strike or lock-
out in breach of the foregoing conditions.

20. For the purposes of the constitution of the Conciliation Committees it would appear to be desirable to group
the different trades into a number of sections. This would
not, of course, prevent a single firm, which did not readily
come within a group, having a Conciliation Committee,
whose operations would be confined to that firm and its
employees. In any trade where there is already in existence
a method of adjusting differences recognised by employers
and workmen, we think it would be undesirable to suggest
that such method should be abandoned or interfered with
unless the parties mutually consider that the proposals we
have made would be an improvement.

21. These proposals, it will be seen, would tend to remove
the necessity for the sudden strike and for the sympathetic
strike or lock-out, without requiring either side necessarily
to abandon their right to adopt either of these expedients if
the conciliation machinery failed.

22. We are not in favour of 'compulsory arbitration,'
and we do not suggest that the ultimate right to strike or
to lock-out should be abandoned. What we do suggest is
that, before the method of strike or lock-out is adopted,
there should be opportunity for impartial discussion and
independent enquiry.

23. We recognise that personal objections to individuals
have entered into the disinclination on the part of some of
those interested to negotiate, and difficult as this subject may
be we think it necessary to deal with it.

24. In ordinary business dealings as well as in private

matters men have the right to decline to associate with people who, for one reason or another, they prefer not to meet ; but in a community such as the City of Dublin, with its interdependent interests, this right is necessarily subject to great limitation. This matter is, however, one for individual consideration and determination, and should not, in our opinion, influence any decision to discuss the proposals which we have made.

25. Charges have been made to the effect that agreements have been frequently broken by both sides, and it has been implied that under these circumstances it would be futile to make further agreements. We offer no excuse for, and have no desire to condone, the breach of agreements, and we recognise the strength of this objection. The subject of the fulfilment of agreements formed part of a long and careful enquiry made recently at the request of H.M. Government by the Industrial Council, and the conclusions unanimously formed then are strengthened by what we have learned here, namely : that the difficulties arising in regard to alleged breaches of agreement can best be dealt with by isolating as far as possible those responsible for the breach. We therefore suggest that it be agreed :—

1. That any complaint as to the breaking of agreements may be referred to the Conciliation Committee for decision as to whether or not there has been a breach.

2. That in the event of the Conciliation Committee failing to agree as to whether or not a breach has been committed the matter shall be decided by the Chairman of the Committee.

3. That in the event of such complaint being held to be substantiated no support whatever be given by the respective Associations or by any affiliated Association to the parties responsible for the breach.

> GEORGE ASKWITH, *Chairman.*
> THOS. R. RATCLIFFE-ELLIS,
> J. R. CLYNES.

H. J. WILSON,
    Secretary to the Court.

October 5, 1913.

II

EMPLOYERS' REPLY TO SIR GEORGE ASKWITH'S FINDINGS

The following is the reply issued by the Employers' Executive Committee to the Government Report printed above.

When the Enquiry held by Sir George Askwith, Sir Thomas Ratcliffe-Ellis, and J. R. Clynes, Esq., M.P., terminated by the reading of their Report, which has been published, the Employers' Executive intimated that they would consult the various bodies of employers whom they represented and obtain their views. This has necessarily taken some time, but they are now in a position to present their reply, and in doing so they take the opportunity to acknowledge the personal courtesy extended to them at the Enquiry by the members of the Court, and where they disagree with their finding, they do so, appreciating the efforts made to arrive at some means which would put a stop to wasteful strife.

Little advantage will now accrue from dealing at any length with the procedure adopted at the Court of Enquiry, but in the interests of the employers at Dublin they feel bound to express their regret that while they were asked to state their case and prove it by witnesses, who were cross-examined, the representative of the workers, on the other hand, made a long series of charges, many of which were obviously untrue, interspersed with attacks on Messrs. Jacob and other respected firms in the city, calculated to seriously injure the businesses of these firms, in support of which no evidence whatever was forthcoming nor opportunity for cross-examination afforded.

In these circumstances they feel that the Court should have called for the withdrawal of these charges, and, if not withdrawn, to have stated in their findings that they were unsupported by any evidence.

The employers are prepared to accept Clauses 1 to 11 of the Report as historically correct, but they think that the Court should have emphasised the fact that the reason the Conciliation Boards were not formed was not the fault of the employers. In 1911 the workers failed even to reply to the communications from Sir J. B. Dougherty (the Under Secretary for Ireland) asking them to nominate representatives for the proposed Board of Conciliation.

With regard to Clause 12, the Court said, ' Statements have been made to us regarding the conditions of labour in the city,' but the Executive Committee beg to point out that none of these statements were proved, and it is unfair to conclude under the circumstances that ' the events which have occurred in the various industries indicate that grievances have existed.'

In Clauses 13 and 14 the sympathetic strike is defined, and Clause 15 expresses the opinion that ' no community could exist if resort to the sympathetic strike became the general policy of trade unionism.' This and the breaking of agreements are the main causes of the existing trouble.

The employers realise that recent acquiescence by other Unions in the methods of the modern sympathetic strike is due to the domination of the legitimate trade unions by the Irish Transport Union. Relieved of this tyrannical control, they are of opinion that the amicable relations heretofore existing would be restored.

Regarding the undertaking referred to in Clause 16, the surmise in the first portion of this clause we agree to be correct. It was a drastic action to meet an extreme case. But when the Court goes on to say that ' whatever may have been the intention of the employers, this document imposes upon the signatories conditions which are contrary to individual liberty,' it seems to ignore its opening remarks in Clause 15, ' No community could exist,' etc. It also ignores the fact that for years past the methods of the Irish Transport Union have imposed conditions which are contrary to the individual liberty of both employers and employees.

Clause 19, although an admirable summary of points for discussion, with a view to arriving at a permanent basis for settlement of future labour troubles does not, in the opinion of the Committee, owing to its complexity, afford any assistance in the present crisis.

The employers, in spite of misrepresentation, maintain the attitude expressed in their letter of September 12, addressed to the Trades Congress Delegates, in the following passage :—

' The employers of Dublin favour trade unionism and collective bargaining, and are ready, as soon as the workers provide trustworthy machinery and trusty men to end the system of sympathetic strikes, to negotiate with them on lines which will secure legitimate claims of labour.'

While it is in no way the province of employers to interfere with the internal management of trade unions, and whilst not desiring to appear to dictate, they, in face of the conclusions come to by the Court regarding sympathetic strikes, broken agreements, and, further, the statements made since in public by the Secretary of the Irish Transport Union, including the declaration in London, ' To hell with contracts,' are compelled again to refuse to recognise this union until :—

(a) The union be re-organised on proper lines ;
(b) With new officials who have met with the approval of the British Joint Labour Board.

When this has been done the Executive Committee will recommend the employers to withdraw the ban on the Irish Transport Union, and to re-employ their workers as far as vacancies and conditions permit ; but until then they regret that existing circumstances compel them to continue to insist on the undertaking referred to being signed.

Apart from any settlement that may be arrived at now, the different stages of the dispute have made it very clear that the difficulty in arriving at any form of guarantees for the keeping of agreements must be the subject of legislation, as it has become of universal importance to the whole trading community.

CHARLES M. COGHLAN, *Secretary,*
Employers' Executive Committee.

OFFICE :—COMMERCIAL BUILDINGS,
DUBLIN, *October* 14, 1903.

III

DUBLIN DISTURBANCES COMMISSION REPORT

BELOW is given, with a few unimportant excisions, the report of the Commission appointed by the Government to inquire into the rioting in connection with the Dublin strikes and the conduct of the police on the occasion of the various disturbances.

To His Excellency the Right Honourable John Campbell, K.T., Lord Lieutenant-General and General Governor of Ireland

May it Please Your Excellency.

On December 19, 1913, Your Excellency issued your Warrant to us whereby, after reciting that in the months of August and September, 1913, during the existence of trade disputes in Dublin, certain disturbances and riots took place in that City, and that allegations of the use of excessive and unnecessary force had been made against the police engaged in the suppression of these disturbances, Your Excellency authorised and directed us to hold an Inquiry at Dublin on January 5 then next, and following days, ' and to inquire into the origin and circumstances of the said riots and disturbances, and into the allegations above mentioned, and to hear and examine all such witnesses as should appear before us with reference to the matters aforesaid, and to Report to Your Excellency thereon.'

In obedience to Your Excellency's Warrant we opened the Inquiry in the Four Courts, in the City of Dublin, on Monday, January 5, 1914, at the hour of 11 o'clock.

.   .   .   .

Mr. J. P. Powell, K.C., and the Hon. Cecil Atkinson (instructed by Mr. Gerald Byrne) appeared on behalf of the police, and Mr. Ignatius Rice, Solicitor to the Corporation of Dublin, appeared on behalf of the Housing Committee of the Corporation, with reference to certain charges made with reference to the conduct of the police on August 31 in certain buildings in the City which are the property of the Corporation.

Our Sittings closed on January 28, 1914, having occupied eighteen days, during which 281 witnesses attended for the purpose of giving evidence. Of these witnesses 202 were members of either the Dublin Metropolitan Police or of the Royal Irish Constabulary, and 79 were civilians.

ORIGIN OF THE DISTURBANCES

On August 30 and 31, and September 1 and 21, 1913, fifteen separate and distinct riots took place in the City of Dublin. Of these five occurred on Saturday, August 30 ; seven occurred on Sunday, August 31 ; two occurred on Monday, September 1, and one occurred on Sunday, September 21.

We shall deal separately with the circumstances of each of these riots, but before doing so it is necessary to report on their origin.

The year 1913 was a period of industrial unrest in Dublin. Between the end of January and the middle of August, 1913, no less than thirty strikes took place in the City, many of which were accompanied by actual violence and intimidation, resulting in prosecutions and convictions in some forty-five cases. On several occasions from the month of March, and particularly in the month of August, speeches containing direct incitements to violence were delivered at meetings of working men, and in many of these speeches, especially those delivered in the month of August, attacks were made upon the police. In the last week of August a strike occurred of a large number of the employees of the Dublin Tramway Company, but as some of the employees of the Company remained in their employment, it was possible, with the assistance of newly engaged hands, to continue a diminished service of the cars. In order to prevent the cars and their drivers and conductors from being attacked in the streets, it was necessary to obtain police protection, and for a considerable time a member or members of the Dublin Metropolitan Police, or of the Royal Irish Constabulary, accompanied each of the cars. The protection afforded to the Tramway Company in running their cars notwithstanding the strike created great resentment, not only against the Tramway Company, but against the police, and two of the earlier riots on Saturday, August 30, and several of the riots on Sunday, August 31, had their origin in organised attacks on tram-cars. All the other riots, with the exception of the riot in Sackville Street on Sunday, August 31, with the origin of which we have dealt separately, had their origin in organised attacks on the police. Although all the riots were directly or indirectly the result of industrial disputes, they were not confined to working men, and in all of them the worst element was supplied by those who seldom or never work, and who may be described as the corner-boys and criminal class in the City.

It is a remarkable feature of the disturbances on which it is our duty to report that between 5 P.M. and 8 P.M. on Sunday evening, August 31, serious rioting occurred in six widely separated districts in the City.

RIOT AT RINGSEND ON SATURDAY, AUGUST 30, 1913

On the afternoon of Saturday, August 30, the first of the riots which we have investigated broke out in the district of Ringsend, near the City.

The Power Station of the Dublin Company is situated here, and it was in the neighbourhood of this building that disorder first showed itself.

Inspector Bannon of the Dublin Metropolitan Police was in charge, and he was assisted by Inspector Chase, who was accompanied by a number of mounted troopers.

During the riot Inspector Chase was struck by a stone, and his horse was knocked down by members of the crowd. The tram-cars were attacked, and when the police sought to protect them, they were received with a volley of stones, bottles, and other missiles, thrown not only from the street, but also from houses. Four members of the force were injured in the course of this riot, which lasted for an hour.

The efforts made by those responsible for the preservation of the peace did not involve the use of any unnecessary violence.

RIOT IN BRUNSWICK STREET, SATURDAY, AUGUST 30, 1913

Later in the same afternoon another riot broke out in Great Brunswick Street, within the City. Superintendent Kiernan and Inspector Barrett were in charge of the district; and the immediate cause of the riot was an attack on a van, the property of the *Independent* Newspapers, which was proceeding from Ringsend towards the City, under the escort of two constables. A crowd of about 250 persons assembled, and blocked the road. The horse was seized, and when the constables forming the escort attempted to protect the driver, they were struck with stones, one of them—Constable O'Callaghan—being knocked down, and kicked while on the ground.

The men who went to the assistance of these constables

were assaulted and struck by stones and bottles, and in the case of some persons who were arrested numbers of stones were found in their pockets.

Men and women joined in the attack, and a prisoner, who had been arrested, was rescued. The men in charge of the tram-cars in the street were also assailed. During the continuance of this disturbance the street was a scene of great violence. The conduct of the police who were chiefly engaged was described in these words by a clergyman who was present : ' It is my distinct opinion that the five or six policemen (D.M.P. and R.I.C.) whom I saw subjected to these insults and violent conduct, behaved with singular self-restraint, and in some cases with actual good humour. There was an absence of violence on their part, except in the last instance, when they only employed such force as was necessary to secure and retain their prisoners. Their behaviour was the only redeeming feature of what was for a Dublin citizen a really humiliating and disgusting spectacle.' This statement, which will be found in the evidence of Sir John Ross, was forwarded by the Reverend Gentleman.

RIOTS IN BERESFORD PLACE, TALBOT STREET, MARLBOROUGH STREET, EARL STREET, EDEN QUAY, AND BURGH QUAY, SATURDAY, AUGUST 30, 1913

On the night of Saturday, August 30, violent rioting took place in the district comprising Beresford Place and the quays adjoining, Marlborough Street, Corporation Street, Talbot Street, and Earl Street.

Inspector Campbell, of the Dublin Metropolitan Police, was on duty in Beresford Place, in charge of twenty men from about 7 P.M. They were stationed outside Liberty Hall, the Head Quarters of the Irish Transport Workers' Union, and about 8 P.M. a crowd which had collected, began to booh and hiss the police, and become violent. The Inspector was struck on the face with a piece of glass, and a large number of his men were also struck. Reinforcements were called for, and Inspector Willoughby, with between twenty and thirty men, shortly afterwards came to the assistance of Inspector Campbell.

Before any charge was made on the crowd at least five constables had been injured, and when the crowd was dispersed by the police, they reassembled at different points from time to time.

The stone-throwing continued, and charges were made during the night along Eden Quay, across Butt Bridge, on Burgh Quay, and in Beresford Place. During part of the disturbance Superintendent Quinn was in charge of a party of men on Butt Bridge, and a number of his men were injured, at least one having to be removed to hospital. This constable, who was hit with a bottle on the head, was unable to return to duty for three weeks.

The riot in this locality went on for a long time, and while it lasted, the throwing of stones and bottles was almost continuous, and many injuries were inflicted.

We regret to say that, as far as we can ascertain, two deaths are attributable to injuries received as a result of baton charges which took place. At Eden Quay, a man called James Nolan, of 8, Spring Garden Street, North Strand, sustained a fracture of the skull, which resulted in his death at Jervis Street Hospital on the morning of Sunday, the 31st. The jury at the inquest found that death was caused by fracture of the skull, and compression of the brain. They also found that the injuries were caused by the blow of a baton, but that the evidence was too conflicting to say by whom the blow was administered. It was proved before us that before the baton charge in question took place, the crowd at the spot in question had been very disorderly, stones had been thrown, and it was quite obvious to any peaceable person that a riot was in progress for some time. No evidence was given before us as to the circumstances under which Nolan became a member of the crowd, but it was beyond all doubt a riotous one.

On the same night a labourer named John Byrne, residing at 4, Lower Gloucester Place, was treated at Jervis Street Hospital for a wound on his head. He died on September 4, and the jury at the inquest found that John Byrne died from fracture of the skull and hæmorrhage. They further found that they had no evidence to show how the deceased received his injuries.

No person gave evidence at the Inquest, or before us, as to the circumstances under which John Byrne sustained the injuries which resulted in his death, and the only account available was the statement made by him to his wife, that he had been struck with a baton at Burgh Quay. It was proved before us that a baton charge had taken place at Burgh Quay on Saturday night, and that the crowd against which this charge was directed was very disorderly and violent, and we have little doubt that in the course of this charge Byrne received the injury which led to his death.

We are of opinion that in the case of both these crowds their conduct towards the police clearly showed to any peaceable persons the danger that they ran by remaining members of them.

Later on on the same night riotous crowds assembled in Marlborough Street, Talbot Street, and Earl Street, and damage was done in many instances to shops and houses. The rioters gathered at the corners of streets, and when charged by the police rushed away, to reassemble later on and again indulge in stone-throwing. In fact during the greater part of the night continuous disturbances existed in this area, and the force engaged were kept busy in dispersing crowds. Unless the officers in charge were prepared to abandon possession of the streets to rioters, they had no alternative but to give the orders to clear the various streets that they did.

THE RIOT IN SACKVILLE STREET ON SUNDAY, AUGUST 31, 1913

The immediate cause of the riot in Sackvile Street on Sunday afternoon, August 31, 1913, was the appearance of James Larkin outside the Imperial Hotel in Sackville Street, for the purpose of addressing a public meeting, which had been proclaimed by the Chief Magistrate of the City of Dublin. Larkin was arrested, and committed for trial on August 28, 1913, and was admitted to bail on the same day. After his admission to bail Larkin publicly expressed his intention of holding a public meeting in Sackville Street on Sunday, August 31. On August 29 a Proclamation, which was extensively posted and circulated in the City, was issued by the Chief Magistrate, prohibiting this meeting. On the evening of August 29 Larkin burned a copy of this Proclamation at a meeting in Beresford Place, and again expressed his intention of holding a meeting in Sackville Street on Sunday, August 31. In these circumstances a warrant was issued for the re-arrest of Larkin, and it became necessary for the police authorities to take steps for the purpose of preventing and dispersing the meeting if an attempt were made to hold it in Sackville Street, on the Sunday. The steps taken for this purpose were described to us in detail by Mr. W. V. Harrel, the Assistant Commissioner of the Dublin Metropolitan Police, and will be found in his evidence annexed to this Report. The length of Sackville Street is 616 yards, and its width from wall to wall a little over 50 yards ; and it was not known in what part of the street the intended meeting would be held. In these circumstances it became necessary to make such arrangements as would ensure a sufficient force of police to prevent and disperse the meeting in whatever part of the street the attempt might be made to hold it, and at the same time to prevent any filling up of the street. With this object in view, Mr. Harrel met all the Superintendents at Head Quarters on Saturday, August 30, and directed them to assemble at 11.30 A.M. on the Sunday in Sackville Street a force of police, which in fact consisted of 5 Superintendents, 9 Inspectors, 23 Sergeants, and 274 Constables, of whom 72 were members of the Royal Irish Constabulary ; to instruct their officers and men that while persons were to be allowed to pass freely along the street about their lawful business, no assembly of persons was to be permitted ; that the police were to advise persons to pass along, and not to remain about ; that small parties of police consisting of a sergeant and a few constables were to move along the sections of the street allotted to each superintendent to keep the people moving when necessary ; that no organised bodies of people were to be allowed to enter the street at any point ; and that James Larkin was to be arrested if he appeared. The superintendents to whom these instructions were given are all men of long experience in the force, and they and the other officers of the Dublin Metropolitan Police who were in command of the various sections of the force in Sackville Street on Sunday, August 31, had frequent previous experience of dealing with crowds and meetings in that street, and were competent to deal with any emergency which might arise in their immediate neighbourhood. In accordance with these arrangements, which were subsequently communicated by Mr. Harrel to Sir John Ross, the Chief Commissioner of the Dublin Metropolitan Police, and approved of by him, the police took up their position in and about Sackville Street at 11.30 A.M. on the Sunday. The force was distributed in the following manner :—One division under Chief Superintendent Dunne, and consisting of Inspector Bannon, six sergeants and sixty-three constables, was stationed in sections at the south side of O'Connell Bridge, at the Ballast Office and at the *Independent* Office at the corner of D'Olier Street. Another division under Superintendent Kiernan, and consisting of two inspectors, five sergeants, and fifty constables, was stationed in three sections on the east side of Sackville Street between Eden Quay and the Pillar. A third division under Superintendent Flynn was stationed at the Bachelor's Walk side of O'Connell Bridge, and a fourth division, under Superintendent Murphy, was posted in sections, one near the corner of Middle Abbey Street, and the other at Prince's Street, near the office of the *Freeman's Journal*. A fifth division, under Superintendent Gordon, had charge of the west side of Upper Sackville Street, from Henry Street to the Rotunda ; and a sixth division, under Inspector Willoughby, had charge of the east side of Upper Sackville Street, from Earl Street to Great Britain Street. Both Sir John Ross and Mr. Harrel arrived in Sackville Street about 1.30 P.M., when the rioting was almost over. They left the Head Quarters at the Castle a few minutes before, without having received any summons, for the purpose of visiting Sackville Street, and as the disturbance actually broke out while they were on their way, they had no knowledge that an attempt had been made to hold a meeting. Recognising the serious state of affairs in Sackville Street, they took immediate steps to summon a troop of Mounted Police, which had been kept in readiness.

Up to 12.30 on the Sunday the state of affairs was normal in Sackville Street ; but from that hour the number of persons in the street increased rapidly until about 1.25 P.M., when there was a considerable though unformed crowd in the street, particularly in the neighbourhood of the General Post Office. About 1.25 P.M. Larkin appeared on the balcony of the Imperial Hotel, and appears to have uttered some words, and to have then retired into the hotel. As soon as he was observed by the people in the street, there was a rush by a crowd numbering 300 to 400, and waving hats and sticks, from the neighbourhood of the General Post Office towards the Imperial Hotel. In order to prevent the rush of this crowd on the hotel, Inspector McCaig with a sergeant and ten men, who were stationed on the foot-way some distance to the south of the hotel door, doubled out into the carriage way ; and simultaneously Sergeant Butler and five men executed a similar movement from the north side of the hotel. These combined movements had the effect of stopping the approaching crowd, who retreated in the direction of the General Post Office in considerable confusion. This result was produced without the use of batons by the police. This crowd reformed in the direction of the General Post Office ; and in the meantime Inspector McCaig and his party of police had been ordered to enter the Imperial Hotel for the purpose of effecting the arrest of Larkin, leaving Sergeant Butler and his men guarding the door of the hotel. As soon as the police were seen entering the hotel, there was a second rush by the crowd, which had greatly increased in numbers, from the direction of the General Post Office towards the hotel. During this rush sticks were brandished, and a missile was thrown from the crowd, which broke a large plate glass window a few feet from the hotel door. Believing that the object of the crowd was to prevent the arrest of Larkin, the police who were guarding the door of the hotel drew their batons, with the result that the rush was stopped, and the crowd again retreated in the direction of the General Post Office, where they again seem to have reformed. In this instance also no batons were used by the police, and none of them came in contact with the crowd. A few moments later Larkin was removed from the hotel under arrest, and, guarded by an escort, was taken to College Street Police Station. As soon as Larkin appeared in the street under arrest a third rush was made by the crowd from the direction of the General Post Office and Prince's Street, diagonally across the street in the direction of the escort. Fearing that the object of the crowd, who were shouting, brandishing sticks, and throwing stones, was to rescue the prisoner, orders were given by Inspector Barrett and other responsible officers to the police to put back and disperse the crowd. In our opinion these orders, and the baton charge by which they were carried out, were justified by the circumstances. The crowd was dispersed by three bodies of police, numbering in all about fifty, who moved out into the street, one from the corner of Lower Abbey Street, another from O'Connell Bridge, and the third from the neighbourhood of the Metropole Hotel. These three bodies of police effectually prevented the crowd from approaching the escort which was guarding Larkin, and turned the crowd back—dispersing them in the direction of the Nelson Pillar and the General Post Office. In the course of the charge by means of which this crowd was dispersed batons were used by many of the police, and a number of civilians were knocked down in the rush back along and across the street, some as the result of blows from batons, and some as the result of collision with and tripping over each other. Owing to the width of Sackville Street, and the fact that the entrances to Middle Abbey Street, Henry Street, and North Earl Street were left open, there was no hemming in of the crowd by the police, and, except for an unfortunate blocking of Prince's Street, there was nothing to prevent the crowd getting away in all directions up the street. Under the police arrangements which we have described, a force of one inspector, two sergeants, and twenty men had been stationed earlier in the day near the junction of Prince's Street and Sackville Street ; and owing to apprehended attacks upon premises in the occupation of the *Independent* Newspapers Company, an order had been given to one of the sergeants with nine men to prevent any crowd passing from Sackville Street through Prince's Street. For the purpose of carrying out this order, the sergeant and nine men to whom it was given were stationed near the office of the *Freeman's Journal*, where Prince's Street becomes a very narrow street, at some distance from the junction of Prince's Street with Sackville Street, and in a position from which it was difficult if not impossible to see the movements of crowds lower down in Sackville Street. During the dispersal in Sackville Street of the crowd which had followed the escort which was guarding Larkin, a large number of persons rushed round the corner of the Metropole Hotel into Prince's Street, cheering and throwing stones at the police in Prince's Street, many of whom were struck. In pursuance of the orders which they had received the sergeant and nine men who were stationed near the office of the *Freeman's Journal* prevented the crowd from going down Prince's Street, and turned them back towards Sackville Street, using their batons for the purpose. Having regard to the orders which he had received not to allow any crowd to pass down Prince's Street, the sergeant had no alternative but to turn back the crowd, and he and his men were justified in using all necessary force in doing so ; and having regard to the numbers and violence of the crowd, the use of batons by this small body of police was necessary. Unfortunately this crowd, as it was being driven back out of Prince's Street, was met by another crowd rushing into Prince's Street and away from the police in Sackville Street, and the two crowds collided, filling up the entrance to Prince's Street, and becoming mixed up with the police who were near the corner of the Metropole Hotel and the police who were putting the first crowd back out of Prince's Street. In the confusion caused by the collision of the two crowds, and in the effort by the police to prevent any crowd going down Prince's Street, a large number of people must have received injuries, not only from the pressure and struggle of the crowd, but also from the blows of batons. As frequently happens in incidents of the kind, there seem to have been several peaceable citizens swept into and along by the riotous mob ; and we have no doubt that some of them were injured during the clearing of the street. In one regrettable instance, that of Mr. O'Donnell, a respectable gentleman carrying on business in Lower Sackville Street received very severe injuries at the hands of the police. There were thirteen police injured during the course of this riot (including the sergeant and nine men who were stationed in Prince's Street—all of whom were injured in discharging their duty).

In dealing with the conduct of the police during this riot it must be borne in mind that the riot was a matter of a few minutes. All the incidents we have described, from the appearance of Larkin on the balcony of the Imperial Hotel until quiet was restored in Prince's Street, took place within three or four minutes.

So far as the movements of the police which turned and dispersed the crowd which was rushing in the direction of the escort are concerned, although batons were freely used, there is no evidence of the use of unnecessary or excessive force up to the moment of the collision of the two crowds at the entrance to Prince's Street. In the confusion of this moment there may have been, and we think that in isolated instances there was, the use of force which in fact was unnecessary. This was due to a misunderstanding on the part of the police who were stationed in Prince's Street as to the object of the second crowd which rushed into Prince's

U

Street, and collided with the crowd which was being driven out of that street. It was in fact an accidental collision between the crowd which they were driving out of Prince's Street and a crowd which had been driven up and across Sackville Street from the direction of Larkin's escort. To the police it very naturally appeared to be a renewed and determined effort by a suddenly and greatly increased crowd to force a passage through Prince's Street, and they dealt with it accordingly. Any unnecessary or excessive force used by the police during the suppression of this riot was due to this misunderstanding.

As some suggestions have been made that the crowd in Sackville Street was driven into Prince's Street for the purpose of being caught and batoned there, we think it right to say that, in our opinion, there is no foundation for these suggestions.

As suggestions were made in cross-examination of the police that some members of the force were seen smoking, and that others of them were under the influence of drink, while on duty in Sackville Street on Sunday, August 31, 1913, we also think it right to say that both these charges were indignantly denied by the police, that there is no evidence whatever to support either of them, and that they are without foundation.

At the hearing of the evidence in connection with this riot Mr. Handel Booth, M.P., attended, and asked to be heard in reply to the speech of Mr. Powell at the opening of the Inquiry. We expressed our desire that he should, in addition to being heard and giving his evidence, have an opportunity of cross-examining the various witnesses produced with reference to this particular riot. Mr. Handel Booth availed himself of this opportunity, and, amongst others, cross-examined Chief Superintendent Dunne, Superintendent Quinn, Superintendent Murphy, and Superintendent Kiernan, who were in charge of the various parties of police engaged in the dispersal of the crowds in Lower Sackville Street, and Inspector Lalor who was in charge of the two sergeants and twenty police who were stationed at or near the junction of Prince's Street and Sackville Street on Sunday, August 31. In the course of the re-examination of Inspector Lalor a charge was erroneously made by Mr. Handel Booth against Mr. Powell of suppressing a material portion of a deposition made by Inspector Lalor. This led to an altercation between Mr. Handel Booth and

Mr. Powell, in the course of which an offensive expression was addressed by Mr. Powell to Mr. Handel Booth, who thereupon withdrew ; and we regret that we had not the advantage of hearing his evidence or receiving further assistance from him.

RIOT IN CORNMARKET, THOMAS STREET, AND ADJOINING STREETS, SUNDAY, AUGUST 31, 1913

This riot commenced about 5 o'clock on Sunday evening, August 31, and continued from time to time up to 10 or 11 o'clock on Sunday night. It originated in attacks by mobs, numbering from 200 to 400 persons, on the tram cars on the line from College Green to Inchicore, One of these cars proceeding from College Green to Inchicore and guarded by three policemen, was held up near the corner of Cornmarket and High Street, about 5 o'clock P.M. by a crowd of 300 or 400 persons coming from Francis Street, and throwing stones and bottles. Two of the policemen who were guarding the tram car and three or four Metropolitan police who were stationed in High Street succeeded in putting back this crowd, notwithstanding a fusilade of stones and bottles, in the course of which every one of the police was struck and cut. In the meantime the windows of the tram car had been smashed by rioters, who had got behind the police, and two of the police who were nearest to the tram car were badly injured, one of them being knocked down with a stave, and the other getting his chin split open with a bottle. Some of the rioters were arrested, and taken with great difficulty to Chancery Lane ; Inspector White, who went in front to keep back the crowd, being struck on the head, and badly cut in Back Lane. On their way back from Chancery Lane to Cornmarket the police were again assailed from the tenement houses in Nicholas Street with stones and bottles thrown from the windows of the houses. A little later in the evening another tram car coming from Inchicore to College Green, and protected by two constables, was attacked and held up by another riotous mob in High Street, throwing stones, bricks, and bottles. The mob numbered about 200, and there were only the two policemen, who were rescued from a position of imminent danger by Father Reilly, who brought them into the Presbytery, followed by about fifty of the crowd, who proceeded to smash the windows of the Presbytery, and tried to force the door. They were relieved by a party of six police from Chancery Lane, who managed to disperse the crowd. From about 5.15 P.M. until 7 P.M., owing to the presence of riotous and disorderly crowds, it was necessary to patrol the streets in the neighbourhood with six members of the Royal Irish Constabulary Troop, who were stoned by the crowd in High Street, and pelted with bricks and bottles from the windows of the houses in High Street and Francis Street. Owing to the condition of this district, it became necessary to requisition a party of thirty-five Royal Irish Constabulary from the Depôt, who arrived about 6.30 P.M. About half of this body were left at Meath Street, and the remainder went on to Cornmarket and Francis Street. In Meath Street the sergeant in charge and eighteen constables were attacked by a mob of about 200 persons, who threw bricks and mineral water bottles, collected for the purpose, at the police. It was necessary to disperse the crowd by means of a baton charge, but none of the police came in contact with the crowd. A similar attack was made in Francis Street on the party of Royal Irish Constabulary who proceeded to Cornmarket by a crowd numbering 600 or 700 persons, stones and bottles being thrown from the houses as well as from the streets. Later in the evening a portion of this last-mentioned party of police were attacked in Pimlico and the neighbouring streets ; and on their way to report themselves at Chancery Lane Barracks about 10.30 P.M., the entire of this party of Royal Irish Constabulary who had come from the Depôt were fiercely attacked, and stoned by a mob of several hundred rioters in Cornmarket. A baton charge was ordered by the sergeant in command, but his men do not seem to have come in contact with the crowd.

This riot, which lasted for several hours, commenced by attacks on the cars of the Tramway Company, which were followed later in the evening by organised attacks on the police in different parts of the district. Eleven policemen were injured—some of them very seriously—they behaved with courage and forbearance, and there was no use of excessive or unnecessary force in dealing with the rioters. Except in the case of rioters who were actually arrested, the police do not seem to have come into contact with the crowds.

RIOT IN AUNGIER STREET, REDMOND'S HILL, CUFFE STREET, AND ADJOINING DISTRICT ON SUNDAY, AUGUST 31, 1913

This riot commenced with an attack, a little before 5 P.M., on one of the outgoing cars of the Tramway Company. The attack came from a crowd which had collected opposite the Transport Workers' Union Hall in Aungier Street. Two members of this crowd attacked and struck the motorman with sticks. The motorman was obliged to leave his car and defend himself with his driving handle. In the meantime the crowd, which had increased to 300 persons, smashed the windows of the car. There were no police in the immediate neighbourhood at the moment, but two men of the ' B ' Division were quickly on the scene, and one of them (145 B) went to the rescue of the motorman. He was at once knocked down, and brutally assaulted while on the ground, and the motorman in attempting to get back to his car was struck with a bottle on the back of the head, and so severely injured that he had to be removed to Mercer's Hospital. One of the policemen went for reinforcements, which soon afterwards arrived, and the crowd was dispersed. Constable 145 B was so severely injured that he had to go off duty for three weeks.

About the same time an in-coming tram car was held up at the same place by the same crowd, who wrecked the car, knocked the conductor down, and took his leather bag containing about £3 in money. The conductor was so badly injured that he had to be taken to hospital, and remained there for ten days. The party of police who were sent as reinforcements to the scene of this riot, consisting of a sergeant and nine men, were received with volleys of stones and bottles from the crowd in Aungier Street. The sergeant ordered his men to draw their batons and clear the street. As soon as the crowd saw the batons drawn they ran up the street and into Great Longford Street, where some of them entered the houses, from which they attacked the police with stones and bottles. An arrest was effected in this street. After taking the prisoner to Chancery Lane this body of police, consisting of ten men, were attacked by four converging crowds, which came out of Longford Street, Whitefriar Place, Aungier Street, and York Street. These crowds,

numbering in all over 500 persons, formed near the Church
in Whitefriar Street, and again fiercely attacked the police
with stones and bottles. The police charged the crowd,
and drove them through Bishop Street to Kevin Street.
During this charge stones and bottles were freely flung at
the police, and a prisoner arrested in Kevin Street was found
to have four stones in his pockets. After bringing this
prisoner to Kevin Street Barracks, the party of police returned
through Lower Kevin Street, and at the crossing of this
street and Redmond's Hill and Wexford Street they were
again surrounded and attacked by converging crowds, numbering several hundreds. The sergeant who had been doing
duty in this district for twenty-five years then stepped out
from his men, and appealed to the crowd not to stone the
police. He was received with a volley of stones, and was
struck four times. In order to effect their escape the sergeant and his men then charged the crowd in Cuffe Street,
and were followed by the other crowds down that street,
from the houses of which the police were stoned, until they
reached Stephen's Green, where they got into a motor car
and returned to barracks for reinforcements. A further
party of fifteen police were sent from College Street to assist
in restoring order, and Inspector Chase and six mounted
troopers were despatched to Aungier Street. Both these
bodies of police were attacked by a crowd of between 200
and 300 rioters outside the Transport Workers' Union
Hall in Aungier Street with stones, bricks, and bottles,
and a number of the men and horses were struck.
The rioters were dispersed by means of baton charges,
and the streets in the district were clear and quiet about
7 o'clock.

No unnecessary or excessive force was used by the police
in dealing with this dangerous riot, in which three policemen
were severely injured, and a large quantity of property was
destroyed.

RIOT AT INCHICORE ON SUNDAY, AUGUST 31, 1913

Between 5 and 6 o'clock on Sunday evening a crowd of
about 150 persons assembled near the Tramway Depôt at
Inchicore, and were hissing and booing at the driver and
conductor of one of the cars. One of the ringleaders of the

crowd being warned to go away, refused to do so, and called upon the crowd to wreck the car. He was then arrested by Sergeant Kincaid (12 A), who, with two constables, was on duty at the terminus of the tramway. He resisted arrest, but was secured with the assistance of the constables, and was then taken in the direction of the Kilmainham Police Station. At the Emmet Hall, which is between Richmond Barracks and Kilmainham Police Station, and is the meeting place of the Transport Workers' Union, a crowd of 150 persons was collected. As soon as the three police with their prisoner came near the Emmet Hall, a crowd of people came out of the Hall, and, with the people already in the street, came towards and met the police, and demanded the release of the prisoner. The crowd then commenced to throw stones, and bricks, and other missiles. The sergeant ordered his two men to draw their batons, and keeping the prisoner between them, with the sergeant behind them, they tried to get their prisoner past the crowd. The crowd closed in on them ; the prisoner was rescued, and the police got separated. Sergeant Kincaid was surrounded, knocked down, kicked, and left unconscious on the ground. He was brought into a neighbouring house by a woman and her family, and only regained consciousness after two hours. He was one month in hospital, and another month off duty as the result of the injuries he received. One of the two constables (Crowley, R.I.C.) was also surrounded, knocked down twice, and kicked each time while on the ground. He escaped with difficulty into the Richmond Barracks, and was confined to hospital for five days. The other constable (Denis McMahon) was struck with a heavy stone on the head while still holding the prisoner, staggered back, and was knocked down, and kicked by the crowd several times about the head and body. He fought his way back to his comrades, but was again knocked down and kicked by the crowd, and lost his helmet and baton. He escaped with his life into a house, the door of which was open, followed by the crowd, who demanded that he should be put out again. The owner of the house, who was in terror of the mob, let him out by the back door, and he got into another house by the back way. He was severely injured and on the sick list for some days. It is some satisfaction to be able to state that the prisoner was re-arrested nine days afterwards at Clondalkin.

A little later in the evening, about 6.30 P.M., a crowd of

about 400 persons collected outside the Emmet Hall for the purpose of hearing an address from one of the windows of the Hall. The speaker told the crowd that the women and children should clear away, and referred to the arrest of the prisoner earlier in the evening, and said, ' The police were sorry for it now.' During the speech two tram cars coming out from the city with broken windows and protected by a sergeant and five constables, reached the outskirts of the crowd. Inspector Wilkinson who, with a party of about ten constables, was already in the immediate neighbourhood of the Emmet Hall, ordered his men to clear the way for the trams. This order provoked the hostility of the crowd, who declined to clear the way. The constables then drew their batons and tried to make a way for the tram cars. Many of the crowd were armed with sticks, and stones were coming freely from all directions, some of them from the windows of the Emmet Hall. In these circumstances, a number of police entered the Emmet Hall and cleared it out, the people who were there rushing out by the back. At the same time a detachment of the West Kent Regiment, who had been sent to the assistance of the police by Mr. Waters (Special Magistrate), arrived on the scene, and escorted the tram cars to the Depôt, and the police were able to disperse the crowd. This is the only occasion on which the services of the military were requisitioned, and their services were confined to escorting the tram cars from the Emmet Hall to the Tramway Depôt, so that they did not come into contact with the crowd.

There was no use of unnecessary or excessive force by the police in dealing with this riot, during which six policemen were injured—three of them very severely.

· · · · · · ·

CORPORATION STREET AND BUILDINGS, SUNDAY, AUGUST 31, 1913

Evidence was also given before us relating to riots which were alleged to have taken place in Corporation Street, and in Corporation Buildings, on the night of Saturday, August 30, and the afternoon of Sunday, August 31. Mr. Rice, solicitor to the Corporation of Dublin, appeared on behalf of the Housing Committee of the Corporation, and called evidence for the purpose of establishing that not only was wilful injury inflicted by members of the police on the property of the Corporation and their tenants, but that excessive and unnecessary violence was in some cases used to such tenants.

Having carefully considered the evidence given on both sides we came to the conclusion that the damage done on the night of Saturday, involving as it did only the breaking of a few windows, was not of a serious character, and we were not satisfied as to the identity of the constables who were alleged to have been guilty of it.

As regards the Sunday, however, we are of opinion that in a number of instances wilful damage was done to the property of the Corporation and their tenants, and we are also of opinion that assaults were committed on some of the occupiers of the buildings for which there was no justification whatever. On this day a number of rioters who fled from the police had taken refuge on the balconies of the Corporation Buildings, and they, assisted by many of the occupants, made an attack on a body of police, who proceeded to enter the buildings for the purpose of dispersing the rioters. With this object they ascended to the balconies, and when there entered a large number of dwellings—some thirty—forcibly. In many of the dwellings damage was caused by the force used on entering, but in some cases, after the entry was made and when no rioters were found inside, some constables proceeded to destroy the property of the tenants. Glass was broken, delph, lamps, and pictures. In some instances furniture and other articles were damaged, and, considering the means of the occupants, substantial damage was inflicted on them. The windows in some houses were also broken.

We make every allowance for the excitement under which the constables were labouring owing to the attacks made upon them from the buildings, but in our opinion in the case of eight or ten dwellings wilful damage was done without justification.

The rooms in which the principal damage was caused were seen on Tuesday, September 2, by Mr. Eyre, the City Treasurer, and his evidence fully corroborated the statements of the tenants of the dwellings, and was fully accepted by us, as was the evidence of Miss Harrison, who saw some of the dwellings. We are also satisfied that in some instances assaults were committed without just cause.

Gloucester Street, Waterford Street, Gardiner Street, and Parnell Street, August 31, 1913

About 5 P.M. on Sunday evening, August 31, extensive rioting prevailed in the district around Gardiner Street, and crowds assembled in that street, and at the corners of streets communicating therewith. In the first instance the police came into contact with the rioters at the corner of Gloucester Street, and dispersed them after being met with a fusilade of stones and bricks, in many cases thrown from houses. A number of troopers were engaged in keeping the crowd moving, but their efforts were greatly hampered by the persistent stone throwing that took place from nearly all the houses in the streets through which they passed. In some of the streets, notably Cumberland Street and Waterford Street, numbers of men were stationed on the roofs of houses, and stripped off slates and tiles for the purpose of throwing them into the street at passing constables. In one case in Waterford Street seven men were discovered on the roof of a house.

Constable Sutton (125 C) was struck in this street with a tile thrown from a roof, and many other constables sustained injuries of a similar kind.

The troopers engaged in patrolling these streets were all hit, some more than once, during the riot, and when arrests had been effected of persons who had been taken on the roofs of houses the escort conveying the prisoners was followed towards the Police Station and freely stoned.

A number of these prisoners were afterwards convicted and sentenced.

This disturbance was spread over the entire district, and the serious feature of it was the readiness of the occupants of the various tenement houses to shelter escaping rioters, and to join with them in attacking the police from the upper stories of many houses. Some baton charges were made, but as a rule these were useless, as the crowds fled before the police and took refuge in houses which were open to receive them.

Riot in Mary Street, Chancery Street, and along the Northern Quays from Chancery Place to Queen Street, on Sunday, August 31, 1913

From about 5 P.M. till 6.30 P.M. the Northern Quays from Chancery Place up to Queen Street, and the streets abutting on these quays, were in a constant state of riot and disorder. Some of the crowds who took part in this disturbance had collected owing to an incident which occurred in Mary Street. A sergeant and two constables of the D Division, on their way from Green Street to Sackville Street between 4 and 5 P.M. came upon a crowd in Mary Street, near the corner of Stafford Street, who were stoning a party of police marching towards Sackville Street. They arrested one of the ringleaders who was inciting the mob to attack the police, and took him to the Bridewell behind the Four Courts. While on their way they were followed by the crowd through Mary's Lane, Michan's Lane, and Chancery Street, and were pelted with bricks, bottles, and stones all the way to the Bridewell—some of the crowd venturing into the Bridewell yard. Before they could leave the Bridewell the sergeant and his two men had to obtain reinforcements from Green Street, and having done so they dispersed this crowd in the direction of Inns Quay and the bridge at Chancery Place, where they re-assembled, and again attacked the police with stones and bottles. One of the police was struck with a bottle, and the man who threw it was pursued and arrested. Later on several tram cars were held up at Church Street and Queen Street bridges by crowds who dispersed up side streets when the police came near them, and re-assembled at some other part of the quays. As soon as the trams ceased running the crowd dispersed and quiet was restored.

No unnecessary or excessive force was used by the police in dealing with the disturbances in this district, during which twelve of the police were injured.

Riot on George's Quay and Moss Street, on Sunday, August 31, 1913

About 8 o'clock on Sunday evening it was reported to the police stationed at the south side of O'Connell Bridge that there was rioting on George's Quay and in Moss Street.

Sergeant O'Donnell and a party of ten constables were sent by Chief Superintendent Dunne to try and suppress it. They found on their arrival at George's Quay that a large fire had been lit on the street near the corner of Moss Street. This fire was surrounded by a collection of loose bricks. The crowd near the fire attacked the police with these bricks and with broken sewer pipes, and they were attacked from the houses with bottles and jam-pots. Sergeant O'Donnell ordered his men to draw their batons and disperse the crowd, and they dispersed the crowd as far as the corner of Moss Street, where the police were again attacked from the houses and in the street, and from a boat or boats on the river. As the crowd numbered over four hundred, the sergeant, seeing that the lives of his men were in danger, brought them back to College Street Station, where he reported the matter to the Superintendent, who ordered out Sergeant Hurley and ten picked men as a reinforcement. Sergeant O'Donnell and his men returned to Moss Street by Townsend Street, and Sergeant Hurley and his men went to Moss Street by Burgh Quay and George's Quay. When Sergeant O'Donnell and party of police got within twenty yards of Moss Street (at the corner of Townsend Street and Moss Street) they were attacked by a crowd of two hundred rioters on the street, and also with bottles, stones, and bricks from the windows and hall doors of the houses in Moss Street. From No. 8 Moss Street in particular missiles were thrown from the hall door, and from the top storey windows, and three of the police were severely injured, one being struck in the mouth, another on the back of the head with a stone, and another on the side of the head with a brick. As one of the persons assaulting the police from 8 Moss Street was identified, the police effected an entrance into the house and made two arrests. Soon after this the crowd in Moss Street was completely dispersed, and quiet was restored about 10 o'clock.

In the meantime Sergeant Hurley and his party of constables had arrived near and been attacked by a fusilade of bricks from the fire which had been lit on George's Quay. They dispersed this attacking crowd down the quays, but never got in touch with them, being themselves stoned by the crowd they were pursuing, and also from a boat in the river. This riotous crowd seems to have reformed many times, and was not finally dispersed for nearly an hour.

The mob with which the police had to deal in this district seems to have been characterised by great violence and lawlessness, and seven policemen were injured during the riots in Moss Street and on George's Quay on this evening.

There was no unnecessary or excessive force used by the police in dealing with this riot.

RIOT AT REDMOND'S HILL AND NEIGHBOURING STREETS ON MONDAY, SEPTEMBER 1, 1913

This riot was really a continuation of the rioting of the previous evening in the same neighbourhood. During the afternoon of Monday, September 1, between the hours of 3 P.M. and 7 P.M. there had been a good deal of desultory stone throwing at the police by crowds which gathered at Redmond's Hill, Digges Street, Aungier Street, Cuffe Street, Whitefriar Street, and Peter Street, but the serious rioting did not begin until after dark. From 9 P.M. until nearly midnight Redmond's Hill, Wexford Street, and Camden Street and the neighbouring side streets were a scene of continuous and dangerous rioting. The crowds collected at the corners of the side streets leading off the main thoroughfares, and kept up a continuous fire of missiles at any body of police who were within range. When the police were out of range, the missiles were directed at shop windows, with the result that a very large quantity of glass was broken. As soon as the police charged any particular mob, it disappeared up or down one of the side streets, and when the police followed in pursuit they were fusiladed with deadly missiles from the windows and even the roofs of houses. At no time were the police actually in contact with any of the many riotous crowds. For more than two hours during this riot Redmond's Hill, Wexford Street, and Camden Street—main thoroughfares of the city—were in possession of the mob, and a deliberate, but fortunately unsuccessful, attempt was made to drive the police off the streets.

This riot was remarkable not only for the ferocity of the attacks upon the police, but also for the wanton destruction of property and the looting of some shops.

There was no use of unnecessary or excessive force by the police in dealing with this riot.

RIOT IN CAPEL STREET AND ADJOINING STREETS ON MONDAY, SEPTEMBER 1, 1913

At 9.30 P.M. on Monday, September 1, Inspector Lowry, with a sergeant and ten men, on their way from Henry Place to Mary Street, were attacked in Capel Street by a mob of 200 to 300 persons, throwing stones, bottles, and pieces of iron. Several of the police were struck. The Inspector deemed it necessary to charge, and they were dispersed up Mary Street, an arrest being made in that street. After bringing the prisoner to the Bridewell the same party of police returned to Capel Street, and found that the mob had re-assembled at the corner of Mary Street. Missiles were again thrown by the crowd, and several shop windows were broken in Capel Street. It became necessary to charge the crowd again, and this time they were dispersed down Capel Street, and over Grattan Bridge, and along Ormond Quay. Later on it was reported to Inspector Lowry that four constables of the Royal Irish Constabulary were being attacked in Capel Street, and on returning there he and his party found the four constables, who were returning to their lodgings at the Hibernian Hotel in Capel Street, surrounded just opposite the hotel by an angry crowd of from 150 to 200 rioters, who were attacking them with stones and bottles. The conduct of the mob was exceptionally brutal, and the position of the four constables was one of extreme danger. Except for the timely arrival of Inspector Lowry and his men, it is difficult to see how they could have escaped with their lives. The mob who were attacking the four constables were driven by the relieving party up Capel Street as far as Little Britain Street, and were there dispersed about 10 o'clock. This was a fierce riot, during which eighteen of the police were injured, and their lives were constantly in danger. In all the instances during this riot in which the police charged the mob, the charge was absolutely necessary, and no unnecessary or excessive force was used by the police in the suppression of the disturbance.

RIOT AT TOWNSEND STREET, SUNDAY, SEPTEMBER 21,
1913

On Sunday, September 21, about 5.50 P.M. a procession,
estimated to contain several thousand people, formed in
Beresford Place and the neighbourhood, and proceeded to
march through the city.   Chief Superintendent Dunne,
with Superintendent Kiernan and Inspector Bannon, and sixty
sergeants and constables, accompanied the procession, which
was led by a crowd of roughs, many of whom were under the
influence of drink.   The Chief Superintendent, who has forty
years' experience in the Dublin Metropolitan Police force,
stated that he had never seen such an assemblage of the
disorderly class.   In the course of their march tram cars
were attacked and wrecked, to the number of nine in all, and
the members of the crowd behaved in a very disorderly fashion.
Stones were thrown at different times during their progress,
but it was not until Townsend Street was reached that the
riot assumed a really serious aspect.   When the procession
reached this street an organised attempt was made by its
members to overwhelm the force which had accompanied
them.   Showers of stones and bottles were thrown, in many
instances from the houses, and a hand-to-hand struggle went
on here for twenty minutes between the police and rioters.
Some of the horses belonging to the troopers were knocked
down ; the men themselves received severe injuries, and in
many instances their lives were only saved by their helmets,
which were broken by stones and missiles.   Pieces of concrete,
iron nuts, and bricks were freely thrown.   Batons were drawn
and used at several points in the street, but for some time
even this measure had not the effect of dispersing the crowd
or restoring order.   Some of the constables were knocked
down and rendered unconscious, and in one instance a member
of the Dublin Metropolitan Police was wounded by a knife.
The total number of constables injured in this riot was thirty-
six.   The entire length of the street for nearly half an hour
was a scene of riot, and the persistent throwing of missiles
from houses added greatly to the dangers incurred by officers
and men.

This was, in our opinion, the most determined and disgraceful riot that took place in Dublin during the disturbances,

and any measures taken by the police for the purpose of suppressing it were amply justified. It was carefully planned, and in the case of many of the houses missiles had been provided some time before for use against the police.

We desire to report, in conclusion, that in our opinion the officers and men of the Dublin Metropolitan Police and the Royal Irish Constabulary, as a whole, discharged their duties throughout this trying period with conspicuous courage and patience. They were exposed to great dangers, and treated with great brutality, and in many instances we were satisfied that, though suffering from injuries which would have fully justified their absence from duty, they remained at their posts under great difficulties until peace had been restored. The total number of constables injured during these riots exceeded 200. Notwithstanding the extent and violence of the disturbances, in no case, save one, and then only for the purpose of protecting two tram cars, was the assistance of the military called for. The riots were dealt with and suppressed by the police, and by the police alone, and had it not been for their zeal and determination, the outburst of lawlessness which took place in the months of August and September would have assumed more serious proportions, and been attended with far more evil results.

We have the honour to remain,
Your Excellency's obedient servants,
DENIS S. HENRY,
S. L. BROWN.
THOMAS PATTON,
Secretary.

9th February, 1914.

IV

BROKEN AGREEMENTS

The following is the text of the agreement of July 23, 1908, referred to in Chapter VIII.

EXTRACT FROM THE 'BOARD OF TRADE LABOUR GAZETTE,' AUGUST 1908

On July 4, 1908, the Dublin Branch of the National Union of Dock Labourers gave notice to their employers that, on and after July 20, no member of that Union would work with any non-union man. The employers replied by issuing notices that any man who objected to work with non-unionists would be discharged, and that no member of the National Union would be employed after July 11.

About 100 members of the Union were paid off on July 10, and the remainder were to have ceased work, in accordance with the above notice, on the following day. On that day, however, negotiations were entered into between the parties and Lord MacDonnell, Sir James Dougherty (Under Secretary of State for Ireland), and Mr. I. H. Mitchell, of the Board of Trade ; and it was arranged that the notices on both sides should be withdrawn, and the *status quo* maintained, pending a further conference to be held on July 18. Accordingly, on the following Monday (July 13), a majority of the members of the Union returned to work ; some difficulties arose, however, by which a number of men were unable to resume work, but these were successfully arranged by Sir James Dougherty.

The adjourned conference took place as arranged on July 18 ; it was presided over by Lord MacDonnell, at the request of the Board of Trade ; and Sir J. Dougherty and Mr. I. H. Mitchell were again present, in addition to representatives of the parties. An agreement was made at this conference for submission to the parties, and on July 30 the following terms of settlement were finally arrived at :—

1. Questions affecting individuals only shall be settled by the individual and the firm concerned.

2. The freedom of the employers as to the persons whom they employ is admitted.

3. No distinction as to work (including the delivery or reception of cargo) between Union and non-union men to be made either by employers or employed.

4. Questions affecting general conditions of employment, hours, rates of wages, &c., shall in the first place be communicated in writing by the men directly affected to the firm or firms concerned. If no arrangement is arrived at, the men, through the General Secretary of the National Union of Dock Labourers, may make further representations on the matter to the firm or firms affected, who will then consider them.

5. If no settlement be arrived at, the question shall be referred to a Conciliation Board consisting of a representative of the employers, a representative of the employed, and an umpire. The umpire to be agreed upon by the two representatives or, failing agreement, to be appointed by the Board of Trade.

6. That no distinguishing badges or buttons be displayed by the men during working hours.

7. All notices and documents, including tariffs issued during this dispute by either side, be withdrawn.

Below are given the terms of the agreement of May 26, 1913. (See Chapter X.)

[AGREEMENT BETWEEN THE IRISH TRANSPORT WORKERS' UNION AND SHIPPING COMPANIES.]

Memorandum of Agreement re Rates of Wages and Conditions of Labour for Quay Labourers (Cross Channel Steamers) at Dublin, between the Representatives of the undersigned Steamship Companies and of the Irish Transport and General Workers' Union. Made on the 26th day of May, 1913.

Constant Men :—
    30s. per Week of 60 Hours.
    8d. per Hour overtime.
    1s. per Hour for Sunday, from midnight Saturday to
        midnight Sunday.
    1s. to be paid for Meal Hour if worked.

Casual Men :—
    5s. per Day from 6 A.M. to 6 P.M. Two Meal Hours.
    3s. 9d. Three-quarter Day. 10 A.M. to 6 P.M. One
        Meal Hour.
    2s. 6d. Half Day. 6 A.M. to 12 noon.
    2s. 6d. ,, ,, 2 P.M. to 6 P.M.

8*d*. per Hour from 6 P.M. to 6 A.M.

Meal Hours, 8 to 9 or 9 to 10 A.M. } If worked 1*s*.

,, ,, 1 to 2 or 2 to 3 P.M. } to be paid.

1*s*. per Hour for Sunday, from midnight Saturday to midnight Sunday.

Handling Slag or Whiting :—

6*d*. per Man for lots of from 20 to 50 Tons.

1*s*. ,, ,, ,, over 50 Tons.

Casual Labour to include working in Ship, on Shore, in Shed or Stores.

Any question as to the interpretation of this Agreement, or any dispute arising between the men and their employers, to be submitted to the latter in writing. No stoppage of work to take place pending negotiations regarding such matters.

This Agreement to be binding on all concerned, and at least One Month's Notice in writing from either side to be given of any intention to terminate it.

The terms of this Agreement to come into force on MONDAY, the 2nd JUNE, 1913.

Signed on behalf of the Shipping Companies :—

TEDCASTLE, McCORMICK & CO., LTD.,
THOS. McCORMICK, Managing Director.
CLYDE SHIPPING CO., LTD.,
CHAS. J. YOUNG, Agent.
For BRISTOL STEAM NAVIGATION CO., LTD.,
A. GOWAN.
DUKE SHIPPING CO., LTD.,
WM. J. DOLLAR, Managing Director.
For BRITISH & IRISH STEAM PACKET CO., LTD.,
D. BARRY, Secretary and Manager.
For DUBLIN, SILLOTH, & ISLE OF MAN STEAMERS,
NICHOLL & FEARY, Agents.

Signed on behalf of the TRANSPORT UNION :—

JAMES LARKIN, Secretary I. T. & G. W. U.
JOHN O'NEILL.
PATRICK NOLAN.

DUBLIN, 26*th May*, 1913.

CARTERS' STRIKE, 1908

Text of Arbitrators' Award

We the Right Honorable Sir Andrew Marshall Porter, Baronet, and Patrick John O'Neill, Esquire, J.P., Chairman of the County Council of the County of Dublin, having been requested to act as Arbitrators to decide upon certain matters (hereinafter appearing) which had arisen and were stated to be in difference between the employers and the employed in connection with the trades and businesses of the Carriers and Carters, and also of Maltsters, in the City of Dublin ; and having acceded to said request, and fully heard the several persons interested and their witnesses ; DO MAKE and publish this as our AWARD AND FINAL DETERMINATION.

We AWARD AND DETERMINE that in respect of the services described in the Schedule hereto there shall be paid the several sums and rates therein mentioned and set out. This applies only to the case of men working ' on their earnings ' as that term is used in the trade. We award no payment in respect of carting the employers' weighing gear.

In the case of men paid by weekly or daily wages, with or without extras, we find it impossible to determine any fixed minimum rate of wages. Many different rates and incidents of employment prevail. No master has indicated any desire to alter the practice of his firm, and no employee has expressed dissatisfaction with the system under which he has served up to the present, and many of the men examined before us have been in the same service for many years.

As regards the hours of working and the question of overtime in the case of men on weekly wages :—

Every hour of work after 6.30 P.M. shall be counted as overtime and paid for at the rate of sixpence by the hour until 11.30, and after 11.30, up to 6.30 A.M. in the next day, at the rate of ninepence per hour. This provision shall apply as well where the employee is detained at railway or steamboat, without default of his own, as on other business. Sunday work is to be paid for at ninepence per hour.

A Saturday closing of work at three o'clock, while very

desirable in itself, cannot be enforced by a strict rule, for the discharge of vessels (at any rate) must go on on that date as on others. The question of allowing meal hours during the day is also one in reference to which, in the case of Carters out with their loads, it would be manifestly unworkable to stop off at a given time. We, however, recommend that if and when it can be done, the men should be allowed a short Saturday and a meal hour ; but for the reasons given this cannot form part of our Award.

As regards the claims of the men employed in the business of Maltsters, we cannot see our way to make any recommendation or award interfering with the existing rates of pay, save as follows:—

It appears that in certain firms (if not all) it has been the practice to allow what is called a ' back shilling ' to be retained by the employer until the end of each season and then given to the workman if his conduct has been satisfactory, or retained in whole or part in the contrary event. We cannot approve of this system, which renders it impossible for the workman to know exactly what he is earning, and which makes him possibly liable to an equal penalty in respect of trivial and important deviations from duty. WE, therefore, AWARD that in all cases where this practice prevails, the ' back shilling ' shall from and after the close of the present malting season cease and determine, and that in lieu thereof one shilling per week shall be added to the weekly wages of the workman.

In addition to the foregoing matters, there are three others in respect of which we have no authority to do more than to offer a recommendation to both parties :—

1. We think it highly unreasonable that it should be in the power of masters or men to determine a hiring without proper notice. In the case of the Maltsters, particularly, it may be ruinous ; and we recommend that both parties should agree, in writing, not to dismiss a man, or to throw up work, without a fortnight's notice, save in the case of a breach of agreement or other misconduct.

2. We strongly advise both masters and men to agree to the establishment of a permanent Court of Conciliation, for the hearing and determining of all trade disputes which may from time to time arise. The Conciliation Act

(59 & 60 Vict. cap. 30) presents every facility for doing this, and we believe that the benefits to be derived from the adoption of its provisions would be of incalculable advantage to all parties.

3. We have to express our hope and expectation that nothing shall be done which would have the effect of punishing or injuriously affecting any of the men concerned in this arbitration, or their comrades, in relation to the recent strike.

A. M. PORTER.
P. J. O'NEILL.

SCHEDULE

	Per load
Storing from ship to stores, with help . . .	8d.
,, ,, ,, ,, ,, without help . .	10d.

Loading boat and schooner, same rate as storing, 8d. and 10d. respectively.

Cashel Point, same rate.

	Per 100 sacks
Carting corn	7s. 0d.
,, wheat or flour to first loft . . .	8s. 4d.
,, ,, ,, ,, ,, second loft . . .	12s. 6d.

		Per 1 ton 5 cwt.
Carting bags of flour or oatmeal within present municipal boundary	first loft	10d.
	second loft	1s. 3d.

	Per sack
Carting barley or oats or malt, first loft . .	$\frac{5}{8}d.$
,, ,, ,, ,, ,, second loft . .	1d.
,, ,, ,, ,, ,, third loft . .	$1\frac{1}{2}d.$
,, pucks, per load	1s. 0d.
Carting empty sacks to or from railway or canal per bundle	$\frac{1}{2}d.$

	Per load
Storing grain to Custom House from either side of way	10d.
Storing grain to Mooney's Mills or North City Mills, same rate	10d.

For carting to or from places outside the present city boundary (together with Pembroke and Rathmines) there shall be allowed at the rate of a load and a half per load in lieu of the rate payable within these limits.

Memorandum

We the aforesaid Sir Andrew Marshall Porter and Patrick John O'Neill, Esquire, do hereby declare and affirm, as a Supplement to our said Award, that the said Award does not, and was not meant to interfere in any way with the relations of the Dublin Granaries Co., Ltd., or the Merchants Carting Co., Ltd., with their respective Carters or servants, it having been expressly stated to us, by and on behalf of the carters and servants of the said two Companies, that they had no cause of complaint whatever, and made no complaint against the said two firms or either of them.

Furthermore, our said Award did not touch, and was not in any way meant to alter or interfere with the special rates agreed upon between Messrs. William Carter & Son, and their men in respect of the carting of grain between their various premises over short distances. These rates remain unaffected.

Dated this 22nd February 1909.

A. M. Porter.
P. J. O'Neill.

In the supplementary Memorandum of February 22, 1909, we stated the reason why the Award was not intended to apply and did not apply to the cases of the Dublin Granaries Company or the Merchants Carting Company. Where there is no complaint there is nothing to arbitrate about.

It appears, however, that there was a misunderstanding as to this, and the men's allegation is that they did not mean to exclude the case of these two Companies. On hearing of this, we at once agreed, if both parties desired, to go into the case of the two Companies. Accordingly, on the 6th inst., we fully heard both sides with their witnesses ; but it is fair to state that the men intimated clearly that they would prefer a decision that the Award covered their case, as they contended it did.

The arrangements of both these Companies with their

carters are substantially the same, and differ from those of the other firms which were before us. There is a fixed minimum wage of £1 per week to each man, whether his earnings would amount to that sum or not. The men are paid in proportion to the work actually done in the week, on a scale which has been in operation for some years without complaint. Under this system the average weekly payments to the Carters have been, up to the present, twenty-six shillings in the one case and twenty-five shillings and sevenpence in the other, during the entire year. These figures have been extracted from the books.

Taking the employment as a whole, and, in particular, bearing in mind the definite minimum of £1 a week always paid, we think these are good wages for unskilled labour in Dublin, and that to add nearly or quite one-third to them would seriously injure and might destroy much of the trade of the city, the consequences of which would fall most heavily upon the working classes.

Therefore, we cannot accede to the requirement of the men to apply the first six items of the Schedule to the Award to these cases in lieu of the existing rates, with which accordingly we do not interfere.

But where the men are required to carry sacks up to second or third loft, we think they should be paid at the rate mentioned in the Schedule to the Award in the case of men working for other firms, and for overtime also beyond their present hours of work at the rate of one shilling per hour.

A. M. PORTER.
P. J. O'NEILL.

16th March, 1909.

[As the result of an arbitration held in Dublin on April 19, 1913, and presided over by the Recorder of Dublin (the Right Hon. T. L. O'Shaughnessy, K.C.) an agreement was come to between the City of Dublin Steam Packet Co. (represented by Messrs. Richard Jones and Michael Dawson), the National Seamen's and Firemen's Union of Great Britain and Ireland (represented by Mr. George Burke), and the Irish Transport and General Workers' Union (represented by Mr. James Larkin), whereby a strike which had occurred amongst the employees was terminated and a fresh start was made on terms duly set out in the compact. In November following, the agreement was flagrantly broken by Mr. Larkin, in circumstances *set out on page 235, and the understanding no longer exists. The author regrets that he has been unable to obtain an authenticated copy of the document and consequently it has been impossible to that extent to complete the list of " broken agreements."*]

V

CHARACTER OF RIOTERS

The following is a return of prisoners arrested and imprisoned in connection with the labour disturbances in Dublin between August 19, 1913, and December 20, 1913, together with a list of previous convictions on various charges, most of which were unconnected with labour disturbances :—

Total number of prisoners arrested 656
Number imprisoned 416
Number previously convicted 184

Prisoners previously convicted—44 per cent. of total number imprisoned.

Number of prisoners once previously convicted			.		.		55
,,	,,	twice	,,	,,	.	.	21
,,	,,	three times	,,	,,	.	.	19
,,	,,	4–10	,,	,,	.	.	43
,,	,,	11–20	,,	,,	.	.	22
,,	,,	21–30	,,	,,	.	.	17
,,	,,	31–40	,,	,,	.	.	4
,,	,,	41–50	,,	,,	.	.	1
,,	,,	51–60	,,	,,	.	.	1
,,	,,	over 60	,,	,,	.	.	1

184

VI

THE CONFERENCES

The following is the employers' statement relative to the Conference held at the Shelbourne Hotel on Saturday, December 6, 1913.

The Conference for the settlement of the labour troubles having proved abortive, the Employers' Executive Committee desire to make the following statement in connection with this important matter :—

As announced in the Press, the Joint Labour Board deputed the following gentlemen to come to Dublin and consider the situation :—Mr. A. Henderson, M.P., Chairman of the Joint Board ; Mr. J. A. Seddon, Chairman of the Parliamentary Committee of the Trade Union Congress ; Mr. H. Gosling, representative of the Congress ; Mr. C. W. Bowerman, M.P., Secretary of the Parliamentary Committee of the Trade Union Congress ; Mr. Tom Fox, Chairman of the National Executive of the Labour Party ; Mr. J. O'Grady, M.P., Chairman of the General Federation of Trade Unions.

At the meeting of the Joint Board delegates and the employers the following agreement was come to :—

' It is agreed that a conference be arranged between employers, Joint Board delegates (six), and representatives of the workmen (eight) engaged in present dispute in Dublin, on Friday, on the following conditions :—

' The Joint Board delegates to meet separately the representatives of men and employers with a view to arriving at an agreed basis for negotiations, this meeting to be held to-morrow (Thursday).

' Failing an agreement being arrived at that would be acceptable to both parties, the Conference with the workmen, tentatively arranged for Friday, will be postponed.'

Dated December 3, 1913.

Basis for Discussion

Proposals were discussed at length between the Joint Board delegates and the Employers' Committee, and the following clauses were finally agreed to as a basis for discussion at a conference between all parties :—

' 1. The abandonment of the sympathetic strike and of the refusal to handle " tainted goods," as recently and at present in force in Dublin, the employers undertaking, when the dispute is over, to confer with the representatives of the workers with a view to forming a scheme or schemes for the prevention and settlement of future disputes.

' 2. Every employer shall conduct his business in any way he may consider advantageous in all details of management, not infringing the individual liberty of the workers, who will obey all lawful orders and work amicably with all other employees.

' 3. No strike or lock-out to be entered upon without a month's notice on either side ; and no strike shall take place without a ballot having first been taken, and the resolution carried by a majority of the workers affected.

' 4. That the representatives of the Joint Labour Board and the representatives of all the Dublin Trade Unions undertake on behalf of the unions they represent that their policy and methods shall be conducted on proper and recognised trade union lines, and that agreements made with employers shall be kept by the unions and their officials. Any union or official failing to comply with the foregoing conditions will be repudiated by the Joint Labour Board and all other unions, and will receive no assistance, financial or otherwise, from them.

' 5. As to re-instatements : while the employers will not undertake to dismiss men who have been employed during the strike, they will re-employ such men as are required as soon as possible ; it being understood that owing to the disorganised condition of trade many firms will be unable to employ a full staff immediately.

' 6. This agreement to apply to all workers, skilled and unskilled, affected by the present labour dispute in the City and County of Dublin.'

At the Conference between all parties, held at the Shelbourne Hotel on Saturday, December 6, Mr. Arthur Henderson, M.P., presiding, the representatives of the workers proposed that Clauses 1 and 5 (the re-instatement of the men) should be considered together. The workers produced the following amendment to Clause 1 :—

' When the present dispute is over the employers undertake to confer with the representatives of the workers with a view to framing a scheme or schemes for the prevention or settlement of future disputes. The workers agreeing, under the same conditions, when the present dispute is over, to handle all goods and to refrain from sympathetic strikes until the said scheme or schemes are in force—the scheme or schemes to be established by March 7, 1914, at the latest.'

But the workers stated that their proposal was conditional on the employers accepting the amended Clause (5), viz.— 'That all men be re-instated.'

The employers, therefore, considering this condition, offered to substitute for their Clause 5 the following clause :—

> 'The employers, while they cannot agree to dismiss men taken on who have been found suitable, will agree that as far as their business permits, they will take on as many of their former employees as they can make room for, and in the operation of their business will make a bona fide effort to find employment for as many as possible, and as soon as they can.'

The workers refused to recede from the position they had taken up in requiring complete re-instatement, a condition obviously impossible of acceptance by the employers, and the Conference came to an end.

Signed on behalf of the Employers' Executive Committee.

CHARLES M. COGHLAN,
Secretary.

COMMERCIAL BUILDINGS, DUBLIN.

The following is the employers' statement relative to the Conference held at the Shelbourne Hotel on Thursday, Friday, and Saturday, December 18, 19, and 20, 1913 :—

'The Executive Committee of the Dublin employers regret to have to report the failure of the Conference held on Thursday, Friday, and Saturday for the purpose of endeavouring to reach a settlement of the industrial crisis which has now lasted four months. Following the break-up of the first Conference on Sunday morning, December 7, the employers were again approached by the Joint Labour Board, and the Conference was resumed on Thursday, 18th, Mr. Arthur Henderson, M.P., again presiding.'

At the sitting of the Conference on that morning the following new proposals were handed in on behalf of the workers :—

> 'That the employers of the City and County of Dublin agree to withdraw the circulars, posters, and forms of agreement (known as the " Employers' Agreement ")

presented to their employees, embodying conditions governing their employment in the several firms as from July 19, 1913.

'That the Unions affected agree as a condition of the withdrawal of such conditions and forms of agreement governing employment in the firms affected, to abstain from any form of sympathetic strike pending a Board of Wages and Condition of Employment being set up by March 17, 1914.

'And the Conference also agrees that in restoring relations, no member shall be refused employment on the grounds of his or her association with the dispute, and that no stranger shall be employed until all the workers have been re-instated.

'All cases of old workers not re-employed on February 1, 1914, shall be considered at a Conference to be held not later than February 15, 1914.'

The Employers' Committee pointed out that this was a resumption of the abortive Conference, and should be taken up where that broke off, viz., on the consideration of the re-instatement offer as follows :—

'The employers, while they cannot agree to dismiss men taken on who have been found suitable, will agree that as far as their business permits, they will take on as many of their former employees as they can make room for, and in the operation of their business will make a bona fide effort to find employment for as many as possible, and as soon as they can.'

And they now offered to add to this the further condition, that

'No worker shall be refused employment on the ground that he is a member of any particular union.'

It was agreed that the clause governing re-instatement was an essential to the settlement of the dispute.

Thereupon the representatives of the workers put a series of interrogatories to the Employers' Committee which they were obviously unable to reply to. The first query required

'A statement of the firms who claim that they cannot re-instate the number so affected, and the proportion of workers the said firms claim they can immediately make room for if a settlement is arrived at.'

Even if this information was obtainable, which it was not, it would be very improper for the Committee to furnish it, in view of the sinister objects for which it was evidently intended.

The next query was whether the statement made by Mr. Murphy in the Press on November 15 last,

'That all but 5 per cent. can return immediately was any idea of the extent to which immediate re-instatement can be guaranteed now,'

to which it was replied that Mr. Murphy's letter, published more than a month ago, referred only to those men out of employment whose places were not filled up, and would be no index.

The next query was for

'A statement from the Employers' Committee of the percentage of workers who will be re-instated.'

The Committee pointed out that they had already replied to this, and further pointed out that it was obvious they could not answer the question, seeing that the dispute had been going on for more than four months, that it affected every trade and every employment in the city 'working under various conditions.'

At this stage on Friday evening the Committee adjourned to enable the representatives of the workers to report the position to the representatives of the National and local delegates now in Dublin.

On Saturday morning Mr. Larkin handed in again the workers' terms, identical with those submitted to the Conference at its opening on Thursday morning, and submitted it as a final judgment.

The Employers' Committee replied that this brought them back to the position in which they stood at the opening, and that as the re-instatement of all workers would involve the victimisation of men employed by them since the dispute began, they could not possibly accede to such a demand.

The employers, looking back on the proceedings at the Conference, taken in connection with the manifesto issued by Mr. Larkin the day preceding, commencing with the remarkable phrase, ' Comrades, a foul and black conspiracy is afoot here,' are forced to the conclusion that there was on the part of at least some of the workers' representatives no real intention to seek a settlement.

CHARLES M. COGHLAN,
Secretary,
Employers' Executive Committee.

COMMERCIAL BUILDINGS, DUBLIN,
  December 21, 1913.

WHAT THE CONFERENCE DISCUSSED

On the Conference opening (on December 18), under the presidency of Mr. Arthur Henderson, M.P., the following was put forward by the representatives of the workers as a basis of agreement :—

' The employers of the City and County of Dublin agree to withdraw the circulars, posters, and forms of agreement (known as the '' Employers' Agreement '') presented to their employees, embodying conditions governing their employment in the several firms as from July 19, 1913.

' That the Unions affected agree as a condition of withdrawal of such conditions and forms of agreement governing employment in firms affected to abstain from any form of sympathetic strike pending a Board of Wages and Conditions of Employment being set up by March 17, 1914.

' And the Conference also agree that in restoring relations no member of any trade union shall be refused employment on the grounds of his or her association with the dispute, and that no new employee shall be engaged until all the old workers have been re-instated.

' All cases of workers not re-employed on February 1, 1914, shall be considered at a Conference to be held not later than February 15, 1914.'

The employers considered the proposals, and replied—

' The employers regret that any misunderstanding should have arisen as to the procedure to be adopted when the Conference re-opened, and are desirous of impressing on the Joint Board and the local representatives that they understood that the Conference was to be continued on the basis previously arrived at.

'The Conference broke up on the subject of re-instatement, and, to avoid further delay, the employers are of opinion that an agreement on this clause is essential before discussing any of the other clauses.

'The employers have, therefore, carefully considered the counter proposal as handed in by the President of the Trades Council this morning in conjunction with the amended Clause 5, which they put forward at the last meeting viz.—

'The employers, while they cannot agree to dismiss men taken on who have been found suitable, will agree that as far as their business permits they will take on as many of their former employees as they can make room for, and in the operation of their business will make a bona fide effort to find employment for as many as possible, and as soon as they can.

'The employers would be prepared, with the object of assisting towards a settlement, to add the following to the foregoing clause :—

'No worker shall be refused employment on the ground that he is a member of any particular union.

'Unless some further suggestions for the amendment of this clause are put forward, of which the employers can approve, they regret that they cannot see their way to depart from the decision which they have already come to, and must, therefore, reluctantly request that this clause be agreed to before proceeding further.'

After discussion, the following question was raised by the representatives of the workers :—

'Are the workers' representatives to understand that the employers agree to withdraw the circulars, posters, and forms of agreement presented to their employees, embodying conditions governing their employment in the several firms as from July, 1913 ? '

The form of agreement referred to is that marked ' No. 1 ' in the employers' letter to Mr. Arthur Henderson dated

December 6, 1913, and any other documents having similar import.

To this the Committee replied :—

'In the event of a settlement, the Committee will advise employers to withdraw any clause in any agreement so far as they relate to any ban on any Union.'

The workers then put the following proposition :—

'We agree that the clause governing re-instatement is essential to a settlement of the dispute, and with a view to assisting to that end we would be thankful if the employers would clarify their position to the extent that they, the employers, would provide us with a statement of the firms who claim they cannot re-instate, the number of workers so affected, and the proportion of workers the said firms claim that they can immediately make room for if a settlement is arrived at.'

The employers replied :—

'The Committee cannot possibly give or get the information asked for. The employers' statement in Clause 5 as amended,

"That they will make a bona fide effort to find employment for as many as possible and as soon as they can,"

very clearly expresses their intentions in this matter.

'It is quite impossible to foresee how soon the disorganised trade of Dublin can or will resume its normal condition, especially in view of the serious injury caused to many of its industries ; but it is obvious that the longer the dispute continues the greater will be the injury to trade, and the greater the difficulty of finding employment for the workers.'

The further query was then submitted :—

'In view of the statement that the employers agree to make a bona fide effort to find employment for as many as possible, and as soon as they can, the workers' representatives feel that this does not give them sufficient data to go upon, and further wish to inquire if the statement of Mr. Murphy in the Press, that " all but 5 per cent. can return immediately," is any index to the extent to which immediate re-instatement can be guaranteed now.'

At this stage it was agreed that the Conference should adjourn till 11 o'clock on Friday morning, when a reply would be given.

On resumption of the Conference on Friday morning the employers replied :—

' On the subject of the numbers for whom employment can be found the Committee, for the reasons already given, cannot give any data of the number that may be re-employed.

' With regard to Mr. Murphy's statement in the Press on November 15 (now more than a month ago), it referred only to those men out of employment whose places were not filled up, and is not any index " to the extent to which immediate re-instatement can be guaranteed now." '

This reply having been considered by the representatives of the workers, the Conference resumed its joint sitting, and the question being put as to the percentage which could be re-employed, the Committee said—

The Committee have very carefully considered the question put forward this morning on behalf of the representatives of the workers, viz. :—

' That the Committee should furnish a statement of the percentages of workers who will be re-instated.

' The Committee replied to this question very clearly and fully yesterday, and they further point out that the present dispute has been going on for more than four months, that it has affected every trade and nearly every employment in the city, working under varying conditions.

' It must be obvious, therefore, that the Committee could not answer the question as to the percentage of men who could be taken back, and they can only repeat their assurance that " the employers will make a bona fide effort to find employment for as many as possible and as soon as they can.

' The Committee trust that the representatives of

the workers will accept this assurance on the part of the employers to act fairly towards their former employees.'

Mr. Henderson and the other Joint Board delegates made a special appeal to the employers to furnish the data, even approximately, so that they might be enabled to get over the difficulty of the local representatives.

The employers having considered the proposal,

Mr. Good, on their behalf, again informed the delegates that the Committee could not possibly give, or get, the information asked for.

The Conference then adjourned to 4 P.M.

On resuming, the delegates handed in the annexed statement, viz.—

' The workers' representatives having been informed by the employers that they had considered the proposals handed in by the President of the Trades Council, and decided that they, the employers, must request that their Clause 5 be again considered, and agreed upon before proceeding further,

' The workers' representatives, in order to under stand Clause 5, submitted the following question :—

' In view of the statements that the employers agree to make a bona fide effort to find employment for as many as possible and as soon as they can, the workers' representatives feel that this does not give sufficient data to go upon, and further wish to inquire if the statement of Mr. Murphy in the Press that all but 5 per cent. can return immediately is an index to the extent to which immediate re-instatement can be guaranteed now. The employers having intimated that they cannot possibly give or get the information asked for, the Joint Board delegates with the consent of the workers' representatives having appealed to the employers for some explanation of their own Clause 5, showing its effect upon the re-instatement of the old workers, and having failed to obtain any further information or data bearing on the subject—the workers' representatives agree, with the concurrence of the Joint Board delegates, that the Conference should adjourn to enable them to report the position to the National and Local Delegates of the respective Unions now in Dublin.'

The employers agreed to the request for an adjournment till Saturday morning at 10.30 o'clock, and the following was handed Mr. Henderson :—

'With reference to the statement handed in by the Chairman. Mr. Arthur Henderson, M.P., at the adjournment of the meeting this evening, the Employers' Committee think it necessary to point out that the precedence given to the question of re-instatement was concurred in by all parties, as it was on that question the previous Conference had broken off.

'The workers' representatives in requiring a reply as to the number of men that could be re-instated, imposed an impossible condition on this Committee in view of the great number and variety of trades involved in the dispute, and the length of time during which it has continued.

'Even if the statement could be supplied no advantage whatever would accrue, as it would not give employment to one man more than the employers undertake to re-instate under their amended Clause 5.

'With regard to Mr. Murphy's letter to the Press, dated November 15 last, we have already dealt with it in a previous communication.'

On the resumption of the Conference on Saturday morning the representatives of the workers presented the following document through Mr. Larkin :—

DUBLIN DISPUTES

'The employers of the City and County of Dublin agree to withdraw the circulars, posters, and forms of agreement (known as the "Employers' Agreement") presented to their employees, embodying conditions governing their employment in the several firms as from July 19, 1913.

'That the unions affected agree as a condition of withdrawal of such conditions and forms of agreement governing employment in firms affected to abstain from any form of sympathetic strike pending a Board of Wages and Conditions of Employment being set up by March 17, 1914.

'And the Conference also agree that in restoring relations no member of any trade union shall be refused employment on the grounds of his or her association with the dispute, and that no new employee shall be engaged until all the old workers have been re-instated.

'All cases of workers not re-employed on February 1, 1914, shall be considered at a Conference to be held not later than February 15, 1914.'

The Chairman of the Employers' Executive Committee read the following in reply :—

'The Committee observe that the proposals put forward through Mr. Larkin this morning are the same as those presented on Thursday morning, and bring us back to the position in which we then stood.

'The clauses submitted again to-day by the representatives of the workers require the full re-instatement by the employers of all the workers. This would involve the victimisation of many who have been employed since the dispute began. The employers cannot agree to dismiss men who have proved suitable, but subject to this condition are willing and anxious to re-employ their old hands as far and as soon as possible.

'The members of the Committee have laboured to try and effect a settlement so much needed and desired, and regret that their labours in conjunction with those of the Joint Board representatives and the Trades Council delegates have not succeeded in arriving at an agreement.'

The Conference was then brought to a close.

INDEX

PRINTED BY
SPOTTISWOODE AND CO. LTD., COLCHESTER
LONDON AND ETON

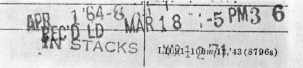

ImTheStory.com

Personalized Classic Books in many genre's

Unique gift for kids, partners, friends, colleagues

Customize:

- Character Names
- Upload your own front/back cover images (optional)
- Inscribe a personal message/dedication on the
  inside page (optional)

Customize many titles Including
- Alice in Wonderland
- Romeo and Juliet
- The Wizard of Oz
- A Christmas Carol
- Dracula
- Dr. Jekyll & Mr. Hyde
- And more...

Emily's Adventures in Wonderland

Ryan & Julia